FIELD GUIDE TO THE
Acacias of Zimbabwe

Richard Barnes [signature]

Jonathan Timberlake
Christopher Fagg
Richard Barnes

with illustrations by Rosemary Wise

Published by: CBC Publishing, PO Box 4611, Harare, Zimbabwe,
with support from the United Kingdom Department for International Development.

February 1999
ISBN 0-7974-1936-5

Acknowledgements

This book has had a long gestation period which started around 1988. During this time, many people, directly or indirectly, have been involved or offered constructive criticism; it is not possible to name them all. The authors particularly wish to thank Tom Müller and Bob Drummond who gave valuable advice and encouragement, including information on localities of unusual species.

The National Herbarium in Harare and its Head, Nozipo Nobanda, allowed us to examine the specimens held there and, at an earlier stage, various staff members of the Herbarium were involved in relevant fieldwork as part of the Communal Lands Vegetation Survey. Specimens were also examined at the Matopos Research Station Herbarium and the Natural History Museum collections in Bulawayo, Oxford Forestry Institute at Oxford University and at the Kew Herbarium in London. Our thanks go to the staff in these places. On the mapping side, much assistance was provided by William Hawthorne and Denis Filer of the Oxford Forestry Institute.

The country round Bulawayo is particularly rich in *Acacia* species and nowhere more so than Umgusa Valley Estates, 25 kilometres north out on the Victoria Falls road. The assistance of the owners, particularly Jenny Bickle, in gathering information and materials for this work is much appreciated. Kit Hustler and Colin Bristow helped with fieldwork at Victoria Falls and Sentinel Ranch, respectively.

Members of the Tree Society of Zimbabwe tried out the key and gave valuable comments on a draft – in particular Tessa Ball, Anthon Ellert, Phil Haxen, Mark Hyde, Ian McCausland, Andy MacNaughtan, Lyn Mullin and Maureen Silva-Jones. Others who provided comments include Gillian Barnes, Mike Bingham, Tom Müller, Jenny Timberlake and Sue Worsley. In particular, thanks are due to Mark Hyde and Peter Mundy for detailed comments on the final draft. Brian Williams provided information on wood properties of some species and Alan Gardiner commented on the use of acacias as food plants by butterflies and emperor moths. Bob Drummond and Ian McCausland helped with information on the origins of names, while Charles Moyo and staff from the Matopos Research Station advised on vernacular names.

The Research and Development Division of the Zimbabwe Forestry Commission has collaborated with the Oxford Forestry Institute and provided a base and logistical support for the fieldwork for a number of research projects on acacias in southern Africa. The authors thank Dr Enos Shumba and his staff for this support.

This publication is an output from two research projects conducted by the Oxford Forestry Institute and funded by the United Kingdom Department For International Development (DFID) for the benefit of developing countries. The views expressed are not necessarily those of DFID. The authors thank DFID for the financial support to conduct the fieldwork and publish this field guide. The authors also thank Professor Jeffery Burley, Director of the Oxford Forestry Institute, for his support in this work and in editing the text.

Jonathan Timberlake[1]
Christopher Fagg[2]
Richard Barnes[2]
Bulawayo & Oxford, September 1998

[1] Biodiversity Foundation for Africa,
PO Box FM730, Famona, Bulawayo, Zimbabwe
[2] Oxford Forestry Institute, Department of Plant Sciences, University of Oxford, South Parks Road, Oxford OX1 3RB, UK

Contents

Acknowledgements ... 2
Introduction ... 4
    Taxonomy ... 4
    Origin and distribution ... 6
    Ecology ... 7
    Uses ... 9
Description of acacias ... 11
How to use this field guide ... 14
Dichotomous key to *Acacia* species ... 16
Collecting *Acacia* specimens ... 21
Character matrix ... 22
Species descriptions ... 24

    Faidherbia albida ... 24
    Acacia abyssinica ... 28
    A. adenocalyx ... 30
    A. amythethophylla ... 32
    A. arenaria ... 34
    A. ataxacantha ... 36
    A. borleae ... 38
    A. burkei ... 40
    A. caffra ... 42
    A. chariessa ... 44
    A. eriocarpa ... 46
    A. erioloba ... 48
    A. erubescens ... 52
    A. exuvialis ... 54
    A. fleckii ... 56
    A. galpinii ... 58
    A. gerrardii ... 60
    A. goetzei ... 64
    A. grandicornuta ... 68
    A. hebeclada subsp. chobiensis ... 70
    A. hebeclada subsp. hebeclada ... 72
    A. hereroensis ... 74
    A. karroo ... 76
    A. kirkii ... 80
    A. luederitzii ... 82
    A. mellifera ... 84
    A. nebrownii ... 88
    A. nigrescens ... 90
    A. nilotica ... 94
    A. pentagona ... 98
    A. permixta ... 100
    A. polyacantha ... 102
    A. rehmanniana ... 106

A. robusta subsp. clavigera ... 108
A. robusta subsp. robusta ... 112
A. schweinfurthii ... 114
A. senegal var. leiorhachis ... 116
A. senegal var. rostrata ... 120
A. sieberiana ... 122
A. stuhlmannii ... 126
A. tortilis subsp. heteracantha ... 128
A. tortilis subsp. spirocarpa ... 132
A. welwitschii ... 136
A. xanthophloea ... 138
Exotic *Acacia* species ... 140
Pods grouped by inflorescence type ... 144
List of *Acacia* species by area ... 148
List of *Acacia* species by habitat ... 149
Glossary ... 150
References and bibliography ... 153
Common and vernacular names ... 157
Index of *Acacia* species with synonyms ... 159
Species matrix ... Inside back cover

List of Boxes

Box 1   Species and provenance trials of African acacias ... 27
Box 2   Nutritional value of *Acacia* pods ... 51
Box 3   Growth rings in the acacias ... 63
Box 4   The glandular acacias ... 79
Box 5   Uses of acacias in communal lands and on small farms ... 87
Box 6   The "*Acacia pennata*" complex ... 92
Box 7   Molecular studies in the African acacias ... 93
Box 8   Conservation of acacias ... 97
Box 9   Gum arabic from the acacias ... 105
Box 10   Germination of *Acacia* seed ... 111
Box 11   Hybridization in the acacias ... 118
Box 12   Nodulation and chromosome numbers of Zimbabwe acacias ... 119
Box 13   Ants and acacias ... 124
Box 14   Bruchid beetles ... 125
Box 15   Episodic regeneration ... 131
Box 16   Wood properties ... 135

Introduction

Acacia is a genus of trees and shrubs, sometimes known as 'thornbushes' or 'thorn trees', widespread in tropical and subtropical Africa. They are particularly dominant over much of the drier and comparatively nutrient-rich savannas of this continent; they also occur in the Middle East and Indian subcontinent, Australasia and central and South America. Acacias are of major ecological and economic importance over much of their range in Africa, owing in part to their contribution to the ecology of an area but also to the range of products they provide to local people and their livestock.

Many species of *Acacia* have significance to both agriculturalists and wildlife managers as indicators of certain environmental conditions and as a primary resource. A good knowledge of the *Acacia* species in the veld therefore can give a manager insight into land potential and condition. Many naturalists, too, are keen to understand the group better.

The genus *Acacia* has often been considered a difficult but fascinating one, especially by field biologists, and a number of field guides have been produced in the region over recent years (e.g. Ross 1971, Bogdan & Pratt 1974, Carr 1976, Timberlake 1980a, Davidson & Jeppe 1981, Coe & Beentje 1991, Steyn 1994) in addition to taxonomic works (e.g. Brenan 1959, 1970, Ross 1975a,1979) and bibliographies and reviews on various individual species (e.g. Fagg & Greaves 1990a, 1990b; Barnes, Filer & Milton 1996; Barnes, Fagg & Milton 1997). Until now, there has not been a comprehensive guide to the acacias of Zimbabwe, nor one that provides details on their distribution and ecology.

This field guide should enable botanists and non-botanists alike readily to identify all species of *Acacia* growing naturally in Zimbabwe from either fertile (i.e. with flowers and/or pods) or infertile specimens. The information on distribution and ecology should help in providing added insights into and understanding of the role these species play in the environment as well as stimulating further research. Additional information on various topics concerning the biology, uses and potential of acacias is given in boxes.

TAXONOMY

The genus *Acacia* was first described by P. Miller in 1754 based on a specimen of *Acacia nilotica* from Egypt. The name is derived from the Greek *akis* meaning a sharp point. It is the largest genus in the subfamily Mimosoideae of the Leguminosae (Fabaceae) or bean family, and the second largest in the whole family. The genus is pantropical with around 1340 described species – 954 in Australia, 230 in the Americas, 129 in Africa, 18 in India, a few species in Asia, and some island endemics. The 129 African species (Lock 1989) are found primarily in the drier parts of the continent from Egypt to South Africa and from Senegal to Somalia.

The study of *Acacia* worldwide by George Bentham at Kew, published in 1842 and refined in 1875, still provides the basis for the taxonomy of the group. He split this large genus into six series, listed below.

Over the last 30 years various attempts have been made to rationalize this classification in light of the many new species described since 1875, current thinking on biogeography, and

---

Classification of the genus *Acacia* (following Bentham 1842, 1875)

Gummiferae	bipinnate leaves and spinescent stipules; mostly African species (some American and about five Australian)
Vulgares	bipinnate leaves and prickles, but no spinescent stipules; mostly American species (some African and Asian and two Australian)
Filicinae	very similar to the Vulgares, but no prickles; only in C. & S. America
Botryocephalae	leaves bipinnate with glands, flower heads in racemes or panicles, stipules (if present) not spinescent; only in Australia
Pulchellae	leaves bipinnate with glands, flowers in heads or spikes or simple peduncles, stipules not spinescent; only in Australia
Phyllodineae	all species with phyllodes; Australian with some species in the Pacific and Madagascar

4   *Acacias of Zimbabwe*

much new anatomical evidence such as pollen grain morphology and chromosome data. Vassal (1972) and Guinet & Vassal (1978) suggested that *Acacia albida* should be removed to a separate genus – *Faidherbia* – and the remaining species grouped into three subgenera, the classification system used in this book. The three subgenera – *Aculeiferum*, *Heterophyllum* and *Acacia* – are defined primarily on pollen morphology, but there is much consistency in other characters such as spinescence, chromosome number and inflorescence type. Thus the divisions are almost definitely natural and not artificial. Only two of these three subgenera are present in Africa, and both are well represented in Zimbabwe. The diagram overleaf shows the Zimbabwe species by taxonomic group (subgenus and series). The species listed under each taxonomic group are also clustered to indicate similarity and natural groupings based on our own ideas, but are not dissimilar in most cases to the arrangements suggested by Brenan (1970) and Ross (1979).

Subgenus *Acacia* has spinescent stipules (paired straight thorns), capitate (globose) inflorescences, and a chromosome number of 2n=52, while subgenus *Aculeiferum* has prickles (hooked thorns) and non-spinescent stipules, capitate or spicate inflorescences, and a chromosome number of 2n=26 (see Box 12, page 119). The division based on stem armature is, with occasional exceptions, supported by differences in inflorescence type, seed morph-

ology and other anatomical features. These subgenera are subdivided further on the basis of arrangement of prickles and type of inflorescence (subgenus *Aculeiferum*), or arrangement of seed in the pods and flower colour (subgenus *Acacia*). It is interesting to note that most of the Australasian species of *Acacia* do not have spines or prickles, and most have phyllodes – a petiole that has expanded and flattened to form a leaf-like structure.

Pedley (1978, 1986) has suggested a similar classification system, but with more attention given to the Australian species. A comparison of the different classification systems is shown below. In 1986 he proposed that Vassal's three subgenera be raised to separate genera. However, this move has not been accepted by the broad botanical community, in part because it would involve the introduction of new generic names with all the confusion that this could bring.

Within Zimbabwe 40 species of African *Acacia* (including *Faidherbia*) have been recorded, although some are very localized and only just enter the country's borders. Some species are subdivided into two or more subspecies or varieties; five of the 40 species have two subspecific taxa present in the country. Much work still remains to be done on the taxonomy of African acacias, and on further research some of these subspecies or varieties may prove to be full species in their own right.

Comparison of *Acacia* classification systems.

Bentham 1842	Vassal 1972	Pedley 1978	Pedley 1986
ser. Gummiferae	sgen. <u>Acacia</u>	sgen. <u>Acacia</u>	gen. <u>Acacia</u>
	sect. Acacia		
ser. Vulgares	sgen. <u>Aculeiferum</u>	sgen. <u>Aculeiferum</u>	gen. <u>Senegalia</u>
	sect. Aculeiferum	sect. Spiciflorae	sect. Senegalia
	sect. Monacanthea		
ser. Filicinae	sect. Filicinae	sect. Filicinae	sect. Filicinae
	sgen. <u>Heterophyllum</u>	sgen. <u>Phyllodineae</u>	gen. <u>Racosperma</u>
			sect. Racosperma
ser. Botryocephalae		sect. Botrycephalae	
ser. Phyllodineae	sect. Uninervea	sect. Phyllodineae	
		sect. Alatae	
	sect. Heterophyllum	sect. Plurinerves	sect. Plurinervia
		sect. Juliflorae	
		sect. Lycopodiifoliae	sect. Lycopodiifoliae
ser. Pulchellae	sect. Pulchelloidea	sect. Pulchellae	sect. Pulchellae

Source: adapted from Chappill & Maslin 1995.

ORIGIN AND DISTRIBUTION

Origin and early dispersal

The earliest members of the plant family Leguminosae were probably in existence in the Cretaceous period 90-100 million years ago, a period when Angiosperm (flowering plant) groups were in a phase of active evolution (Raven & Axelrod 1974). It was at this time that the super-continent Gondwanaland, of which the major components were present-day Africa, South America, Madagascar, India, Australia and Antarctica, was splitting apart. Although the split started about 130 million years ago, it is thought to have been completed only about 90 million years ago when Africa was finally separated from South America. But there was probably still plant migration between the two continents up to the Palaeocene period of the Early Tertiary (60 million years ago) owing to their physical closeness and the presence of chains of volcanic islands.

The subfamily Mimosoideae, to which *Acacia* belongs, probably had a western Gondwanaland origin, that is, it evolved in the portion of the ancient continent that comprises present-day Africa and South America, perhaps in a tropical lowland forest setting (Vassal 1972, Raven & Axelrod 1974). There has been much debate on the origins and relationships of the three subgenera of *Acacia*. One view (Pedley 1986) suggests that the two subgenera, *Acacia* (Pedley's genus *Acacia*) and *Aculeiferum* (Pedley's genus *Senegalia*), evolved separately from a proto-*Acacia* (the earliest plants recognizable as *Acacia* in the broadest sense) in the tribe Ingeae, which includes *Acacia* and related genera. He suggests that both subgenera were present in Africa and South America before the continents finally separated around 90 million years ago, hence their wider distribution. At around this time, subgenus *Heterophyllum* (Pedley's genus *Racosperma*) was actively evolving from subgenus *Aculeiferum* and dispersing into northern Australia, taking advan-tage of arid conditions there. Pedley goes on to say that at least the acacias with phyllodes (Bentham's series Phyllodineae) were present in Australia as part of the original Gondwanaland stock, but that the other typical Australian groups (Bentham's series Botryocephalae and Pulchellae) may have evolved later. Recent serological work on *Acacia* seeds

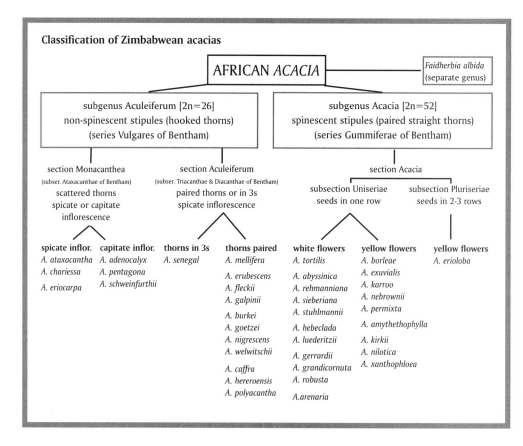

Classification of Zimbabwean acacias

AFRICAN *ACACIA* — *Faidherbia albida* (separate genus)

subgenus Aculeiferum [2n=26]
non-spinescent stipules (hooked thorns)
(series Vulgares of Bentham)

subgenus Acacia [2n=52]
spinescent stipules (paired straight thorns)
(series Gummiferae of Bentham)

section Monacanthea
(subser. Ataxacanthae of Bentham)
scattered thorns
spicate or capitate
inflorescence

section Aculeiferum
(subser. Triacanthae & Diacanthae of Bentham)
paired thorns or in 3s
spicate inflorescence

section Acacia

subsection Uniseriae
seeds in one row

subsection Pluriseriae
seeds in 2-3 rows

spicate inflor.	capitate inflor.	thorns in 3s	thorns paired	white flowers	yellow flowers	yellow flowers
A. ataxacantha	A. adenocalyx	A. senegal	A. mellifera	A. tortilis	A. borleae	A. erioloba
A. chariessa	A. pentagona		A. erubescens	A. abyssinica	A. exuvialis	
A. eriocarpa	A. schweinfurthii		A. fleckii	A. rehmanniana	A. karroo	
			A. galpinii	A. sieberiana	A. nebrownii	
			A. burkei	A. stuhlmannii	A. permixta	
			A. goetzei	A. hebeclada	A. amythethophylla	
			A. nigrescens	A. luederitzii	A. kirkii	
			A. welwitschii	A. gerrardii	A. nilotica	
			A. caffra	A. grandicornuta	A. xanthophloea	
			A. hereroensis	A. robusta		
			A. polyacantha	A.arenaria		

(Brain 1987) also suggests that subgenus *Aculeiferum* and the mainly Australian subgenus *Heterophyllum* (now generally called *Phyllodineae*) are actually more closely related than are the two African groups – subgenera *Acacia* and *Aculeiferum*.

Today, the most widespread group in Africa is subgenus *Acacia*, with spinescent stipules. The most species-rich group worldwide, however, is subgenus *Heterophyllum*, most of which have phyllodes. In general, the drier parts of Africa have more species of subgenus *Acacia*, while the moister or forested areas contain more species of subgenus *Aculeiferum* (Ross 1981).

Africa's biological history has been marked by periods of aridity which have led to a marked impoverishment of the flora compared to that of tropical South America and Asia (Raven & Axelrod 1974). It appears that dry climates developed and spread at the end of the Oligocene period (30 million years ago), which would probably have led to diversification in the arid-adapted genus *Acacia*. There is also evidence of major climatic shifts in the Quaternary period over the last 2.5 million years, probably leading to major changes in plant distribution patterns. This may be the reason for some of the odd distributions seen for species such as *A. stuhlmannii* and the subspecific differentiation within *A. mellifera*, *A. nilotica*, *A. robusta* and *A. senegal*.

It is probable that the armature of African acacias, particularly the long spinescent stipules found in subgenus *Acacia*, has evolved as a defence against large herbivores, which have been an integral part of the African evolutionary scene for millions of years (Coe & Beentje 1991). Herbivores have not been a major evolutionary factor in Australia or, for the last few million years, in South America. Quite a few *Acacia* species also have seeds with adaptations for large mammal dispersal, illustrating how the two groups, plant and animal, have evolved together (Coe & Coe 1987).

Present distribution

The area of greatest *Acacia* species diversity is the arid savanna and semi-desert scrub of east and northeastern Africa stretching from southern Tanzania northwards to Somalia, Ethiopia and Eritrea – the Somalia-Masai regional centre of endemism as described by Frank White in his monumental work on the vegetation of Africa (White 1983). Maps developed under the African *Acacia* projects at the Oxford Forestry Institute (Fagg 1997) show that on a continental scale

there are two areas of particularly high species diversity – one in S. Kenya/N. Tanzania, and the other in the Limpopo Basin (E. Botswana, S. Zimbabwe, northeast South Africa, Swaziland and S. Mozambique). A "hot spot" analysis, indicating the proportion of species in any area with very restricted distributions, shows that although northeast Africa (N. Tanzania to Somalia) has the greater concentration of such species, there are also significant areas in southeastern Africa associated with the Limpopo Basin south to Maputaland.

An analysis of the continental distributions of the *Acacia* taxa (including *Faidherbia*) found in Zimbabwe (below) shows that although many (38%) have broad tropical distributions, there is a significant proportion (30%) that is confined to southern Africa alone (Angola, Zambia, Malawi and Mozambique southwards). In addition to the 13 taxa of broad southern Africa distribution, six are confined to the Limpopo Basin, two to the Zambezi Basin and five to the broadly-defined Kalahari Basin – a total of 26 taxa or almost 60% of the total found in the country. There is only one *Acacia* species endemic to Zimbabwe (*A. chariessa*), but a second has its main populations here (*A. rehmanniana*) and a third is confined to a small total area with a significant portion in Zimbabwe (*A. eriocarpa*).

Distribution patterns of *Acacia* taxa found in Zimbabwe (including *Faidherbia*).

Distribution pattern	no. taxa	%
Widespread tropical	17	38
Afromontane	1	2
Broad southern Africa	13	30
Limpopo Basin	6	14
Zambezi Basin	2	5
Kalahari Basin	5	11
TOTAL	44	100

ECOLOGY

There are African acacias that will tolerate hot and arid, hot and wet, and cold and arid environments, but none can tolerate cold and wet conditions (Ross 1979). Therefore the genus is found throughout tropical Africa except in high Afromontane areas. Between them they are adapted to an extraordinary range of climatic conditions, growing in regions of extreme aridity, through savanna woodlands to the fringes of tropical forest. Their tolerance of soil conditions is no less remarkable. There are species that will grow on coastal dunes, some that will grow on shifting desert sands, others that are adapted to acid soils in high rainfall areas, and yet others that thrive on black cracking clays. The combined tolerance of climatic and edaphic (soil-related) extremes often makes them the only trees that can regenerate and survive in such environments, either as pioneers or as climax species.

The ability of acacias to capture difficult sites rapidly has resulted in many of them being regarded as invasive species both in indigenous and in exotic situations. However, their occupation is but a step in the succession that occurs on cleared or degraded land. It is significant that these attributes are found in most tree species that have become successful exotics.

Acacias in vegetation

Over a great part of Zimbabwe the rainfall is too high and the soils too poor for acacias to dominate the vegetation. There are few species in the wetter parts of the country, and they are generally confined to clay-rich soils such as along drainage lines or vleis. It is on the red clays derived from rocks of the Basement Complex that acacias start to become important or dominant members of the vegetation, particularly in areas too dry for the establishment of miombo woodland dominated by *Brachystegia* or *Julbernardia* (Timberlake *et al.* 1993). Typical species here include *A. karroo*, *A. nilotica*, *A. gerrardii* and *A. rehmanniana*, with *A. galpinii* along the drainage lines. At lower altitudes *A. nigrescens* is an important component of extensive areas of woodland on well-drained clay or stony soils, while *A. tortilis* subsp. *spirocarpa*, *A. robusta* subsp. *clavigera* and *Faidherbia albida* form closed canopy woodland on the alluvium flanking larger rivers.

Most of the other species of *Acacia* found in Zimbabwe are only locally common and are restricted to certain habitat types, although they may be of ecological importance there. As a group, acacias do not have the same ecological prominence here as they do in, for example, Botswana, Namibia or the Sudan.

Soils

Acacias are generally found on richer soils with a higher nutrient status (eutrophic) and few are adapted to soils poor in nutrients (dystrophic). Such eutrophic soils in Zimbabwe are usually clay-rich or found in depositional sites. Under higher rainfall conditions those nutrients present tend to get leached out, a factor compounded by the ancient nature of many of Zimbabwe's soils.

Many acacias appear to require reasonable levels of calcium and other nutrients in the soil to establish themselves. Interestingly, it is on the calcareous alluvium of some river valleys, such as the Limpopo, Gwayi and Save, that acacias are most prevalent and at their most diverse. In the Umguza Valley just north of Bulawayo, for example, 17 species of *Acacia* are found in an area of just a few hundred square kilometres.

Plant succession

Although the invasion of cleared or disturbed land by many *Acacia* species is generally a transitory phase, succession to broad-leaved woodland of varying density and composition can be arrested. This may be because the soils have been modified through excessive loss of nutrients, erosion or surface capping, or through continued suppression of succession through fire or utilization by browsers or the axe. Most of the major mining areas are situated in areas underlain by Basement Complex rocks because it was here that gold was found. Mining in the early years of the century necessitated the cutting of large quantities of wood for fuel, mine props and construction in these areas. There was also widespread clearing for agriculture and the introduction of heavy concentrations of cattle. These practices often resulted in soil erosion and soil capping, and a greatly reduced capacity of the soil to receive and store moisture. Such areas are possibly now not able to support the vegetation originally found there, and the stands of low acacia woodland and scrub that currently occupy them are probably here to stay.

Bush encroachment

Some species of *Acacia* are of major economic concern owing to their invasiveness in grazing areas, a phenomenon termed bush encroachment. This is a particular problem with *A. karroo* in the Eastern Cape of South Africa, with *A. mellifera* in parts of the northern Cape and in central Namibia, and with *A. tortilis* in parts of Botswana, but it has not caused similar concern in Zimbabwe. However, *A. karroo* and *A. nilotica* do invade heavily grazed or frequently burnt rangeland in parts of Midlands Province and Matabeleland, and *A. polyacantha* can be a major invader in old fields in parts of Mashonaland.

Rooting habits

Probably the major environmental factor determining plant species distribution in Zimbabwe is the amount of available soil moisture (Timberlake *et al.* 1993). Apart from rainfall, temperature, topographic position and soil type, moisture availability is also affected by soil depth and the rooting depth of the species concerned. Many acacias, such as *A. nigrescens* and *A. erioloba*, rapidly put down a deep taproot in their first year or two to tap reserves of moisture deep in the soil, and this enables them to obtain moisture for a longer period of the year. They can therefore establish themselves away from rivers or run-on situations. Other species, such as *A. polyacantha* and *Faidherbia albida*, have a much shallower rooting system and are confined to riverine or moister situations, while shallow rooted species such as *A. fleckii* and *A. ataxacantha* have adapted to the long dry season by coming into leaf only during the rains and losing their leaves early. Further work is needed on rooting systems as this is probably a major factor in determining where certain species will grow.

Nitrogen fixation

Acacias, like most legumes, have symbiotic bacteria (*Rhizobia* spp.) associated with their roots. These bacteria, which live in small outgrowths of the roots called nodules, can convert atmospheric nitrogen into a form that the plant can take up – a process termed biological nitrogen fixation. Nearly all species of the legume subfamily Caesalpinioideae (including *Brachystegia*, *Julbernardia* and *Colophospermum*), however, do not nodulate, and neither do all Mimosoideae, the subfamily to which *Acacia* belongs.

Nodulation under greenhouse conditions has been reported for 37 of the 44 taxa of *Acacia* (including *Faidherbia*) found in Zimbabwe (see Box 12, page 119). Data are not yet available for *A. eriocarpa* and *A. hebeclada* subsp. *chobiensis*. One group of acacias, represented in Zimbabwe by *A. adenocalyx*, *A. pentagona* and *A. schweinfurthii* (sometimes termed the "*A. pennata* complex", see Box 6, page 92), does not nodulate at all and is believed to be a primitive group with its origins in tropical rainforests. Recent research (Barnes *et al.* 1997) has shown that *A. erioloba*, an aberrant *Acacia* in other respects, also does not normally nodulate.

Biological nitrogen fixation is particularly prominent in young establishing individuals, which have a greater nutrient requirement, in order to allow them to grow taller and out-compete grasses and herbs. It is thought that this may be a family adaptation to low-nutrient soils or early succession niches. However, under extreme environmental stress, plants often fail to form nodules and, even when nodulated, active nitrogen fixation appears to occur only when moisture is available.

Animals and acacias

Some *Acacia* species are closely associated with various species of birds and mammals, and such animals may indeed be dependent on them. For example, weaver birds often use acacias for nesting (presumably the thorns act as a defence against predators) as do some vultures, secretary birds and eagles, possibly as the trees offer a broad platform with a clear view. As has been well documented, giraffe feed extensively on acacia trees (Du Toit *et al.* 1990), to which their feeding has become adapted. Such associations may have other hidden benefits for the acacias. In the open savannas of East Africa, for example, species of *Acacia* that can survive heavy browsing pressure obtain a competitive advantage over other non-thorny woody plants. The obligate relationship between some Central American *Acacia* species and ants, described by Janzen (1966), has not been noted in Zimbabwe (see Box 13, page 124).

The change in associated fauna is often noticeable when one moves from broad-leaved savanna to acacia savannas, although this may be due primarily to the nutrient status of the soil rather than to the presence of *Acacia* species as such.

USES

Acacias in Zimbabwe have been used for a multiplicity of purposes – some because of special properties intrinsic to a particular species, others just because of availability. As expected, acacias tend to be most used where they are most common.

Browse

The utilization of leaves, pods and young shoots from acacias by both domestic livestock and wildlife is most prevalent in the drier parts of the country where grass growth is less favoured. Although all acacia leaves are probably edible, of particular value are those species, such as *A. karroo*, that retain their leaves into the long dry season or flush early before the rains – the most critical times for forage availability.

Owing to their nitrogen fixing ability, the leaves of acacias are often comparatively rich in crude protein, with figures of 10-20% commonly quoted. Although some secondary compounds such as tannins, which greatly reduce protein digestibility, are sometimes present in leaves, this does not seem to deter livestock much. The main line of defence is probably the thorns, which become better developed in the face of heavy browsing. It is the young leaves that appear to have the highest concentration of phenolics (including tannins), whereas values are much lower in mature leaves and pods (Ernst *et al.* 1991). There is also a suggestion that severe browsing can actually increase palatability at times (Du Toit *et al.* 1990).

Acacias are possibly best regarded for their pods, particularly those species with indehiscent pods such as *A. erioloba*, *A. nilotica*, *A. tortilis* and *Faidherbia albida* (see Box 2, page 51). It is the seeds, rather than the pod itself, that contain most protein and, in indehiscent pods, these are retained inside, not scattered. However, such seeds are adapted to herbivore ingestion, and many of them survive the digestive process and pass out intact. There are many stories of cattle in southern Africa surviving droughts by supplementary feeding with ground-up pods, often mixed with molasses and sulphur to encourage ingestion and neutralize any prussic acid (cyanide) which might be present. This practice also helps reduce loss of condition in cattle during the long dry season. There is generally more prussic acid in the leaves and immature pods than in the mature pods (Steyn & Rimington 1935), but some species such as *A. karroo* have no trace of it.

Wood

Utilization of acacias for their wood or timber is very widespread, but there are only a few species that are highly regarded for one or other purpose. It is the density, strongly linked to durability and size, that determines suitable uses.

Although some species (e.g. *Faidherbia albida* and *A. sieberiana*) have very light wood of little value for construction or firewood, others (e.g. *A. nigrescens* and *A. erioloba*) have very heavy wood that is both durable and suitable for outside construction (see Box 16, page 135) as well as providing excellent firewood. *A. nigrescens* in particular, which is widespread in suitable habitats, grows comparatively straight and has a reasonable quantity of heartwood when pole-sized; thus it is much used for fencing.

Owing to hardness, small sizes, deformation of the trunks, and a tendency to crack, most acacias do not make fine woodworking material. There are, however, some that are very suitable for this purpose, such as *A. galpinii* and *A. polyacantha*, while the limited quantity of wood available from *A. amythethophylla* is said to be of exceptional beauty.

Some of the best firewood available in rural areas comes from *A. erioloba*, *A. nigrescens* and *A. nilotica*, which burn slowly without too much smoke and provide good coals. *A. karroo*, although not so good, is much more readily available.

Edible products

Gum is produced by many acacias as a defence against fungal and insect attack, particularly where the wood is exposed, as at a wound. The sticky exudate, consisting of complex polysaccharides, possesses both anti-fungal and anti-bacterial properties (Coe & Beentje 1991) and is also edible and nutritious for human and other primates. The best known gum is from *A. senegal* var. *senegal* (see Box 9, page 105), a taxon not found here, but it is very similar to gum from *A. karroo*. In southern Africa it is this gum that enters commerce (Barnes *et al.* 1996).

The flowers of some acacias contain good quantities of nectar and are produced early in the season, thus making them locally important sources for honey bees. Acacia honey tends to be more liquid than that from some other species and it has a strong taste. It is not known how important acacia species are for honey production in Zimbabwe.

Medicines

Relatively few medicinal uses of acacia have been recorded in the country. This may partly be a reflection of the limited range of species available in Mashonaland, from where most traditional medical usage has been documented (Gelfand *et al.* 1985), but it is also likely to reflect the limited range of secondary compounds present. Many of the medicinal uses recorded seem to be based on the astringent property of tannins present in the roots and bark. Decoctions from various species, principally from the roots, have been used for a range of ailments such as stomachache and convulsions, and as emetics, stimulants and aphrodisiacs. The roots of *Faidherbia albida* have been used as a fish poison and those of *A. polyacantha* are used both to repel snakes and as a treatment for snake bite. A decoction of the bark of *A. karroo* is used against "tulp" (*Moraea* sp.) poisoning in cattle.

Below is a brief discussion of some features of acacias that are of assistance in species identification.

Life form

Most species of *Acacia* are small to medium-sized trees 2 to 8 m high, although stunted and multi-stemmed individuals are not uncommon on certain soils. In disturbed areas some species that are normally trees have a shrub-like habit, e.g. *A. karroo* and *A. rehmanniana*. The only true low shrub species (consistently less than 2 m high) are *A. arenaria*, *A. chariessa*, *A. hebeclada* and *A. stuhlmannii*. Other acacias are climbers or scramblers, e.g. *A. ataxacantha* and *A. schweinfurthii*, while *A. pentagona* is the only true woody climber or liana. The tallest species in Zimbabwe (over 30 m at times) is *A. galpinii* when growing alongside rivers, but the largest tree in terms of girth and canopy spread is probably *Faidherbia albida*.

The habit of many species, that is the form of branching and canopy profile, is often distinctive, particularly when individuals are not crowded and growing in the open. A typical profile is shown on each illustration. It is often possible in a given area to identify species by their characteristic shapes, but caution must be exercised when moving to a new region.

Trunk and bark

The form of the trunk in acacia trees, and the colour and texture of the bark, are quite varied. Trunks are often not particularly straight and fork low down. However, some species, such as *A. galpinii* and *A. nigrescens*, can have a rather straight and tall trunk, while *A. senegal* var. *leiorhachis* has a typically tall, thin 'whippy' stem rising above basal branching.

The bark can be smooth, flaking or peeling, or deeply fissured, with colours ranging from yellow (*A. xanthophloea* and *A. senegal* var. *leiorhachis*), green (*A. kirkii*) or whitish (*A. polyacantha*, *A. fleckii* and *Faidherbia albida* when young) to the more common dark brown or black. Some species (*A. karroo* and *A. rehmanniana*) have a powdery reddish underbark on younger growth. The colour and texture of the bark and the colour of the underbark can be important field characters. Another notable feature of a few acacia species is the presence of hooked thorns on raised bosses (or "knobs"), seen in *A. nigrescens* and *A. goetzei*.

A few of the more rapidly growing species such as *A. karroo* can "weep" a gummy exudate from wounds or insect holes, or from what appear to be splits in the bark, which inhibits the entry and growth of pathogens such as fungi and the activities of wood-boring insects. While not a diagnostic character, it is commonly encountered in senile individuals of some species. This gum often attracts various species of *Charaxes* butterfly and fruit chafers.

Young twigs

The shape, colour, hairiness and arrangement of thorns and leaves on young twigs are a very useful set of criteria in identification. Some species have leaves in "tufts" or "cushions" (e.g. *A. robusta* and *A. gerrardii*), some are very hairy (e.g. *A. stuhlmannii* and *A. permixta*), and some are somewhat shiny (e.g. *A. karroo*). Generally the diagnostic characters are clearer on twigs from the last two seasons than they are on older growth. In some species the thorns are greatly reduced or lost on older twigs, especially those higher up in the canopy where defence against mammalian herbivores is presumably no longer required, while, by contrast, saplings can have very long dense thorns, e.g. *A. tortilis*. The descriptions given here refer to the current season's growth.

Thorns

Acacia thorns are of two types – modified stipules and superficial prickles. This characteristic, and the variation in arrangement within the superficial prickles group, have been used as the basis for subdivision in the genus. In addition, differences in inflorescence type, flower colour, seeds, seedling morphology and chromosome number follow this division. True spines, not found in *Acacia*, are actually woody branches with sharp tips, seen from the buds along their length, e.g. in *Dichrostachys*.

Stipules are small leaf-like outgrowths at the base of the leaf. In some species they fall off soon after the leaf expands, but in one group of acacias, subgenus *Acacia*, they persist, elongate and become woody to form the classic long, straight (or sometimes curved) thorns, e.g. in *A. tortilis*. These thorns are part of the leaf structure and are not superficial.

In the other group of African acacias, subgenus *Aculeiferum*, the prickles arise from the epidermis just below the nodes or are scattered along the internodes, and so are superficial. This group can be subdivided into three: those with paired prickles just below the nodes, those with prickles in groups of three just below the nodes, and those with scattered prickles along the internodes.

The arrangement of thorns or prickles is perhaps the most useful character in preliminary identification of acacias as it can be seen throughout the year, even when the plant is leafless. In many cases the arrangement is characteristic of a species or small group of species. For example, in Zimbabwe only the two varieties of *A. senegal* have three prickles at the nodes.

The well-known "ant-galls" of some African acacias (e.g. *A. drepanolobium* of East Africa and *A. seyal*) are not found in Zimbabwe, for unknown reasons. In places certain individuals of *A. karroo*, or sometimes just certain branches on a single tree, have greatly enlarged or thickened thorns up to 8 cm long. These thorns can split open along one side and occasionally support small colonies of *Crematogaster* ("cocktail") ants. It is not known what causes this or if it is under genetic or environmental control. Only the thorns on the later part of a season's growth appear to show the phenomenon. Thorns of *A. erioloba* are sometimes inflated at their fused bases and when the leaves have fallen a small hole at the leaf insertion remains. Occasionally ants are found living in here. Although "ant-galls" are absent in Zimbabwe, ants are not uncommonly seen "patrolling" the younger twigs and presumably can defend the plant against some herbivore attacks in return for secretions from the leaf glands, on which they feed (see Box 13, page 124).

Leaves

The leaves of all the African acacias are bipinnate, that is they are divided into paired pinnae which in turn are divided into leaflets. In many cases the leaflets are small and elongated, but in some of the acacias (e.g. *A. nigrescens* and *A. mellifera*) the leaflets are quite large and more rounded. The whole divided leaves of *A. amythethophylla* are very large although the leaflets are comparatively small, while in other species the whole leaf may be comparatively small even when the leaflets are of medium size, e.g. *A. nebrownii*. In the descriptions leaves have been described as small, medium and large with normal (not extreme) measurements given in brackets.

Most acacias are deciduous, that is they lose their leaves for part of the year. Many start to sprout new leaves with the warmer weather in September/October and slowly lose them into the cold dry season of June/July/August. However, the aberrant *Faidherbia albida* comes into leaf around May and only starts to lose its leaves around November, the opposite of other species. The most useful browse species are obviously those that retain some leaves during the dry season when livestock need them. Species such as *A. erioloba* and *A. karroo* have only a very short leafless period in August/September, whilst others, such as *A. erubescens* and *A. fleckii*, are leafless longer than most. Within a single species some individuals can retain leaves for longer depending on the site and access to soil moisture and on the particular season.

Glands

Most species have small glands near the base of the leaf stalk (or petiole) and/or between the pinnae pairs. The shape of these glands can be diagnostic for certain species and very useful in separating them, e.g. *A. galpinii* and *A. polyacantha*, or *A. fleckii* and *A. erubescens*. The function of the leaf glands is not clear. However, they are known to secrete small amounts of nectar which attract ants, and it is possible that this attracts the attention of nectar robbers away from the flowers.

On the young twigs and pods of species of the "glandular complex" (see Box 4, page 79) there are numerous minute reddish glands, so small they can only be seen with a hand lens and are often mistaken for specks of dirt. Similar red or brown glands are also found on the pods of *A. caffra*, *A. hereroensis* and *A. tortilis* subsp. *spirocarpa*. In the "glandular complex" these glands secrete a gum which apparently attracts ants, and may assist in keeping the plant free of insect herbivores. It is not clear what the function of the glands is in the other species.

Flowers

The flowers of acacias are actually very small and without showy petals, although they have conspicuous stamens. The individual flowers are grouped together into clusters, the inflorescence, commonly termed the "flower". There are three types of inflorescence in acacias – globose heads ("balls") of yellow individual flowers, globose heads of white or cream flowers, and elongated heads ("spikes") of white or cream individual flowers. The yellow-flowered species have long, straight thorns, as do many species with globose white inflorescences, while the species with white spikes have hooked prickles (except *Faidherbia albida*). As the inflorescences are present only for a month or so each year, their colour and type have not been used as a primary diagnostic characteristic in the main key.

Some *Acacia* species flower before the rains (August to October) as daily temperatures rise. The most notable of these are the white spikes of *A. nigrescens* and the yellow-cream spikes of *A. galpinii*, both of which flower in September before the leaves appear, and the abundant, white, sweet-scented balls of *A. robusta* subsp. *robusta* in the Bulawayo area. Other species, such as the yellow-flowered *A. karroo* and *A. nilotica*, flower after the first good rains. *A. karroo* often flowers after a wet spell and can bloom several times in a season.

Presumably, flowering patterns are linked to availability of pollinators. Most acacias are insect-pollinated, thus it is likely that different insects are responsible at the different seasons in which inflorescences appear. On the other hand, it could be that different flowering times have evolved to avoid competition for the attention of bees, which appear to be the major pollinators.

Flowering periods have not been well recorded and more information on relative phenology and what environmental factors may trigger them is required. An interesting study of comparative phenology of acacias was done in Nylsvley, north of Pretoria in South Africa (Milton 1987).

Pods and seeds

Pods are often important for field identification. Although there may be none left on the tree or shrub at first look, careful searching will often reveal one or two on a protected branch or half buried on the ground underneath.

The pods, which may be thick and woody (e.g. *A. sieberiana* and *A. hebeclada*) or thin and papery (e.g. *A. mellifera* and *A. senegal*), normally contain one row of seeds similar to a bean pod. *Acacia* pods can be divided into those that generally split open on the tree to drop their seeds (dehiscent, e.g. *A. karroo*), and those that do not split open and are dispersed intact with seeds inside (indehiscent, e.g. *A. erioloba*). The indehiscent species are dispersed by animals in their droppings; their seeds are rounded, rather than flattish, and they have harder seed coats.

This field guide incorporates four different ways to identify a specimen. The user can go through the illustrations, distribution maps and descriptive text until he or she is confident that the specimen, whether a living individual in the field or a dried twig, has been correctly named, or one of the three keys can be used. An effort has been made in the keys to base identification primarily on vegetative characters, present during much of the year, rather than on inflorescences or pods which are only seasonally present.

Dichotomous key

The first and main key is a dichotomous key. This uses vegetative characters and incorporates pods and flowers only where necessary. Obviously, any identification using this key should be confirmed with the full description and illustrations. As it is the only key in the book that separates out *Acacia* species from similar non-*Acacia* species (such as *Dichrostachys* and *Albizia*), as well as separating out the introduced Australian acacias, care should be taken when using the other keys to exclude such species. All indigenous *Acacia* species included in this book have thorns (sometimes they have to be looked for as some twigs may be without) and bipinnate leaves. The only other species in Zimbabwe that have this combination of features are *Dichrostachys cinerea*, *Pterolobium stellatum* and *Caesalpinia decapetala*.

At each step in the dichotomous key one or other of the given options should be chosen, leading on to the next step. A range of twigs should be looked at in case some characters are better expressed elsewhere on the plant or on a neighbouring individual. Pods are most useful in identifying acacias and occasionally they are found still on the plant long after the main crop has fallen, generally where they are protected from animals and wind, or on the ground underneath.

Character matrix

The other two keys are different types of character matrix. In the species matrix at the end of the book, any of the readily-noted field characters shown can be chosen, and those species showing that character (usually, if not always) are shown by a dot. A solid ● signifies the character is nearly always present; an open ○ signifies the character is only occasionally present. To reach a firm identification, which should be checked against the description in the text, a combination of characters should be used. For example, if a specimen has scattered hooked thorns it can be rapidly noted that it must be one of seven species. If it occurs on clay soils but not in forests it can be readily deduced that it is most likely to be *A. chariessa*.

The character matrix (pages 22-23) lays out a selection of easily noted vegetative characters (thorns, leaflet size, habit, etc.) along the top axis, with inflorescence and pod characters along the side. Any species with that combination of characters is mentioned where column and row intersect; citations in brackets indicate an unusual character combination for the species. If inflorescences and/or pods are present this matrix rapidly leads to a small group of species that can then be checked against the individual entries. The matrix is only indicative, not diagnostic.

Illustrations

The illustrations are all drawn from Zimbabwe material and show a flowering branch, leaves, flowers and a mature pod. Enlarged drawings of glands, leaflets and seeds are included. An inset drawing shows the habit of a typical individual, drawn from photographs taken in Zimbabwe.

Descriptions

All 40 species of African *Acacia* found in Zimbabwe, covering 45 taxa (including subspecies, varieties and *Faidherbia albida*), are described and arranged alphabetically. In every case (except *A. goetzei*) all recognized subspecies or varieties are given a separate entry. Brief descriptions of the seven non-native species naturalized in various parts of eastern Zimbabwe are given after the species descriptions.

Scientific names by which each species has previously been known in Zimbabwe are mentioned and are also listed in an index at the end. The common names in languages used in Zimbabwe for each species are given, and a full alphabetical list is given on pages 157 and 158. These names have been taken from literature concerning Zimbabwean plants and checked by local authorities. Minor differences in spelling and incorrectly-applied names have been ignored. Some names in common use apply to a group of acacias (i.e. hooked thorned or straight thorn *Acacia*) and not to individual species. Only English names that appear to have widespread usage in the country are included.

The description of each species follows the order: growth form, bark, stem, young twigs, thorns, leaves, flowers, fruits. They are compiled from Zimbabwean specimens and field notes, so may differ from those seen elsewhere, but draw heavily on the descriptions in Brenan (1970) and Ross (1979). The descriptions are orientated towards field use and therefore detailed measurements are usually omitted, except where they are diagnostic. If needed, such details can be obtained from the taxonomic works referred to above. Bark refers to that on mature trunks. Young twigs refers to those from the current season. Leaf sizes and number of pinnae refer to mature leaves. Flowering times, as far as possible, are taken from field notes and specimens, but these can vary substantially depending on the season. Some species, for example, may flower after a rainy spell.

The major field characters are listed after the main description. This is followed by details on characters differentiating the species from others with which it might be confused. Such differences sometimes require the use of a hand lens and careful observation to see clearly.

Distribution of the species in Africa is given, followed by a more detailed account of its distribution in Zimbabwe. These notes have been compiled from available herbarium specimens (National Herbarium, Harare (SRGH); National Botanical Institute, Pretoria (PRE); Royal Botanic Gardens, Kew (K); Forest Herbarium, Oxford (FHO); Matopos Research Station Herbarium (MRSH); Natural History Museum, Bulawayo (BUL); and the field herbaria at Hwange National Park and Matetsi Safari Area) and extensive field trips to most parts of the country. Data were recorded on the herbarium database program BRAHMS (Filer 1999) and latitude/longitude noted for each record. The associated mapping program MUSICA (Hawthorne 1998) was used to produce the distribution maps, and apparent aberrant records were checked. The small outline map showing the network of major roads has all confirmed records (both sight records and herbarium specimens) plotted on it as dots. A blank area does not necessarily mean the species does not occur there, simply that it has not been recorded.

Ecological notes are primarily derived from the authors' own field observations in Zimbabwe over some years, coupled with notes from regional literature and observations by various people in the country (see Acknowledgements). Suggestions as to factors determining or causing the distribution of each taxon are included, but some are not supported with solid evidence and remain speculative. The authors welcome any further observations on distribution and ecology, particularly for those species with localized distributions.

The final section under each description gives details on the general biology and nomenclature of the species, as well as related species outside Zimbabwe. This is followed by details on its various economic uses obtained from both local literature and local observations, including timber characters, forage value and medicinal uses. Economic uses elsewhere in Africa that have not been recorded from Zimbabwe are mostly omitted. Growth rates and notes on cultivation are given. Finally, the origin of the name is mentioned, most having been derived from Greek or Latin.

Included towards the end of the book are illustrations of pods from all indigenous acacias, grouped under spicate and globose flowered species; a list of species found in various geographical areas and vegetation types in the country; a glossary of technical terms used (some of which are illustrated); and a list of common names. Also included is a comprehensive bibliography of sources of information used in preparation of the book. To improve readability specific references have not been included in the text, except in the introductory section and in the boxes. Finally, an index lists all scientific names by which the various species (indigenous and exotic) are, or have previously been, known in the country.

Dichotomous Key to Acacia Species

The starting point of this key is woody plants with bipinnate compound leaves. The first five couplets eliminate other genera of the Mimosoideae (e.g. *Albizia* and *Dichrostachys*), and other species such as *Burkea* and *Jacaranda*, from the main key and also separate out the two main naturalized Australian acacias found in the country. Two species of Caesalpinioideae (*Pterolobium stellatum* and *Caesalpinia decapetala*), both scrambling shrubs with scattered hooked thorns on the stem and leaf rachis, are separated out in the main key. If one is sure that the specimen in hand is an indigenous *Acacia*, start at couplet 6.

The main key divides the taxa into five groups, A to E, on the basis of arrangement of thorns. Throughout, vegetative characters (mostly thorns and leaves) are used, most of which do not need a hand lens. Sometimes the character is not found on a particular twig, such as straight and hooked thorns in *Acacia tortilis*, so it is necessary to look at a range of twigs. The leaf characters are based on mature leaves and, as both leaves and leaflets are used, it is important to distinguish between pairs of pinnae and leaflets (see Glossary). As acacias are very variable, it is important to check determinations with the descriptions and illustrations.

Note: There are many Australian acacias that only produce bipinnate leaves on young plants or coppice shoots, and later develop round or strap-like pseudo-leaves (phyllodes), or produce bipinnate leaves at the apex of the phyllodes. Seven species of *Acacia* introduced into Zimbabwe are described in this field guide (see pages 140-143), but only two are included in the keys.

Bipinnate compound leaves

1a.	Armed plants	2
1b.	Unarmed plants	3

2a.	Plant armed with single straight thorns (strictly a short branch), often leaf-bearing or with leaf buds	*Dichrostachys cinerea*
2b.	Plant with thorns in pairs or threes; if thorns single then hooked	6 [main key]

3a.	Plants with some phyllodes present	Australian *Acacia* spp.
3b.	Plants without phyllodes	4

4a.	Flowers in small yellow globose heads; narrow pods dehiscing along one margin only	5
4b.	Flowers not as above; pods not dehiscing along one edge only	non-acacias

5a.	Leaves with glands along leaf rachis, both at junctions of pinnae pairs and in-between; leaves dark green; pods constricted between seeds	*A. mearnsii* (introd.)
5b.	Leaves with glands along leaf rachis only at junctions of pinnae pairs; leaves silvery-grey in colour; pods not constricted between seeds	*A. dealbata* (introd.)

Zimbabwe Acacia Key (Woody plants armed with thorns)

6a.	Plant with only straight thorns at nodes	**Group A**
6b.	Plant with both straight and hooked thorns at nodes	**Group B**
6c.	Plant with only hooked thorns, not necessarily at nodes	7

7a.	Plant with scattered hooked thorns along the stem	**Group C**
7b.	Plant with hooked thorns at nodes (rarely occasional thorn on stem in between)	8

8a.	Plant with only paired hooked thorns at nodes	**Group D**
8b.	Plant with 1 or 3 hooked thorns at nodes	**Group E**

Straight thorns   Paired hooked thorns   Thorns in threes

Scattered hooked thorns   Inflated thorns   Knob thorns

Group A: Paired straight thorns at nodes

| 9a. | Mature leaves with 15+ pinnae pairs (usually more than 20) | 10 |
| 9b. | Mature leaves with 1-14 pinnae pairs | 13 |

| 10a. | Young growth not obviously hairy; low spreading shrub with ascending shoots (sometimes zig-zag in shape) | *A. arenaria* |
| 10b. | Young growth clothed in spreading hairs; small or large trees | 11 |

| 11a. | Leaves with less than 20 pinnae pairs; thick indehiscent woody pods | *A. sieberiana* |
| 11b. | Leaves with more than 20 pinnae pairs; dehiscent leathery pods | 12 |

| 12a. | Rusty-red bark on branches; small tree not found above 1500 m | *A. rehmanniana* |
| 12b. | Pale yellow papery bark on young tree, becoming smooth brown to black; large flat-topped tree restricted to the Eastern Highlands above 1500 m | *A. abyssinica* |

| 13a. | Powdery bright yellow bark, or peeling bark with a green underlayer | 14 |
| 13b. | Bark not with above characteristics | 15 |

| 14a. | Tree with distinctive yellow powdery bark; leaves with 3-6 pinnae pairs; flattish pods; restricted to Limpopo/Save Basin | *A. xanthophloea* |
| 14b. | Tree with peeling bark over distinctive green underlayer; leaves with 6-14 pinnae pairs; 'warts' on pods; not found in Limpopo/Save Basin | *A. kirkii* |

| 15a. | Shrub with red-brown glands on young stems; glossy shine to youngest growth | 16 |
| 15b. | Tree or shrub without glands on stem; youngest growth not glossy | 19 |

| 16a. | Twigs with conspicuous spreading (1-2 mm·long) hairs | *A. permixta* |
| 16b. | Twigs not hairy | 17 |

| 17a. | Leaves consistently with 3 or more pinnae pairs, conspicuously crenulate along leaflet margins; found on black clays | *A. borleae* |
| 17b. | Leaves generally with 1-5 pinnae pairs, leaflets not crenulate on margins; found on sandstone soils | 18 |

| 18a. | Leaves generally with 2-5 pinnae pairs; pods long and curved almost into a circle, not glandular, constricted between the seeds | *A. exuvialis* |
| 18b. | Leaves generally with 1-2 pinnae pairs; pods small and broad, not markedly curved, covered with small red glands, not constricted between the seeds | *A. nebrownii* |

| 19a. | Plant with distinct white colour to twigs; tree loses leaves during wet season; spicate inflorescence | *F. albida* |
| 19b. | Plant without the above characters | 20 |

| 20a. | Leaves large 10-37 cm long, 10-20 cm wide; flattened spines, often inconspicuous; inflorescences borne in a terminal panicle | *A. amythethophylla* |
| 20b. | Leaves less than 10 cm long; conspicuous spines, not flattened; inflorescences axillary | 21 |

| 21a. | Plant with some stout thickened thorns fused at base | 22 |
| 21b. | Plant without stout thorns, but if enlarged then not thickened and fused at base | 23 |

| 22a. | Young growth zig-zag in shape; thorns sometimes fused basally; glands between all pinnae pairs; pods large, woody, pale grey and velvety; on sandy soils | *A. erioloba* |
| 22b. | Young growth straight; robust thorns not distinctively fused at base; glands only between top 1-3 pinnae pairs; pods brown, glabrous and not woody; on clay soils | *A. grandicornuta* |

| 23a. | Obconical shrub; restricted to Beitbridge region; young growth and pods covered in long (up to 3 mm) grey-white spreading hairs | *A. stuhlmannii* |
| 23b. | Usually a tree, if a spreading shrub not found in Beitbridge area; young growth and pods not covered in long spreading hairs | 24 |

| 24a. | Large straight thorns commonly pointing slightly backwards; distinctive blackish pods constricted between the seeds | *A. nilotica* |
| 24b. | Plant without above characters | 25 |

| 25a. | Leaves up to 2 cm long | 26 |
| 25b. | Leaves longer than 2 cm | 27 |

| 26a. | Tree with distinctive flat-topped crown; youngest growth pubescent; loosely curled pods hairy, with reddish glands | *A. tortilis spirocarpa* |
| 26b. | Tree with more open and rounded crown; youngest growth without glands and hardly pubescent; pods tightly curled, smooth, waxy, without glands | *A. tortilis heteracantha* |

| 27a. | Young shoots densely pubescent | 30 |
| 27b. | Young shoots not densely pubescent | 28 |

| 28a. | Leaf rachis slightly pubescent; usually a riverine tree of lower altitudes | *A. robusta clavigera* |
| 28b. | Leaf rachis glabrous; often found away from rivers | 29 |

| 29a. | Leaflets up to 2.5 mm wide with a similar colour each side; bark dark brown with a reddish layer beneath; narrow curved pods | *A. karroo* |
| 29b. | Leaflets over 2.5 mm wide, lighter in colour underneath; grey to dark brown bark without reddish layer beneath; pods broad, thick and woody | *A. robusta robusta* |

| 30a. | Leaflets same colour on both surfaces; pods erect on shoots, late-dehiscent | 31 |
| 30b. | Leaflets darker in colour on upper surface; pods hanging from branches, dehiscent | 32 |

| 31a. | Large riverine shrub, only along upper Zambezi River; pods over 2.5 cm wide | *A. hebeclada chobiensis* |
| 31b. | Low shrub, not riverine, associated with old dunes in N Tsholotsho/S Hwange area; pods under 2.5 cm wide | *A. hebeclada hebeclada* |

| 32a. | Widespread, but not found on Kalahari sands; thick ascending branches | *A. gerrardii* |
| 32b. | Restricted to the Kalahari sands in Hwange area; branches not robust or ascending | *A. luederitzii* |

Group B: Pairs of long straight and/or short curved thorns at nodes

33a.	Leaves up to 2 cm long	34
33b.	Leaves longer than 3 cm	35

34a.	Tree with distinctive flat-topped crown; youngest growth and loosely curled pods pubescent and with minute reddish glands	*A. tortilis spirocarpa*
34b.	Tree with more open and rounded crown; youngest growth with no glands and hardly pubescent; pods tightly curled, smooth and waxy, without glands	*A. tortilis heteracantha*

35a.	Plant with distinctive ascending robust branches and grey wrinkled bark; younger trees clothed in tufted leaves; widespread, but not found on Kalahari sands	*A. gerrardii*
35b.	Young growth less robust; restricted to Kalahari sands in Hwange area	*A. luederitzii*

Group C: Scattered hooked thorns along stem and leaf rachis

36a.	Leaflets >3 mm wide	37
36b.	Leaflets <3 mm wide	39

37a.	Young twigs and pods hairy	*A. eriocarpa*
37b.	Young twigs and pods glabrous	38

38a.	Flowers whitish, in spikes; pods ovate, conspicuously red, clustered at tips of shoots	*Pterolobium stellatum*
38b.	Flowers yellow, large and showy; pods leathery, not acacia-like	*Caesalpinia decapetala* (introd.)

39a.	Petiole <2 cm long	40
39b.	Petiole >2 cm long	42

40a.	Young stems blackish brown with minute brown glands; leaflets with midrib subcentral; flowers globose; only known from lower Mazowe Valley	*A. adenocalyx*
40b.	Young stems pale grey to brown, without glands; leaflets with midrib and lateral nerves invisible; flowers in spikes	41

41a.	Leaves mostly longer than 4.5 cm and with more than 8 pinnae pairs	*A. ataxacantha*
41b.	Leaves shorter than 4 cm and with less than 8 pinnae pairs	*A. chariessa*

42a.	Young branchlets light green; widespread in riverine woodland below 1000 m	*A. schweinfurthii*
42b.	Young branchlets red brown, older stems 5-angled; restricted to evergreen forest in Eastern Highlands	*A. pentagona*

Group D: Paired hooked thorns at nodes

43a.	Leaves with 1-2 leaflet pairs	44
43b.	Leaves with 3 or more leaflet pairs	45

44a.	Twigs with transverse white lenticels; trunk without prickly knobs; leaflets mostly <1 cm wide; straw-brown papery pods	*A. mellifera*
44b.	Twigs without distinctive lenticels on twigs; trunk usually covered with persistent prickly knobs; leaflets mostly >1 cm wide; dark brown leathery pods	*A. nigrescens*

45a.	Leaves exceeding 15 cm in length with more than (13)15 pinnae pairs	54
45b.	Leaves less than 15 cm long with less than 15 pinnae pairs	46

46a.	Leaves with 6 or fewer leaflet pairs, leaflets rounded to oblong	47
46b.	Leaves with 10 or more leaflet pairs, leaflets more than 3 times longer than broad	50

| 47a | Leaflets <3 mm wide; only in Beitbridge area | *A. mellifera* hybrid |
| 47b | Leaflets >3 mm wide | 48 |

| 48a. | Leaflets symmetric at base, without hairs | *A. welwitschii* |
| 48b. | Leaflets asymmetric at base, with or without hairs | 49 |

| 49a. | Leaf rachis distinctly pubescent, pods <2 cm wide; only known from Gonarezhou area | *A. burkei* |
| 49b. | Leaf rachis without hairs or only sparsely pubescent; pods >2 cm wide; widespread | *A. goetzei goetzei* |

| 50a. | Petiole less than 1.2 cm long | 51 |
| 50b. | Petiole longer than 1.2 cm | 52 |

| 51a. | Petiole with large squat gland and no glands along rachis; stems pale; pods almost hairless; on sandy soils in Matabeleland | *A. fleckii* |
| 51b. | Petiole with stalked gland and glands along the top end of the rachis; stem purple-brown; pods pubescent; on clay/stony soils in Bulawayo/Matopos area | *A. hereroensis* |

| 52a. | Shrub or small tree; leaves ± broad as long, pinnae pairs often markedly drooping below rachis; pods <2 cm wide | *A. erubescens* |
| 52b. | Tree; leaves markedly longer than broad, pinnae pairs not markedly drooping; pods >2 cm wide | 53 |

| 53a. | Often a large tree >10 m high; leaves mostly with more than 8 pinnae pairs; no thorns on rachis; pods with thin valves | *A. galpinii* |
| 53b. | Not a large tree; leaves with 4-8 pinnae pairs; thorns often present on rachis; pods with thick leathery to woody valves | *A. goetzei microphylla* |

| 54a. | Leaflets less than 1.5 mm broad; pale bark peeling off in flakes; large squat petiolar gland; widespread | *A. polyacantha* |
| 54b. | Leaflets greater than 1.5 mm broad; dark brown bark, not peeling; small or absent petiolar gland; very rare (only Harare) | *A. caffra* |

Group E: Hooked thorns in threes (sometimes only one) at nodes

| 55a. | Shrub or small tree with 1 or 3 downward-pointing thorns; leaflets ovate; in Beitbridge area | *A. mellifera* hybrid |
| 55b. | Shrub or tree with 3 thorns, the two outer pointing upwards | 56 |

| 56a. | Tall spindly shrub or tree; peeling yellowish bark; pods more than 3 times longer than broad; flowering in late dry season | *A. senegal leiorhachis* |
| 56b. | Multi-stemmed funnel-shaped shrub; pods less than 3 times as long as broad; flowering in early/mid rainy season | *A. senegal rostrata* |

Collecting Acacia Specimens

Although sight records, as recorded in checklists or reports, are valuable indicators of the distribution of a species, there is no substitute for confirmed, repeatable identifications. This is particularly the case for some of the taxonomically-confusing species of *Acacia* of the glandular and *A. goetzei* complexes. For such species careful identification is required based on a collected specimen which can be checked by a specialist or matched in a herbarium – a voucher specimen. Voucher specimens are also required for confirmation of records of unusual distribution or unusual features and to support particular information such as use, as they can be confirmed or revised later. In the course of writing this book we occasionally came across published information, especially on distribution, that seemed very odd. At times there was a voucher specimen in the herbarium which we could use for confirmation (assuming that the locality was recorded correctly – we believe there were a few cases where the collector had got specimens mixed up!), but in its absence we often felt the information was incorrectly recorded. Such voucher specimens are normally kept in a herbarium and also form the basis on which future workers can re-evaluate or describe a taxon. The importance of herbarium specimens in providing the raw material for taxonomic work is often grossly under-estimated.

Generally the material required for a voucher specimen is a twig or shoot with both current and past season's growth, leaves and thorns, and inflorescences and/or pods. This material should be large enough to fit into a folded sheet of newspaper (c.45 x 30 cm). It is a good idea to collect two or three specimens of particularly interesting species or occurrences; these are termed duplicates. The collected material can be cut in the field with a pair of secateurs or a sharp knife. The specimen is then arranged inside the folded sheet of newspaper with the leaves spread out and flattened. If necessary the stem can be bent. Straight thorns often pose a problem. Although crude, a practical way to deal with them is to place the newspaper and specimen on a flat surface, put a sheet of wood or metal on top, and then crush it flat. In this way most thorns are bent flat in the plane of the rest of the material. Specimens need to be dried fairly quickly over a day or two, but not subjected to a high heat. Sheets of absorbent paper should be placed in between the specimens and then removed once or twice a day for drying in the sun or in an oven before being used again. Further details on plant collecting techniques are given by Bridson & Forman (1992).

If acacias are dried too slowly, the leaflets form an abscission layer at the junction with the rachis, and fall off. Because of this, specimens can end up as bare twigs and a lot of loose leaflets, easily lost or mixed up with others. One way to overcome this is by dipping the leaves in, or spraying, with petrol, killing them and so stopping the formation of an abscission layer. However, this can lead to blackening of the specimen which destroys the natural colour of the foliage and flowers.

Perhaps the most important part of collecting is often not given sufficient attention – the recording of notes. Each specimen should be clearly and unambiguously labelled, normally by using a serial number following the collector's name (e.g. Fagg 1234). Ideally, a jeweller's tag with the number should be attached to each specimen at the time of pressing in case specimens become separated from their papers. The serial number should be recorded in a notebook and the following information recorded under it: date of collection, locality of collection (place name, distance and direction from a point found on a map sufficient for someone else to find the site; ideally, longitude/latitude from a detailed map or GPS), soil type (e.g. loose sand, black clay), ecology and associated species. In addition, any details on the plant not visible on the specimen (e.g. height of tree, branching, habit, colour of bark) should be recorded. It should be remembered that a well-preserved specimen with very poor locality data (e.g. only "Hwange District") is of limited value.

Dried, labelled specimens can be deposited at the National Herbarium in the National Botanic Garden, Fifth Street Extension, Alexandra Park in Harare. They can also assist in identification. The collection of *Acacia* specimens at the National Herbarium is good, but additional specimens are still required of some species with limited distribution and of individuals found out of their recorded geographical range. Such information will assist greatly in improving our knowledge of Zimbabwe's acacias.

Acacia character matrix

FLOWERS/PODS			LEAVES/TWIGS → thorns in threes	scattered thorns: climber	scattered thorns: shrub/tree	hooked thorns — thorns paired at nodes; leaflets large (> 4mm broad): knobs on stems	leaflets large (> 4mm broad): no knobs on stems	leaflets small (< 4mm broad); Bark pale or peeli...: large tree	leaflets small (< 4mm broad): small shru...
WHITE SPICATE INFLORESCENCE		pods hairy			eriocarpa				
		pods smooth	senegal		ataxacantha chariessa	goetzei nigrescens	burkei welwitschii	polyacantha	erube... flecki...
WHITE GLOBOSE INFLORESCENCE	pods straight	pods hairy			adenocalyx				
		pods without hairs		pentagona schweinfurthii			mellifera		
	pods curved	pods hairy							
		pods without hairs							
	pods coiled	pods with or without hairs							
YELLOW GLOBOSE INFLORESCENCE	pods straight or ± curved	pods hairy							
		pods without hairs							
	pods curved through 90°	pods hairy							
		pods without hairs							

		mixed hooked & straight thorns		straight thorns					
				twigs/pods with red glands		twigs/pods without glands			
						twigs smooth		twigs hairy	
(tree)	small tree/ shrub	thorns white	thorns grey	twigs smooth	twigs hairy	bark pale, green or yellow	bark dark	small tree/shrub	large tree
	hereroensis								
i	caffra					Faidherbia			
			hebeclada					stuhlmannii	abyssinica sieberiana
			luederitzii					rehmanniana	luederitzii
			(gerrardii)					gerrardii	
							arenaria grandicornuta robusta	rehmanniana robusta	
		tortilis					tortilis		tortilis
								(nilotica)	
				nebrownii		kirkii xantho- phloea	amytheth- ophylla	nilotica	
							erioloba		
				borleae exuvialis (karroo)	permixta		karroo		

(left margin label: dark, not peeling)

1

FAIDHERBIA ALBIDA *(Delile) A.Chev.*
(= *Acacia albida* Delile)

Common names: winterthorn, white thorn, apple-ring acacia; anaboom (Afrikaans); umpumbu, umtungabayeni (Ndebele); hlofungu, mukalaunga (Shangaan); mutsangu (Shona, Tonga); mujagwe (Tonga)

Faidherbia albida is a large tree characteristic of lowveld rivers, with a broad spreading crown and coiled fleshy pods, relished by elephants and other animals. One of its oddest features is that it remains leafless for much of the wet season, only coming into leaf in the early dry season. Formerly called *Acacia albida*, the species has sufficient differences from other acacias for it to be placed into a genus of its own.

Description *F. albida* is a large spreading tree up to 16 m high in the open, rising to 25 m high in riverine woodland. The diameter of mature trunks is normally 70-100 cm, but can reach 150 cm. Canopy can be as broad as the tree is high. **Bark** is whitish on younger stems, and greyish on mature trunks; the slash is fibrous. **Young twigs** are pale to whitish, zigzag in shape and smooth. **Thorns** are paired at the nodes and straight, stout and strong, up to 2 cm long, pointing up and outward. The shoots of young plants differ somewhat and have whiter stems and more numerous thorns. **Leaves** are medium-sized (3-8 x 2-8 cm) with 3-6 pairs of pinnae, each with blue- or grey-green leaflets. Trees are generally leafless in the wet season and come into new leaf around April-May. **Inflorescence** is a long spike of yellow-white flowers, appearing in the axils of the leaves on young growth around May-July, after the leaves. **Pods** are distinctive, reddish brown to bright orange, fleshy, thick and indehiscent. They are coiled and twisted, looking like the peel from an orange or apple, and fall from August to November.

Field characters Large riverine tree; in leaf during dry season; whitish zigzag twigs; pods orange coloured, coiled and fleshy.

F. albida is unlikely to be confused with species of *Acacia* owing to its habit, habitat and "reverse" phenology. The fleshy coiled pods are distinctive.

Distribution and ecology *F. albida*, the only species in the genus, is found throughout dry tropical Africa as far south as KwaZulu-Natal in South Africa and also in the Arabian peninsula and Middle East. In Israel it is found below sea level (-270 m) and in Sudan it is found as high as 2500 m altitude. In Zimbabwe it is a species mostly of lower altitudes below about 900 m, although some (perhaps introduced) populations are found as high up as 1200 m.

The species is found in a variety of habitats and demonstrates various ecological attributes, but in Zimbabwe it is primarily a species of sandy alluvium along large seasonally-flooded rivers. It is common to see even-sized stands on old floodplains with little regeneration and few associated tree species, and also to see mini-forests of young plants on sandbanks of large rivers. Old stands have the appearance of parkland and are one of the well-known sights of the floodplains at Mana Pools in the Zambezi Valley. In parts of Binga and Omay districts, subsistence cultivation is practised under such stands. Occasional catastrophic flooding would appear to be necessary to create the silty sandbanks for new establishment sites. Regeneration is mostly episodic, not continual.

Notes The species was named *Acacia albida* by Delile in 1813 and was accepted as an *Acacia* for over 100 years, although it always stood apart in having unusual phenology and different vegetative characters. In 1934, after a study of the wood anatomy, the French botanist Auguste Chevalier proposed that it should be transferred to a separate monospecific genus which he named *Faidherbia*. However, general acceptance of this name really came about only in the early 1980s when pollen and molecular studies started to provide an overwhelming weight of evidence for the species' removal from the genus *Acacia*.

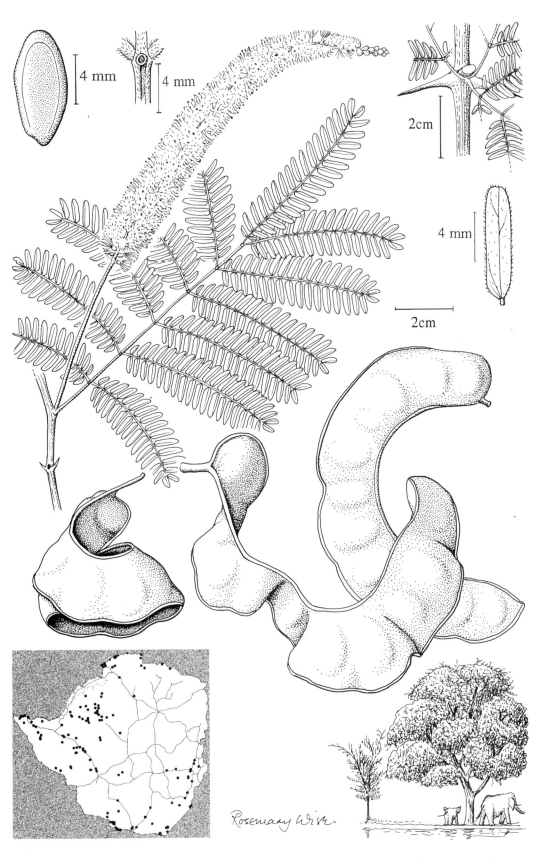

4 mm

4 mm

2cm

4 mm

2cm

Rosemary With

FAIDHERBIA ALBIDA

In eastern and southern Africa two well defined geographical races of *F. albida* are recognized. Race A has glabrous twigs and small leaflets and is found from central Tanzania northwards to Ethiopia, while Race B has pubescent twigs and larger pubescent leaflets and occurs from central Tanzania southwards. However, in West Africa the trees often combine the characters of both races, for instance they have large glabrous leaves, and so the races are not distinguished taxonomically. There also appear to be two distinct ecological groups, with populations from West Africa tending to be very deep-rooted where they occur on the sandy plains, while populations from eastern and southern Africa are shallow-rooted and confined to riverine situations or where there is a high water table. Seedlings from West Africa also develop much more root growth than shoot growth compared with ones from southern Africa. Genetic diversity studies also indicate two major groupings in the species correlated with the above groups, with the highest diversity found in the West African populations. The well-known situation found in West Africa of extensive cropping under *F. albida* is less feasible here, except perhaps with introduced ecotypes.

The sapwood and heartwood are not clearly differentiated, and both have a coarse, even texture with no visible growth rings. The wood is light (540-560 kg/m³), medium-soft and pale, and requires seasoning to prevent splitting. Large trunks were hollowed out by fire to make dugout canoes along the Zambezi River and it has been used as light structural timber, crates, wood wool, etc, but not for outdoor application.

The outstanding attributes of *F. albida* are its nutritious pods and foliage, its soil-improving properties, and its reverse phenology. This allows grain crops to be grown beneath its canopy in the wet season when the tree is leafless and does not cast shade or compete for moisture. The pods are much relished by cattle and wildlife, including elephant who frequently knock against trees to dislodge the fruits. The pods are particularly useful to livestock, not only because of their high protein content but also because they are produced at the very end of the dry season when they are most needed. Fruit quality is said to diminish if there is late wet season rainfall. Some rural people have used the seeds as a famine food although they are reputed to contain prussic acid (cyanide). The seeds are boiled and the skins removed, then boiled again and the water discarded. Large trees possibly produce up to 350

kg of pods in a good season, although quantities vary greatly. An average pod yield is probably 50-160 kg per tree. Other studies suggest an average pod yield per hectare of 300 kg (fresh weight) in a good year.

Bark, roots and powdered pods have been used as a fish poison, and there are various medicinal uses reported from other countries.

Seeds are easy to germinate (suggested treatment is to soak in water for 24 hours) and plants establish readily under frost-free conditions. A deep taproot is formed in the first year. Growth rates are fast in the absence of competition from grasses and, once established, plants are tolerant of cold but not frost. The trees found in the highveld, for example on the Umguza and Khami rivers near Bulawayo, probably established themselves during a series of frost-free years from seed left in the dung of wide-ranging herbivores. The seed is adapted for dispersal by herbivores, being hard and tolerant of the digestive process. Young trees coppice well.

It has been suggested that the reason for its reverse phenology may be that it has become adapted to having its roots saturated with water and effectively asphyxiated during the wet season. The tendency to leaf loss during the rains is certainly less marked on trees growing in drier situations, and the leaf production period is shorter on heavier soils.

There has been much concern expressed in Zimbabwe over low regeneration rates of *Faidherbia* in the Zambezi Valley and over the damage to trees by elephant, particularly along the Mana floodplain. Regeneration is known to be episodic and follows on the occasional creation of bare, open habitats after large floods. Such floods do not occur now since the regulation of catastrophic floods by Kariba Dam, thus extensive new habitats are not being formed. The species is, however, colonizing small sandbanks and the margins of many sandy low altitude rivers. As the present extensive mature stands of *Faidherbia* become senescent and die, it is likely such parklands will become rare in Zimbabwe, but the species itself will probably remain relatively common but local.

The genus is named after a French general, Faidherb, who campaigned in West Africa, although the species was first described from Egypt. The specific name is Latin for "whitish" (*albidus* - whitish) and refers to the pale colour of the stem and thorns.

BOX 1 - SPECIES AND PROVENANCE TRIALS OF AFRICAN ACACIAS

Human progress has been largely the result of success in increasing the production and quality of food, fibre and fuel crops through improved agricultural methods. Genetic improvement, at first through the process of simple selection and later through the science of plant breeding, has been the principal contributor to this success because, unlike the development of cultural methods, the results of selection and breeding can be fixed in each generation and can be accumulated over time. From historical records we know that steady gains have been made in crop plants over many centuries and that the principal domestic species now represent vast improvements over their wild progenitors. There is also sound reason to believe that there is still enough genetic variation left in these species for selection and breeding to make even greater contributions to productivity in the future.

Trees are no different from crop plants and most have just as much plasticity in their genetic make-up. In fact few tree species are more than one or two generations removed from the wild undomesticated state and therefore most contain an immense amount of variation with which to work. This potential has already been shown in breeding programmes for the pines and eucalypts where the value of the crop can be doubled or more in a single generation of selection. The African acacias are important contributors to agricultural production even in their wild state, where they are conspicuous for their resilience under minimal management. It is also known that they are extremely variable over their natural range in all their important traits. They are, therefore, ideal subjects for rapid genetic improvement through modern methods of selection and breeding. This has been recognized by international agencies and national institutions (Armitage *et al.* 1980, Palmberg 1981) and a series of projects has been undertaken to explore, assemble and evaluate the genetic resources of four Africa-wide species, *Acacia nilotica*, *A. senegal*, *A. tortilis* and *Faidherbia albida*, and also of two important southern African species, *A. erioloba* and *A. karroo* (Barnes & Fagg 1995). All these species occur naturally in Zimbabwe.

Under these projects, undertaken by the Oxford Forestry Institute, the distributions within Africa of these six species were comprehensively sampled with seed collected to cover their likely genetic variation as indicated by geography, climate, soils, ecology, phenotype and molecular genotype (Fagg & Barnes 1995). This work was carried out in consultation, cooperation and collaboration with international agencies and national research institutes throughout Africa who have contributed to the unique assembled resource of seed of 141 provenances of the six species. The Zimbabwe Forestry Commission have provided a

centre for the first field trials that have been established over 14 different sites in Matabeleland (Barnes *et al.* 1996), where the acacias play an important part in the rural economy.

Genetic variation both between and within species in the trials has been greater even than expected, that is to say the difference in growth rates and growth patterns between species and provenances at the same site is very great. Likewise, the interaction of the seed source with environment is very variable, i.e. the comparative performance of the different seedlots varies with site (rainfall, soil, altitude, etc.). One of the most crucial factors in the Matabeleland trials has been frost which has had a severe affect on most provenances from the lower-lying and more tropical parts of Africa. Nevertheless, there has been surprisingly rapid growth among the best performers. It has also become apparent that trees are affected by competition with each other, and with grasses and weeds, from an early age and that growth potential can only be realized if wide spacings are used and clean weeding practised. At three years from planting, the largest trees in the trials are three to four metres tall on the better sites. Where frost has been present, it is generally the southern African sources that have performed best, as would be expected because they have evolved in frosty winters. Among the best overall performers so far under these conditions have been the Chivu (Zimbabwe) provenance of *A. nilotica* subsp. *kraussiana*, the Maun (Botswana) *A. tortilis* subsp. *heteracantha*, the Devure (Zimbabwe) *A. tortilis* subsp. *spirocarpa* and the Jedibe Island (Okavango, Botswana) *A. karroo*. A close negative correlation between performance and latitude of seed source is seen with the frost-resistant *A. erioloba*, with the best performers coming from Zambia and the worst from the northern Cape Province of South Africa. The high altitude provenances of *F. albida* from Ethiopia have done best on the cold sites whereas some of the local provenances of this species, such as Gonarezhou (Zimbabwe) and Kapula (Zimbabwe), have done best where there is no frost.

A great deal of information is coming from these trials and over the next ten years it will be possible to make increasingly precise recommendations on which provenance of which species should be planted in which agricultural niche and in which environment in order to provide a particular product or service. The trials also provide an opportunity to determine which characters of interest are under most genetic control and therefore how to select most effectively when carrying out improvement thinnings in natural stands. The next step will be to devise methods to integrate the superior genetic material from selected trees within the best populations into existing agricultural systems.

2

ACACIA ABYSSINICA *Benth.*

Common names: Nyanga flat-top

The table-like flat tops of *Acacia abyssinica*, especially when they occur in groves on mountain footslopes, are one of the typical sights of the Eastern Highlands.

Description *A. abyssinica* is a conspicuously flat-topped tree up to 10-16 m tall, usually with more than one main stem. **Bark** of young trees is pale yellowish-brown, peeling off easily in papery wads like the pages of a book; turning brown to nearly black, rough and fissured in older trees. **Young twigs** are covered with grey to yellowish hairs. **Thorns** are paired at the nodes, straight and variable in size up to 7 cm long, whitish or grey in colour. Older specimens can be practically thornless. **Leaves** are long (8-10 cm) with 20-40 pinnae pairs, each bearing many, closely-spaced and very small leaflets. **Inflorescence** is an axillary cluster of white globose heads, reddish in bud, appearing from October to December. They can occur singly or in clusters and are concentrated towards the ends of the twigs on both current and previous seasons' growth. **Pods** are dehiscent, straight or slightly curved, grey to brown and leathery in texture with longitudinally wavy striations, ripening from February to June.

Field characters Flat-topped canopy; thick, pale, papery bark; many pinnae and very small leaflets; at edge of gullies and at bases of hills at high altitudes.

Dried specimens can be confused with *Acacia rehmanniana* or *A. sieberiana*, but in the field the typical growth form and distinctive flat crown, the more yellowish peeling bark, and the leathery, not woody, pods of *A. abyssinica* should help to distinguish it. *A. sieberiana* nearly always has fewer than 20 pairs of pinnae and larger leaflets (3-4 mm long), although there is some overlap between the two. Leaves and pods of *A. rehmanniana* are very similar to those of *A. abyssinica*, however the mature leaves of *A. abyssinica* are generally longer (around 8-10 cm long) than those of *A. rehmanniana* (6-8 cm long), the young growth of *A. rehmanniana* is much more densely and velvety pubescent, the flowers are in terminal clusters, and the bark is distinctively red-brown, not yellowish as in *A. abyssinica*. The major ecological differences are the distribution (*A. abyssinica* is found only above 1500 m and *A. rehmanniana* below this) and habitat – *A. abyssinica* is confined to gravelly or well-drained slopes.

Distribution and ecology *A. abyssinica* is a true Afromontane species and is found from Ethiopia southwards through Kenya, Uganda and Tanzania to Malawi, eastern Zimbabwe and central and northern Mozambique; it is not found in South Africa or Zambia. The species is associated mostly with the Eastern Arc mountains and the East African Rift Valley. In Zimbabwe it is confined to montane situations above 1500 m altitude in the Nyanga, Mutare, Vumba and Chimanimani areas.

A. abyssinica is found in montane grassland and open woodland often at the edge of wooded gullies, but rarely in dense woodland or forest. It is locally common but with a disjunct distribution. The species appears to colonize old land slips and coarse colluvial soils such as screes at the base of hill slopes. It normally occurs in groups and not as isolated individuals.

Notes Previously the species was divided into two subspecies – subsp. *calophylla* Brenan with smaller, more closely-set pinnae – and subsp. *abyssinica,* which is confined to Ethiopia. Recently, this subspecific distinction has been shown to be untenable and no difference is now recognized.

The occurrence of the species in apparently even-aged stands with little regeneration underneath suggests that establishment is episodic, possibly following an event such as land slippage.

The larvae of the butterflies *Azanzus* *natalensis, Uranothauma nubifer* and *Triclema nigeriae* breed on the foliage.

Because of its arresting shape, light shade and the favourable environment it creates for other plants to grow under its canopy, this tree has become popular in gardens. Although reputedly slow growing, it is widely grown in Harare where its growth rate can be more than 1 m per year.

The specific name refers to the country Ethiopia, formerly Abyssinia, from where the species was first described.

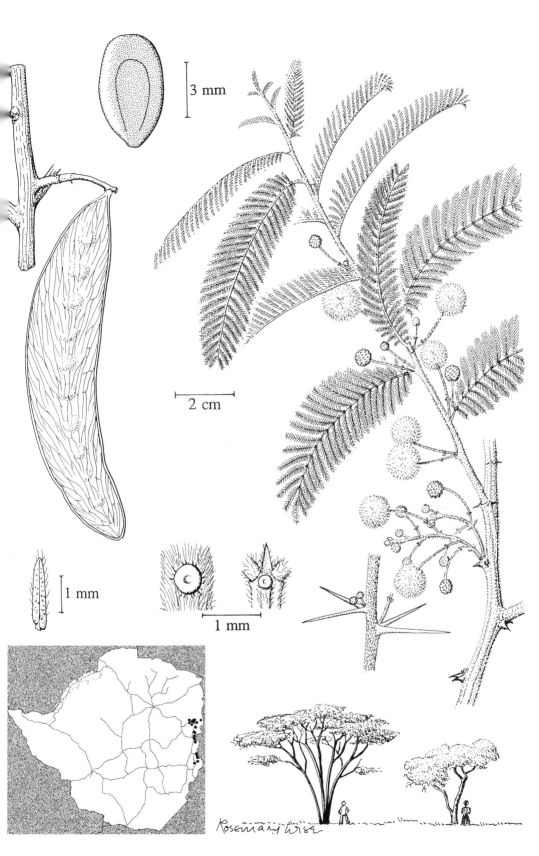

ACACIA ABYSSINICA

3

ACACIA ADENOCALYX *Brenan & Exell*

Common name: pfurura (Shona-Pfungwe)

Acacia adenocalyx, a rather nondescript scrambling shrub, is known only from one area in Zimbabwe. It is normally associated with lowland and coastal areas in East Africa, but may well be found in other rocky gullies in the lower Mazowe valley area.

Description *A. adenocalyx* is a scrambling shrub up to 10 m high, often climbing trees. **Stems** are slender and often characteristically coiled to aid climbing, unlike any other *Acacia* in Zimbabwe except *A. pentagona*. **Young twigs** are pale brown with many conspicuous whitish pustular lenticels and are often coiled at the ends to grasp the branches of supporting trees. They are covered in very short brownish hairs with scattered small brown glands. **Leaves** are moderately large with 8-16 pairs of pinnae, each with many small leaflets. **Thorns** are small, hooked and scattered along the stem, arising from darker epidermal bands. **Inflorescence** is a terminal panicle of white globose heads appearing on young growth. **Pods** are dehiscent, broad, oblong and stiffly papery, with raised margins. They are covered with many minute brown glands and are sometimes slightly pubescent.

Field characters Climbing shrub; scattered thorns; blackish brown twigs; brown glands on twigs and pods; short petiole; only found in thickets in Pfungwe.

A. adenocalyx looks like *A. schweinfurthii*, but is generally more delicate in appearance with darker, slender stems covered in small lenticels, smaller thorns, shorter petioles with only a small gland at the base and discolorous non-pubescent leaflets.

Distribution and ecology *A. adenocalyx* is a species of the East African coastal belt bushlands and thickets, occurring from southern Kenya to central Mozambique. In Zimbabwe it is known only from two gullies among gneiss boulders at the base of Chibvudza Hill near the Nyandire bridge in Pfungwe communal land, Rushinga, at an altitude of 650 m. The Zimbabwe and central Mozambique locations are outside its normal range. Very little is known of its ecology or distribution here, where it is found in thickets.

Notes The species forms part of the aberrant "*A. pennata*" complex (see Box 6, page 92), the only acacias that are reported not to nodulate. The affiliations of the group appear to be to moist forests and coastal thickets rather than to the dry savannas.

There are no recorded uses.

The specific name is derived from the Greek and means glandular calyx (*adeno* - gland; *kalyx*- calyx).

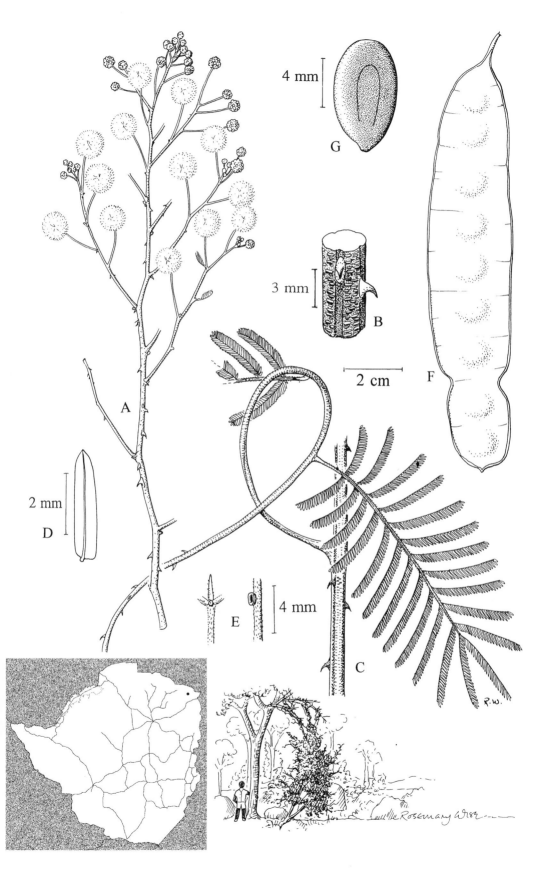

G

4 mm

3 mm

B

2 cm

F

2 mm

D

E

4 mm

C

A

ACACIA ADENOCALYX

4

ACACIA AMYTHETHOPHYLLA *A. Rich.*
(= *A. buchananii* Harms, *A. macrothyrsa* Harms)

Common names: large-leaved acacia; umtsungadzi (Ndebele); chitatsunga, chiungatsikidzi, mumengami, mutandanyoka (Shona)

A leafy, green shrub or small tree found in moderately high rainfall areas, *Acacia amythethopylla* is rather unlike most other acacias. The terminal panicles of golden-yellow flowers are very distinctive.

Description *A. amythethophylla* is a bushy shrub to small tree up to 7 m high with a rounded crown. The stem diameter can reach 30 cm. **Bark** is dark grey to almost black, rough with longitudinal and horizontal fissures. **Young twigs** are glabrous, brown to grey-brown, smooth at first but developing a roughness with age. **Thorns** are straight but short and flattened, the stipular origin being fairly clear, dark coloured and inconspicuous giving the impression of a thornless tree. **Leaves** are large (15-30 cm long), the largest of all Zimbabwe acacias, with 7-14 pairs of pinnae each with many medium-sized leaflets. There is an elongated gland above the pulvinus. Although retaining leaves for much of the year, plants are generally leafless towards the end of the dry season. **Inflorescence** is a terminal, much-branched panicle of many, golden- to orange-yellow sweetly scented globose heads. These appear on new growth later than most acacias in January-March. Flower heads are often galled. **Pods** are leathery, flat, straight and oblong, up to 20 cm long. They are dehiscent and mature around May-July, when they are often seen hanging in clusters from the branch ends.

Field characters Small tree or shrub; large broad leaves with many pinnae and leaflets; inconspicuous flattened thorns; conspicuous terminal panicles of golden-yellow flowers.

Although common, shrubs often occur singly and are inconspicuous until they produce their golden-yellow flowers in the latter part of the rainy season. It is unlikely to be easily confused with other species of *Acacia* but, at a distance, can be mistaken in habit for *Peltophorum africanum*. However, *Peltophorum* is thornless, has fewer and larger, more rounded leaflets, and large, showy yellow petals. The pods are also much smaller and ellipsoid in shape.

Distribution and ecology *A. amythethophylla* is widespread from West Africa to southern Sudan and Ethiopia and southwards to Angola, Zambia, Zimbabwe, Malawi and Mozambique. Within Zimbabwe it is found in the wetter parts of the highveld north and east of Gweru above an altitude of around 1000 m. It is a constituent of some types of miombo woodland, and is commonly associated with *Brachystegia boehmii* and *B. spiciformis*. *A. amythethophylla* occurs on relatively nutrient-poor soils in stony or rocky areas, possibly under frost-free conditions.

Notes Until recently, the name *A. amythethophylla* was used for a variant (found only in Ethiopia and Angola) that lacked the large panicled inflorescences of *A. macrothyrsa* (found from West Africa, across to Sudan and down to Zimbabwe and Mozambique). However, in 1979 the two species were combined and the older name, *A. amythethophylla*, was retained.

The wood is not well known but said to be of exceptional beauty. However, owing to the small size of the bole, possibly due to fire damage, very little is available. The sapwood is a pinky-white contrasted with a heartwood that is a dark red-brown with orange streaks. The heartwood is very heavy (1170 kg/m³), strong and durable, but the proportion is small and therefore it is useful only for carving, turnery and inlay work.

An infusion of the roots is used by some Shona traditional healers against convulsions, snake bite and female infertility. It has also been used to wash the body as a cure for madness. The larvae of some species of *Charaxes* butterfly are said to feed on the foliage, although this has not yet been noted in Zimbabwe.

The species is readily grown from seed, is fast growing and frost-resistant.

The specific name comes from the Greek (*amuthos* - without words or countless, *phyllon* - leaf) and refers to the large number of leaflets. The previous name, macrothyrsa, comes from the Greek (*makros* - large, *thyrsos* - wand), and refers to the large panicles of conspicuous flowers.

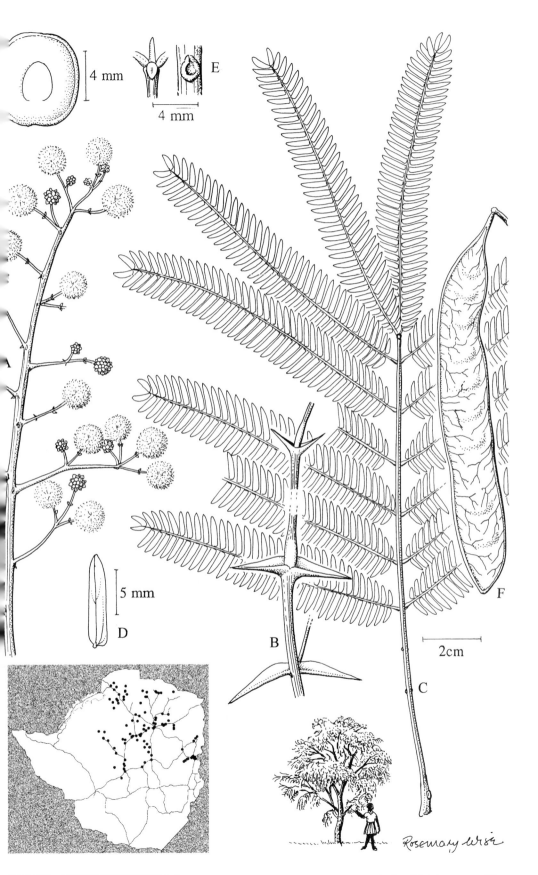

E

4 mm

4 mm

5 mm

D

B

C

2cm

F

Rosemary Wise

ACACIA AMYTHETHOPHYLLA

ACACIA ARENARIA *Schinz*
(= *A. hermannii* Baker f.)

Common names: sand acacia; sanddoring (Afrikaans); ivikani (Ndebele)

A low spreading shrub with large leaves like ostrich feathers, *Acacia arenaria* is often seen invading roadsides and old fields on red clay soils in Matabeleland.

Description *A. arenaria* is an obconical shrub up to 2 m high, multi-stemmed from the base with ascending spreading branches; rarely a small tree. **Bark** is grey, sometimes grey-brown or almost black, usually smooth, and has a greenish inner layer. **Young twigs** are pale grey, brown to reddish brown, longitudinally striated and sparingly pubescent. They are generally zig-zag in shape. **Thorns** are in pairs at the node, straight, slender, widely divergent, each pair arranged at right angles to the pair before, pale coloured and up to 7 cm long. **Leaves** are feathery, tapering and up to 20 cm long, with a very short petiole and 15-35 pairs of pinnae. There is a raised gland at the base of the petiole. **Inflorescence** is a series of axillary white globose heads on short peduncles, appearing on the current season's growth from December-February. The inflorescences are clustered towards the tips of the growing shoots so as to appear almost terminal. **Pods** are narrow and dehiscent, curved through 90° and slightly constricted between the seeds The valves are pale to deep reddish brown in colour, glabrous to slightly pubescent and glandular. They are often found clustered on the shrub for many months.

Field characters Low shrub with ascending shoots; slender shoots zig-zag in shape; long divergent slender thorns; large feathery tapering leaves; long slender curved pods.

Distribution and ecology *A. arenaria* is found in southern Angola, Namibia, northern Botswana and western Zimbabwe, but is surprisingly absent from Zambia. There are outlying populations in central Tanzania with a gap between these populations and those in southern Africa. In Zimbabwe it is found from Bulawayo (including urban areas) and Inyati west towards Botswana, mostly at an altitude of 1000-1200 m, with only a few outliers on the Kalahari sands. Despite its name, it is usually found in previously cleared or disturbed areas on red clay soils derived from metavolcanic rocks of the goldbelt, but is also recorded from vlei margins. It is unusual here to see it on particularly sandy soils, its preferred habitat in Botswana. *A. arenaria* is often seen in stands by roadsides and can be quite gregarious. It generally occurs in association with other *Acacia* species.

Notes There is evidence that *A. arenaria* is spreading on bare soils in Matabeleland; in many respects it behaves as a pioneer and is often an indicator of previous disturbance and soil erosion. It is said to live for only about 15 years.

No particular uses have been recorded for this species. Goats relish the flowers, which are generally within their reach, and pick the flower heads from between the long sharp thorns.

The specific name is Latin for growing on sand (*harena* - sand), its typical habitat in Botswana, although not in Zimbabwe.

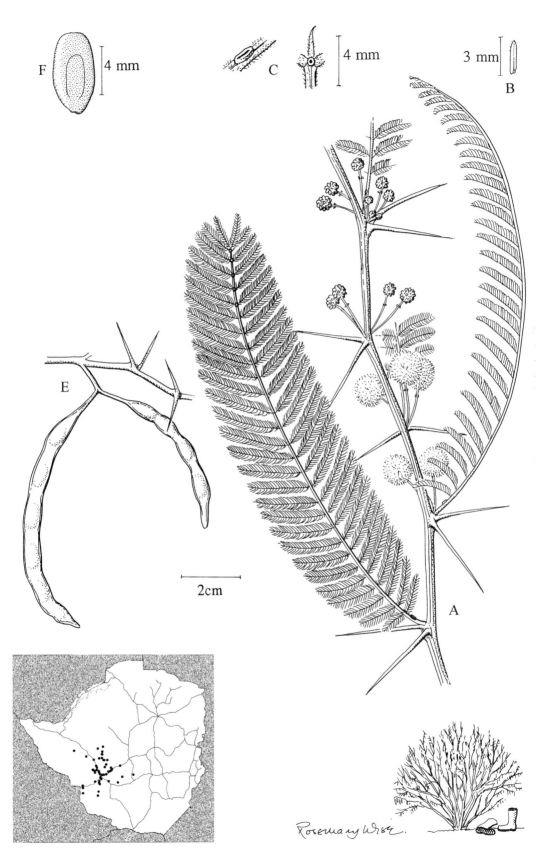

F

4 mm

C

4 mm

3 mm

B

E

2cm

A

Rosemary Wise.

ACACIA ARENARIA

6

ACACIA ATAXACANTHA *DC.*

(= *A. lugardiae* N.E. Br., *A. senegal* sensu Wild 1952)

Common names: flame acacia; vlamdoring (Afrikaans); ulutatu, umbambangwe, umqaqawe, uthathawu (Ndebele); kato (Shangaan); muchanga, mugowa, mukakanyuro, mukombonkunono, mukomborakombora, musavamhanga, rukato (Shona); lubamfwe, mugowa konono, mukobonkunono (Tonga).

An untidy scrambling bush with scattered thorns, *Acacia ataxacantha* often forms thickets on sandy soils in the west and far north of the country.

Description *A. ataxacantha* is a multi-stemmed shrub up to 3-5 m in height, often scrambling, and occasionally a small tree with a stem diameter up to 10 cm. It is generally lax and rather formless in shape. **Bark** is grey to dark grey, sometimes with a brownish tinge. **Young twigs** are brown and finely hairy with darker longitudinal striations. Older growth is grey to pale grey. **Thorns** are hooked, dark brown, up to 0.8 cm long and scattered along the stems and leaf rachis. **Leaves** are medium to large in size (5-12 x 3-6 cm wide) with 8-15 pairs of pinnae. A stalked gland is present at the base of the petiole. Two leaf-like stipules, which soon fall, can also be found at the leaf base. **Inflorescence** is a long axillary spike, or clusters of spikes, of cream white flowers appearing on new growth from December to March, often clustered towards the end of shoots. **Pods** are reddish to red-brown, straight, slender and papery. They are brittle and early dehiscent.

Field characters Scrambling shrub; scattered hooked thorns; stalked gland on petiole; reddish papery pods.

A. ataxacantha can be confused with *A. schweinfurthii*, also a scrambler. However, *A. ataxacantha* has smaller leaves, a stalked gland at the base of the short petiole, flowers in spikes, and the pods are smaller and pointed. It is also more commonly found on sand or rocky soils, while *A. schweinfurthii* is a riverine species. *A. chariessa*, *A. hereroensis* and *A. adenocalyx* have similarities to *A. ataxacantha*, but the combination of scattered thorns and the stalked petiolar gland should help distinguish it.

Distribution and ecology *A. ataxacantha* is widespread in tropical and subtropical Africa from Senegal in the west to Sudan in the northeast and southwards to Namibia, the former Transvaal and KwaZulu-Natal. There is an apparent disjunction in Tanzania and eastern Zambia. In Zimbabwe it is a species of drier areas, being particularly widespread in Matabeleland below 1200 m, where it is locally common on Kalahari and similar sands. It is also found in the Zambezi Valley and occasionally in the south-eastern lowveld, where it is confined to riverine areas. *A. ataxacantha* has a tendency to form thickets, particularly in areas of disturbance, and is typical of the margins of jesse bush and dry forest. It may have a preference for acidic soils. In Kalahari sand woodlands it is found on the redder sands higher up the catena, and not on the pale sands.

Notes Although stems are quite thin, the wood is said to be heavy (930 kg/m³) with good durability, but is prone to splitting. The sapwood is wide and creamy white while the heartwood is deep brown red. It is said to be resistant to decay owing to gum deposits. Because of the small size of the stems it is used only for tool and implement handles and baskets.

A. ataxacantha was planted in parts of northern Zimbabwe as an effective barrier along drainage lines during the liberation war, where it still persists. In Hwange National Park it is killed back by severe frosts, but often sprouts again from the base in the following season.

The roots are used by some Shona traditional healers against constipation, abdominal pains and to protect infants from witchcraft. The leaves are moderately high in crude protein (14-20%, figures from Hwange National Park), and are larval food for the butterfly *Charaxes zoolina*.

The specific name comes from the Greek for "unarranged thorns" (*taxis* - arrangement, *akantha* - thorns), referring to the scattered thorns.

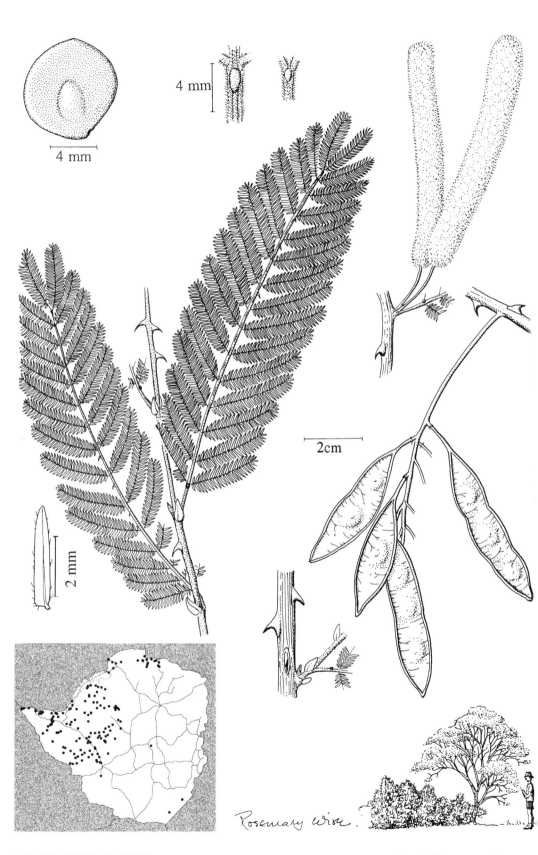

4 mm

4 mm

2cm

2 mm

Rosemary Wise.

ACACIA ATAXACANTHA

7

ACACIA BORLEAE *Burtt Davy*

Common name: sticky acacia

Acacia borleae is a small shrub, showy when in flower and with wavy-margined pods, found on black clay soils in the far south of the country.

Description *A. borleae* is a small shrub from 1 to 3 m in height with many slender stems from the base. **Bark** is grey and sometimes peeling, with a greenish underbark. **Young twigs** are green, somewhat shiny, often reddish tinged, and with many small sticky pustular red glands. **Thorns** are long, white, slender and straight, and paired at the nodes; on young growth they can be up to 7 cm long. **Leaves** are medium-sized (to 6 cm long), often clustered, with 2-10 pairs of pinnae, each with bright yellowish green leaflets with a rounded tip. The leaflets have small glands on the surface and margins giving a crenulate appearance, particularly when dry. **Inflorescence** is an axillary cluster of attractive bright yellow globose flowers appearing on young growth from December to March. **Pods** are small (to 8 cm long), dehiscent, curved, sometimes almost forming a circle, constricted between the seeds, and turning grey-brown at maturity. They are covered in small sticky reddish glands.

Field characters Sticky young growth; up to 10 pairs of pinnae; crenulate margins to leaflets; curved glandular pods with constricted margins.

An attractive and easily noted species when flowering, it can be confused with *A. nebrownii* and other glandular species. However, the glandular leaflets, crenulate leaf margins, leaflets without a mucronate tip, more pairs of pinnae and habitat clearly differentiate it.

Distribution and ecology *A. borleae* is one of the shrubby glandular species (see Box 4, page 79) found at lower altitudes from Botswana through the former northern Transvaal and southern Zimbabwe to southern Mozambique, Swaziland and KwaZulu-Natal, and is always associated with basalt or similar extrusive rocks. In Zimbabwe it is locally common on basalt-derived black clays below 600 m altitude from Tuli east to Gonarezhou and up the lower Save Valley to Chisambanje, often with shrub mopane. An isolated population has been found on black clay soils in the Sengwa Research Area in western Gokwe – it is not clear if this is an introduction. *A. borleae* is a good indicator of deeper basalt soils, but is also found on black montmorillonitic clays of alluvial origin. In some black clay areas it is common on roadsides and in fallow fields, where it forms small thickets.

Notes Named after the botanist Jeanne Borle who collected the type specimen near Maputo.

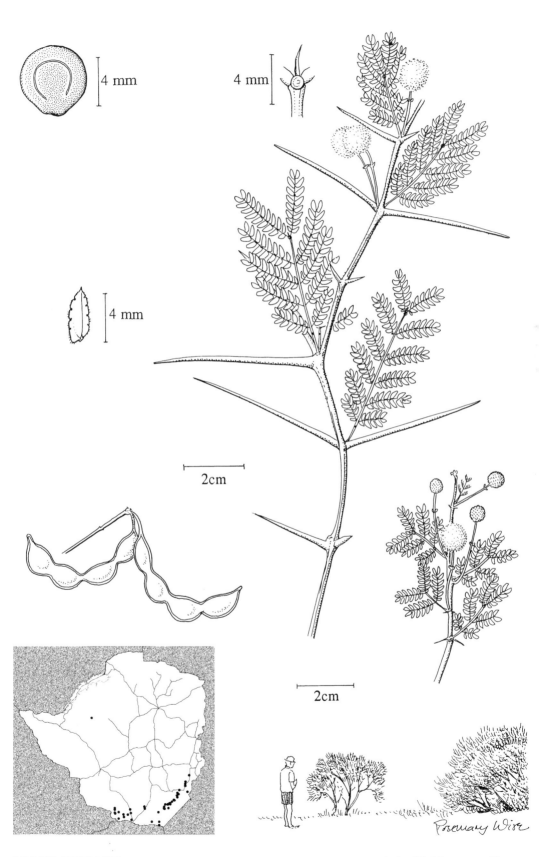

ACACIA BORLEAE

8

ACACIA BURKEI *Benth.*

Common names: black monkey thorn; mukaya (Shangaan)

Acacia burkei is not an easily recognized tree, appearing very similar to both *A. nigrescens* and *A. goetzei*. It is confined to sandy soils in the Gonarezhou area of the southeastern lowveld.

Description *A. burkei* is a medium-sized tree to 10 m with a rather narrow crown. **Bark** is grey-brown, deeply fissured and flaking, with a yellowish tinge underneath. **Young twigs** are greyish-brown, sometimes pubescent, and with orange or white pustular lenticels. **Thorns** are paired at the nodes and strongly hooked, brown to blackish, often persisting on the trunk. **Leaves** are medium-sized (4-10 cm long) with 3-5 pairs of pinnae, each with a few pairs of rounded grey-green leaflets, much smaller than those of *A. nigrescens*. The rachis is pubescent and often has scattered thorns. **Inflorescence** is spicate and white, produced on new or old wood with the leaves in October-November or earlier. **Pods** are medium sized (8-12 cm long), straight, apiculate, black-brown in colour and dehiscent.

Field characters Hook thorns on knobs; many rounded leaflets; hairy calyx; sandy soils.

In many aspects *A. burkei* is similar to *A. nigrescens*, but it has more and smaller leaflets, the bark has a yellowish tinge, it comes into flower with the leaves, and the flowers have a hairy calyx. *A. burkei* generally has more leaflets than *A. welwitschii*, and both leaflets and rachis are pubescent. The habitat is also quite different, although in appearance from a distance they can be easily confused. It is often very similar to *A. goetzei* but differs in always having a pubescent leaf rachis, narrower pods, and a pubescent calyx. Their distributions are not known to overlap in Zimbabwe.

Distribution and ecology *A. burkei* is a southern African species found in KwaZulu-Natal, Swaziland and the former eastern Transvaal north and westwards to southern Zimbabwe, central Mozambique and southeast Botswana. In Zimbabwe it has not been much collected and is apparently very local, confined to Cretaceous sandy soils, often with *Terminalia sericea* and *Guibourtia conjugata*, in the Gonarezhou area of the southeast lowveld. The habitat of *A. burkei* is distinct from that of *A. nigrescens* which often occurs nearby, as it is invariably on sandy, not loamy, soils.

Notes *A. burkei* is part of the confusing *A.nigrescens–A.goetzei–A.burkei–A.welwitschii* complex. It does not appear to be a particularly well-defined species (see *A. goetzei*) and is possibly derived from *A. nigrescens*, although its ecology is somewhat different. In KwaZulu-Natal *A. burkei* is particularly variable with "big leaflet" and "small leaflet" forms; all Zimbabwe specimens appear to be of the "big leaflet" form.

The wood is very hard and heavy (900 kg/m³) and yellow-brown in colour. It is difficult to work but has been used in South Africa for furniture and household items. There it has a reputation of being similar to the wood of *A. galpinii*, but slightly denser. It is reportedly a slow-growing and cold-sensitive species.

The emperor moths *Heniocha dyops* and *H. marnois* feed on the foliage of *A. burkei* and some other *Acacia* species.

The specific name is derived from the botanist Burke, who collected the type specimen in the Magaliesberg range in northern South Africa.

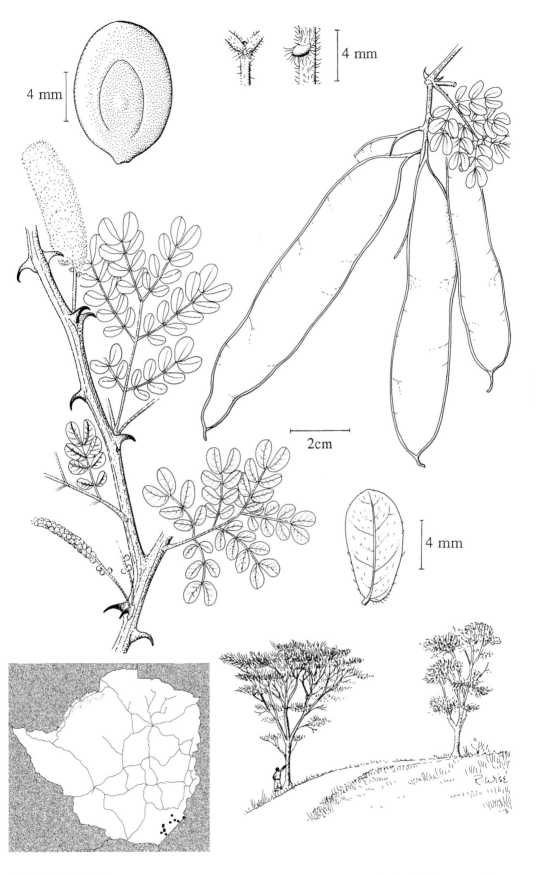

ACACIA BURKEI

9

ACACIA CAFFRA *(Thunb.) Willd.*

The one known population of *Acacia caffra* in Zimbabwe, at what was maybe an old outspan site near Harare, has probably arisen from an introduction many years ago. The tall, narrow-crowned tree is not readily separated from some other Zimbabwe species at first glance.

Description In Zimbabwe *A. caffra* is a shrub or tall thin tree to 14 m in height, with a crooked stem and shapeless narrow crown. **Bark** is greyish and fissured. **Young twigs** are red-brown with longitudinal grey striations. **Thorns** are large, hooked and mostly in pairs below the nodes, although a few can be found scattered along the stem. Thorns also persist on the branches. **Leaves** are large (15-20 x 6 cm) with 10-20 pairs of pinnae. The moderately long petiole (1.5-3 cm) has a petiolar gland near the first pair of pinnae. **Inflorescence** is a spike of creamy white flowers clustered at the junction of the previous and current seasons' growth, appearing early in the season in September-October, or as early as July. The dehiscent **pods** are brown and straight, often with constricted margins and small red glands.

Field characters Only known from Harare; paired hooked thorns with occasional scattered thorns; large drooping leaves.

Elsewhere in its range *A. caffra* has been confused with both *A. hereroensis* and *A. ataxacantha*. It differs from *A. ataxacantha* in the thorns, which are nearly always paired, not scattered. *A. hereroensis* has smaller leaves and shorter petioles, and the larger leaves of *A. caffra* tend to droop. Owing to restricted geographic distributions in Zimbabwe, they are unlikely to be confused here.

Distribution and ecology *A. caffra* is a southern African species, only found in southeast Botswana, the northern and eastern parts of South Africa, the eastern Cape, and in southern Mozambique, with an isolated population in Zimbabwe. This latter, aberrant, population is from a vlei margin at Tynwald on the western outskirts of Harare. The location, now a construction camp, is said to be an old outspan site dating from ox-wagon transport days, and it has been suggested that *A. caffra* is an introduction dating from then. If so, the population, which is regenerating but confined to only tens of individuals and a small area, has persisted for almost a century. There is a further, unlikely and as yet unconfirmed, report of *A. caffra* occurring on Hwedza Mountain south of Marondera (Robertson 1991). The Harare population is found on clay loam soils; outside of Zimbabwe it is a species of open woodland on rocky hills and dry river valley bush.

Notes In South Africa *A. caffra* is a very variable species. The form found in Harare is more robust than normal, with larger leaflets and broader pods, and corresponds to the form found in the Rustenburg-Waterberg area of northern South Africa. This lends credence to the suggestion that it was brought in from there on ox-wagons in the early part of the century. *A. caffra* is considered to be very closely related to *A. hereroensis*, although they can be distinguished where they grow together in northern South Africa. They may eventually be combined.

Not surprisingly, there are no uses recorded from Zimbabwe. But in South Africa the wood is heavy (980-1060 kg/m^3) and hard, with dark brown heartwood and off-white sapwood. The texture is medium to slightly coarse, and the wood seasons without defects. It is used there for fencing poles and firewood, and is said to be good for ornamental work. The foliage and pods are considered good fodder for livestock and wildlife.

The species is said to grow fairly fast and to be cold resistant. It coppices well. The trees in Harare are probably over 50 years old and are still sound.

It is thought the specific name comes from Kaffraria, a former name for part of the Eastern Cape Province in South Africa.

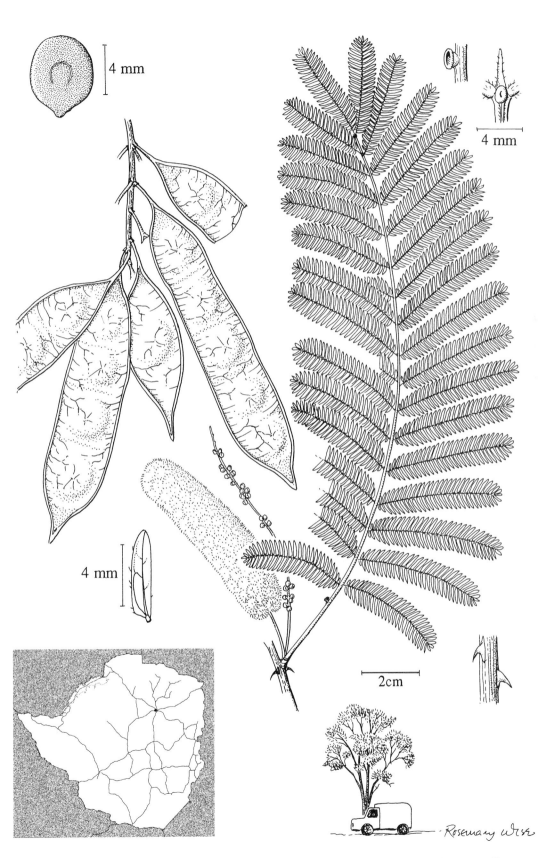

ACACIA CAFFRA

10

ACACIA CHARIESSA *Milne-Redh.*

Common names: ulutatau (Ndebele)

A low, slender shrub with ankle-grabbing hooked thorns, *Acacia chariessa* is endemic to Zimbabwe and is found only on soils from some rock types of the Basement Complex in the central part of the country.

Description *A. chariessa* is a low, spreading or sub-erect shrub 0.3-1.5 m in height with slender shoots; much more slender than normal *Acacia* shrubs. **Young twigs** are glabrous and purplish-brown. The very small, hooked **thorns**, sometimes almost straight, are not paired but scattered along the shoots. **Leaves** are small (2-4 cm long) with 4-8 pairs of pinnae, each with many small grey-green leaflets which do not persist into the dry season. **Inflorescences** are axillary, short cream-white spikes appearing on young growth around December to February. The small (4-5 cm), thin, papery **pods** are dehiscent, purplish to red-brown in colour, oblong to oval with a pointed tip, and have a long stalk.

Field characters Small shrub, almost a woody herb; small scattered thorns; glabrous shoots; small thin papery pods.

The species is unlikely to be confused with others owing to its small size, although superficially it looks like a small *A. ataxacantha*.

Distribution and ecology *A. chariessa* is endemic to Zimbabwe. It is found on a range of substrates derived from schistose goldbelt rocks on the central watershed from Mvuma to Bulawayo at altitudes of over 1000 m. Although reported to be confined to serpentine and pyroxenite soils (indeed it is sometimes termed the "Dyke Acacia"), it also occurs on other soil types. The normal habitat is open bushland or low woodland on rocky shallow soils, often with *Combretum* or other *Acacia* species. It is normally only noticed when in flower or when the small thorns catch the ankles or lower leg. The species is often recorded from open disturbed sites such as those associated with road construction, and it would appear to be shaded out in more mature vegetation. It may also be encouraged by fire.

Notes *A. chariessa* was first described in 1933 from a specimen collected in Bulawayo. In some early publications from Zimbabwe it was mistakenly called *A. verek* Guill. & Perr., a synonym of *A. senegal*.

An infusion of the roots is said to have been used by some Ndebele traditional healers for blood purification and to protect newly-born children against disease.

The specific name comes from the Greek and means "graceful" or "elegant".

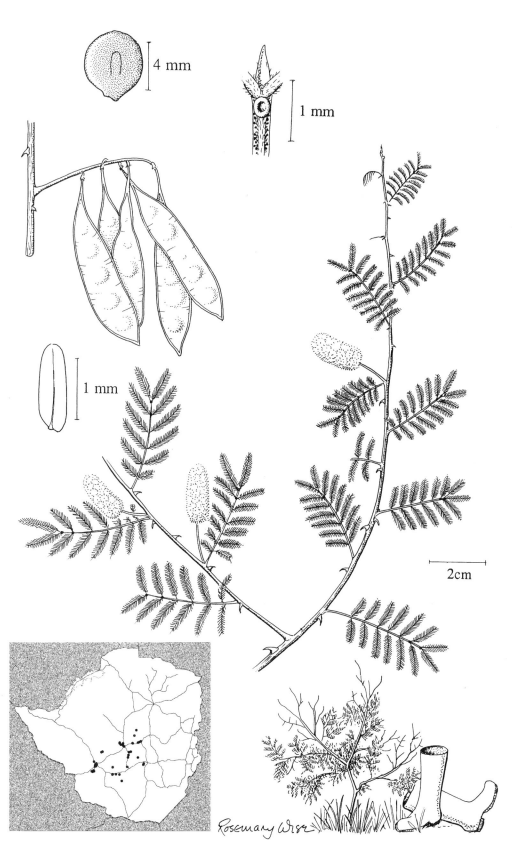

ACACIA CHARIESSA

11

ACACIA ERIOCARPA *Brenan*

Common names: woolly-podded acacia

Acacia eriocarpa is a distinctive straggly shrub only found in the Zambezi Valley, where it occurs in shrubland or thickets on loose sandy soils. The large leaves and leaflets and the hairy pods help to distinguish it.

Description *A. eriocarpa* is a shrub or small, usually multi-stemmed, tree 2-4 m high, sometimes a scrambling shrub. The **stem** is light grey. **Young twigs** are softly yellow- to grey-velvety pubescent, but lose these hairs with age, and have distinctive pustular lenticels; they break easily. The medium-sized **thorns** are hooked and scattered along the stems, including the main stem and on the leaf rachis. **Leaves** are large (10-16 cm long) with 4-7 pairs of pinnae, each with many large, grey-green, softly pubescent rounded leaflets, much darker above than below. There are large foliar stipules on the young growth and a prominent flattened petiolar gland near the base. **Inflorescences** are axillary spikes of white flowers appearing on new growth around December to February. **Pods** are dehiscent, densely hairy and yellow-brown in colour. They are moderately large (6-12 cm long), broad and linear-oblong in shape, and have thickened margins; many are often clustered together.

Field characters Scattered hooked thorns; large pubescent leaflets; large foliar stipules; hairy pods; found in jesse bush in the Zambezi Valley. Significantly different in appearance from other scattered-thorn acacias, thus unlikely to be confused with them.

Distribution and ecology *A. eriocarpa* is confined to the middle sections of the Zambezi Valley and its major tributaries below about 900 m altitude, and is recorded from northern Zimbabwe, southeastern Zambia and the Tete area of Mozambique. In Zimbabwe it occurs from Hwange and Gwayi River through Binga and Omay to Dande. It is generally found on unconsolidated sandy deposits, often colluvial in origin and possibly acidic, and also on rocky soils derived from Upper Hwange Sandstone. Where these sand areas are relatively extensive, as in northern Dande, *A. eriocarpa* is a typical constituent of the vegetation, but it is generally localized in its distribution. It can form thickets in places. The species can be regarded as a typical element of some types of "jesse bush", a dense woodland or thicket vegetation type that is more open than true dry layered forest. Typical associates include *Terminalia brachystemma* and *Combretum* species. Unlike most acacias, *A. eriocarpa* seems to require acid soils.

Notes The species was first described in 1957 from a specimen collected near Chirundu.

It is a shallow-rooted species, as are many in jesse bush, and in drought periods it appears to be prone to terminal dieback of the shoots.

The specific name is Greek for "woolly fruit" (*erion* - wool, *karpos* - fruit).

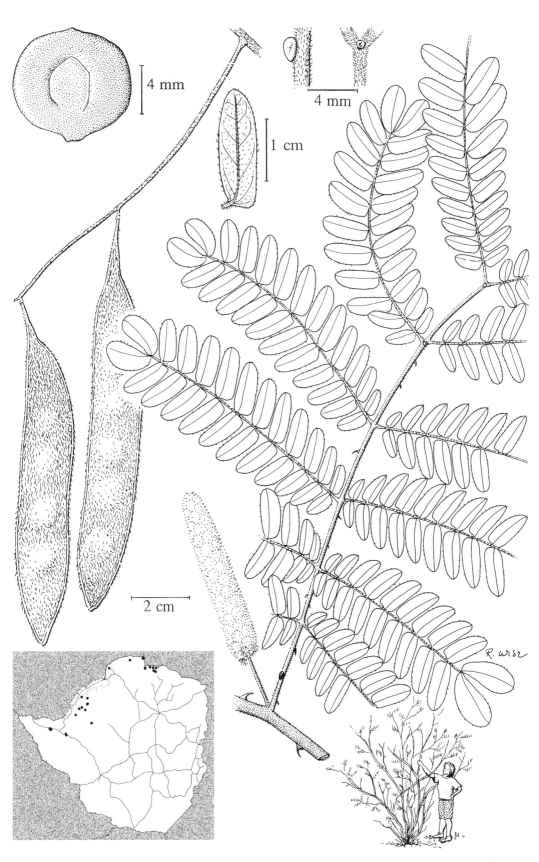

4 mm

1 cm

4 mm

2 cm

R. WISE

ACACIA ERIOCARPA

12

ACACIA ERIOLOBA *E. Mey.*
(= *A. giraffae* Willd. [*A. erioloba* x *A. haematoxylon*])

Common names: camel thorn, giraffe thorn; kameeldoring (Afr); umwhohlo (Ndebele)

When mature, *Acacia erioloba* is a majestic tree of the Kalahari sands of western Zimbabwe. The large, grey-hairy, kidney-shaped pods are greatly relished by both game and livestock.

Description *A. erioloba* is a large spreading tree with a broad crown, generally 8-12 m high and with drooping branches; one of the largest *Acacia* species in Zimbabwe when mature. **Bark** is rough, blackish and fissured. Trunks can exceed 100 cm diameter, but most large specimens are around 60-80 cm. A shrub or sucker form, looking a bit like a chanterelle fungus, has ascending shoots and many long thin thorns. **Young twigs** are characteristically zigzag in shape and young woody growth is often tinged purple with a translucent epidermis. **Thorns** are paired at the nodes, large (2-5 cm long), robust and straight, often inflated at the base and whitish in colour; each pair is divergent and points in the opposite direction to the previous one. Young thorns are thin and sharp. **Leaves** are of medium size (2-4 x 2-5 cm wide), broader than long, with 2-5 pairs of pinnae. Leaflets are moderately sized and somewhat blue-green in colour. There are no petiolar glands, but glands are found on the rachis. The tree often remains green through much of the dry season. **Inflorescence** is a ball of bright golden-yellow flowers that often appear before the rains from late August to October, rarely later. They are usually solitary or in twos and scattered along the twigs of the previous season's growth. **Pods** are distinctive, large and woody. They are thick, densely covered in short grey hairs and shaped like an ear or half moon. The large seeds are only released as the indehiscent pod disintegrates on the ground or when eaten by animals. The seed is fat with a thick tough coat.

Field characters Large spreading tree on sandy soils; zigzag shape of young twigs; large thorns often with inflated bases; large woody, grey, velvety ear-shaped pods.

All but very young specimens are unlikely to be confused with other species. The fused swollen thorns, dark green foliage and large grey pods are distinctive.

Distribution and ecology *A. erioloba* is a southern African species found from southern Angola and Namibia across Botswana to southwest Zambia, western Botswana, the north and west of South Africa and just into southwest Mozambique. It is typical and characteristic of large areas of the Kalahari sandveld. In Zimbabwe it is mainly found in northern Matabeleland where it is associated with shallow, possibly calcareous, sands at the margins of vleis and pans on the Kalahari sands, and can be locally dominant. *A. erioloba* in Zimbabwe is rarely found on deep sand. However, in the south of Hwange National Park, it is found on the crests of fossil sand dunes, and in the Umguza Valley near Bulawayo it is common on old alluvial sands. The species is found as far east as Nkayi, but is particularly common in the Hwange National Park /Gwayi/Nyamandhlovu areas. Outlying populations occur on the Cretaceous sands of Sentinel Ranch near Tuli and in Gonarezhou National Park.

Stands often appear to be even-aged suggesting periodic establishment at intervals of many years. In some cases this can be attributed to previous clearing or cultivation followed by cattle grazing. Elephant are known to pull down branches and damage trees, e.g. around Hwange Safari Lodge. The fruits and seeds are browsed by wildlife and livestock, and this is probably the major means of seed dispersal. The seeds can pass through an animal's digestive system unharmed and are often seen in the dung.

In many instances *A. erioloba* can be considered a secondary colonizer, and stands of the shrub form are sometimes encountered on drying or eroding vlei margins. Such encroachment is occurring in some parts of Hwange National Park. These stands are slowly taken over by trees more typical of the Kalahari sand plateau

→

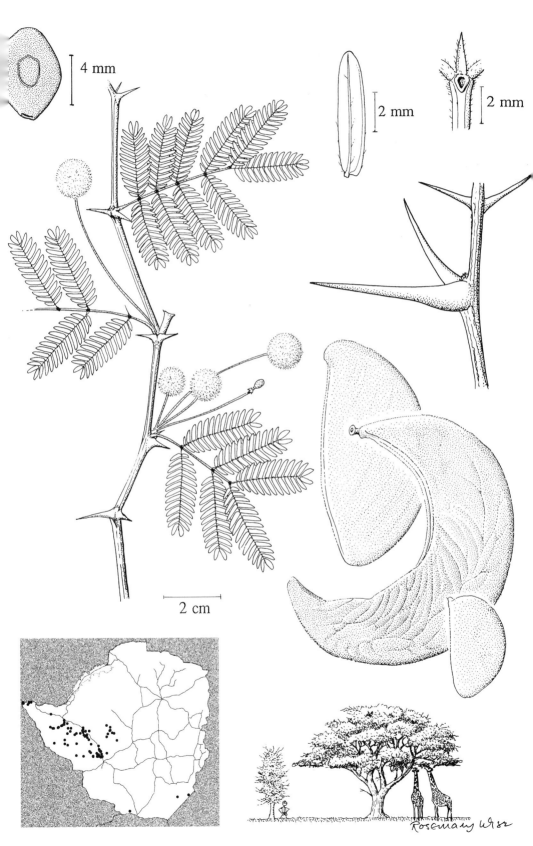

4 mm

2 mm

2 mm

2 cm

ACACIA ERIOLOBA

Rosemary Wise '82

as the sand cover increases. Where the species occurs it is distinctive and often ecologically important. Old specimens can be quite majestic.

Notes The species was first described in 1809 as *A. giraffae*, but in 1975 Ross recognized that the type specimen from the northern Cape was in fact a hybrid, with *A. haematoxylon* as one of the parents. Thus another, later, type specimen had to be found. This specimen was described by Meyer in 1836 as *A. erioloba*, the name now given to the species. *A. erioloba* is taxonomically a rather aberrant species of *Acacia*. It has been suggested that, along with *A. farnesiana* (L.) Willd. (present in Africa but probably introduced) and *A. caven* (Mol.) Mol. from South America, these three species should be separated into a separate genus called *Vachellia* (Ross 1973).

Although it was reported to nodulate under greenhouse conditions when inoculant was provided, *A. erioloba* has not been observed to nodulate naturally. Recent research which looked at relative isotope proportions of nitrogen suggests that the species gets most of this nutrient from groundwater, not from biological nitrogen fixation.

The sapwood is wide and pale while the heartwood is uniformly deep dark red to purple-red. The wood is dense and very heavy (1230 kg/m³) with a medium to fine texture, and the tree is often large enough to provide reasonable sized planks. Heartwood durability is excellent, and it is immune to fungus, borer and termite attack, but prone to splitting. It requires sharp blades and produces an excellent finish with only oils and waxes. The wood is used for firewood, fenceposts and hut poles. However, it is usually too twisted to be much used for furniture or turning.

A. erioloba is a very important source of browse in the areas where it grows. The main source is the pods, which, when crushed with the seeds, can contain 10-20% protein. The yield can easily attain 1-2 tonnes/ha/year, although data from the Umguza Valley near Bulawayo indicate up to 600 kg/ha (see Box 2, page 51). A single, large, free-standing tree at Umguza has produced 500 kg of pods a year. Pods are eaten by eland, kudu, elephant and cattle. In times of drought the pods are collected by some ranchers, milled with some sulphur to neutralize the prussic acid (cyanide) often found in them, and fed to cattle. On many occasions this has allowed herds to survive which would have otherwise died. Flowers are also eaten by livestock and wildlife. The gum is also edible. Larvae of the emperor moth *Gynanisa maja* feed on the foliage, and these are sometimes eaten by humans.

A. erioloba grows slowly for the first three or four years, but thereafter can be surprisingly fast for a long-lived species. The species is tolerant of frost (a late frost, however, can greatly reduce flowering), but is intolerant of fire. It coppices freely, unlike many acacias. The species does not appear to do well when planted on clay soils, and does not transplant well owing to the deep taproot formed within the first year. The longevity of *A. erioloba* is not known, but large specimens are probably at least 100 years old and could reach 300 years.

The specific name is Greek for "woolly lobe" (*erion* - wool, *lobos* - lobe), referring to the shape of the pods. The common name is a corruption of the Afrikaans name which means "giraffe thorn", presumably referring to use of it by these animals. The old specific name, giraffae, refers to the Afrikaans name.

BOX 2 – NUTRITIONAL VALUE OF ACACIA PODS

Many acacias produce nutritious pods that are an important forage for livestock and wildlife. They are especially valuable because many ripen and fall in the dry season when there is no green grass. At this time they also improve the utilization of the low quality roughage, all that is available at that time of the year when draft animals must work their hardest.

There is great variation both between species and between individual trees in the time of the year that the pods mature and fall. For example, the pods of *Acacia nilotica* ripen from April to September, those of *A. erioloba* ripen from June to August, those of *A. tortilis* ssp. *spirocarpa* from August to September, and those of *Faidherbia albida* from September to November. Both small-scale and commercial farmers in various parts of Zimbabwe now regularly collect pods of these four species and feed them either whole or milled (to release the rich source of protein in the seeds) as a supplement at the end of the dry season. The most useful *Acacia* species in this regard are those with indehiscent pods. These fall to the ground entire and are much more readily picked up by livestock.

The level of crude protein, one of the main determinants of feed quality, in *A. erioloba* pods is around 10% compared to only 4% crude protein in maize stover. The crude protein value of the ground pods (around 15%) is considerably higher than that of maize grain (around 10%) and, as it is the protein that is costly in a feed, the value of the pods is clear. One drawback is that some unripe pods of this and other species contain concentrations of toxic prussic acid (cyanide), which can affect or kill livestock (Steyn & Rimington 1935). Feeding of crushed pods with sulphur locks up any of this compound present into a non-toxic form.

It has been estimated that a parkland with 15 *A. erioloba* trees per hectare can yield an annual pod crop with a crude protein equivalent of 372 kg/ha, higher than the maximum expected from small-holder grain crops in the same area. There are no input costs associated with this production, except a minimal amount for collection of the pods; shade, browse and the beneficial effect on the grass production beneath the trees are added benefits.

13

ACACIA ERUBESCENS *Oliv.*
(= *A. dulcis* Marloth & Engl.)

Common names: blue thorn; gowe (Ndebele); chibatamondoro, chisosampotolo (Shangaan)

A small straggly tree of poor shallow soils in hot, dry places, *A. erubescens* has distinctive pale, peeling, papery bark.

Description *A. erubescens* is a small to medium-sized multi-stemmed tree up to 10 m in height, often shrubby and branching low down, and with a straggly appearance. **Bark** is grey to yellowish or whitish, papery and often flaking. **Young twigs** are yellowish to greyish brown or purplish, often peeling and slightly pubescent. The strong hooked **thorns** are paired at the nodes and up to 6 mm long. **Leaves** are medium sized (6 x 4 cm) with 4-7 pairs of pinnae. The petiole is over 1 cm long (usually over 1.3 cm on mature leaves) to the first pinnae, and a small raised gland is present on the lower petiole. The leaflets are not particularly small and are often slightly curved, as is the leaf rachis when viewed from the side. **Inflorescence** is an axillary spike of white flowers appearing on both older and young growth early in September and October, before or at the same time as the leaves. **Pods** are dehiscent, straight and oblong in shape, conspicuously veined, and pointed at the end. They are greyish brown when mature and leathery in texture, but tinged purple when young. The tree often has young pods when other acacias are starting to flower.

Field characters Small multi-stemmed tree; pale peeling bark; long petiole and gland; early pods.

Closely related and similar to *A. fleckii*, *A. erubescens* can be separated on the basis of its longer petioles (greater than 1 cm to first pinnae pair), small raised petiolar gland, glands between the pairs of pinnae, fewer pairs of pinnae and larger leaflets. It also occurs in a different habitat, and is generally not found on sandy soils.

Distribution and ecology *A. erubescens* is a savanna species occurring from Angola, Democratic Republic of Congo and Tanzania south to Namibia, Botswana, northern South Africa and Mozambique. In Zimbabwe it is a species of dry woodlands and bush at medium and lower altitudes, generally below about 900 m. It is found across the country, but is particularly common in areas with less than 800 mm annual rainfall. The species is especially noticeable in southern Matabeleland and the lowveld on gneissic soils. The normal habitat is shallow and gravelly soils or red clays, where it is often associated with mopane and other *Acacia* species, not light-textured soils. It is only locally common, rarely forming stands, and is not an important component of any vegetation type.

Notes The wood is heavy (1070 kg/m^3) but difficult to work. The sapwood is yellow or off-white and the heartwood is dark brown.

The emperor moths *Heniocha dyops* and *H. marnois* feed on the foliage of *A. erubescens* and some other *Acacia* species.

Growth rate is fairly slow, and the species is moderately cold-tolerant. No seed pretreatment is required for germination.

The specific name is Latin for "becoming red" or "blushing" (*erubescere* - to blush) and possibly refers to the reddish colour of the young pods.

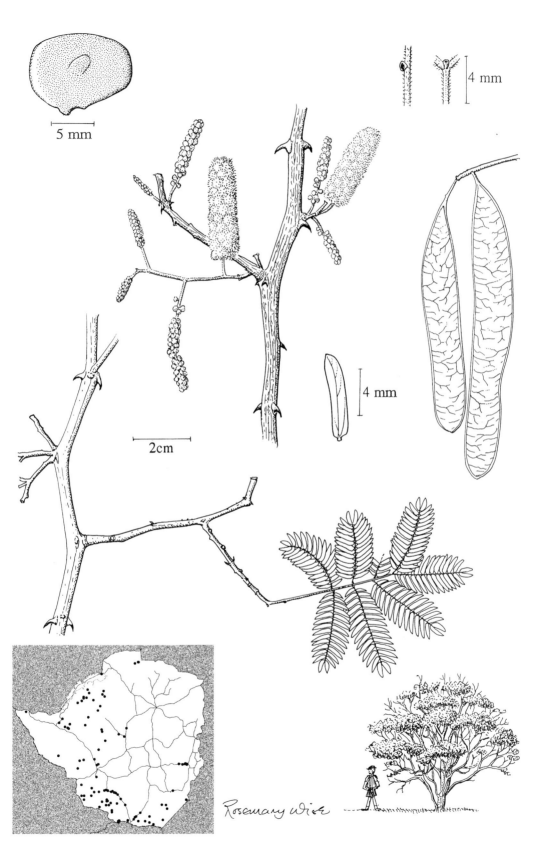

ACACIA ERUBESCENS

14

ACACIA EXUVIALIS *Verdoorn*

Acacia exuvialis is one of the slender-stemmed glandular acacias found in the southeastern lowveld. The Zimbabwe population appears to be different from those in South Africa, and is possibly a different species.

Description *A. exuvialis* is a small shrub to 2 m with slender grey-brown shoots. The stems have an oily appearance and are not flaking. **Young twigs** are grey-brown or red-brown to purplish, with scattered sticky reddish glands. **Thorns** are straight, white and paired at the nodes. **Leaves** are small (3 x 2 cm) with 1-5 pairs of pinnae, each having a few yellow-green leaflets with mucronate tips. There are no or very few glands on the leaves. **Inflorescences** are generally solitary axillary globose heads of bright yellow flowers, appearing on young growth around February. **Pods** are small, dehiscent, grey-brown in colour and constricted between the seeds, but without glands.

Field characters Oily appearance to stem; few pairs of pinnae; eglandular leaflets; involucel more than halfway up peduncle; pod constricted between seeds.

A. exuvialis is separable from *A. borleae* by the fewer (generally 2-5) pairs of pinnae, and more-or-less eglandular mucronate leaflets and pods. It is separable from *A. nebrownii* by generally possessing more pinnae pairs and leaflets, the position of the involucel which is at least half way up the peduncle, and the pod which is constricted between the seeds.

Distribution and ecology *A. exuvialis* is one of the glandular species (see Box 4, page 79) found at lower altitudes in southeastern Zimbabwe and the former northeast Transvaal. Within Zimbabwe it has not been well collected but appears to be confined to gravelly soils derived from Cretaceous sandstone in the Gonarezhou area. All records are from in and around Gonarezhou National Park. It is commonly associated with shrub mopane.

There is a certain amount of ecological separation between *A. borleae*, *A. nebrownii* and *A. exuvialis*, with *A. borleae* principally confined to basalt clays, *A. nebrownii* to shallow Karoo sandstone soils and *A. exuvialis* to shallow Cretaceous sandstone soils.

Notes The shrub form of *A. exuvialis* found in Zimbabwe is distinctly different from the larger form with peeling bark found in the former northeastern Transvaal, but until more collections are made it is referred to this species.

The specific name means "stripping off" and comes from the Latin (*exuviae* - that which is taken off) referring to the peeling bark.

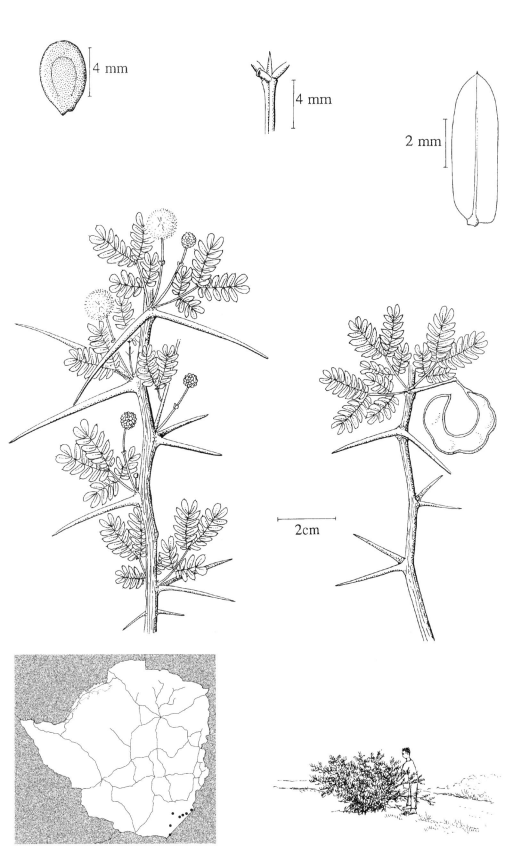

4 mm

4 mm

2 mm

2cm

ACACIA FLECKII *Schinz*
(= *A. cinerea* Schinz, *A. caffra* var. *tomentosa* sensu O.B. Miller 1952)

Common names: blade thorn

Confined to western Zimbabwe and sandy substrates, *Acacia fleckii* has pale grey stems and loses its leaves early.

Description *A. fleckii* is a shrub to 3 m, or a small to medium-sized tree to 10 m (occasionally more), usually multi-stemmed. The canopy is generally rounded and comes close to the ground. Trunk diameter is normally 20-30 cm but can be larger on mature specimens. **Bark** is pale and greyish, sometimes tinged with yellow, and is generally smooth but can be peeling. **Young twigs** are also pale and often densely short-pubescent when young. **Thorns** are hooked and paired at the nodes. They are strong, moderate to large in size, broad-based, and markedly blackish. **Leaves** are medium sized (5 x 3 cm) with 5-15 pairs of pinnae, each with many small bluish green to greyish pubescent leaflets. The petiole is short (0.3-1.0 cm) with a large squat, saucer-shaped gland near its base. **Inflorescence** is a long axillary spike of white flowers generally appearing from November to January after the first rains, and sometimes before the leaves. They are often clustered towards the end of the current season's growth. The large handsome inflorescences make the plant quite noticeable when flowering. **Pods** are medium sized, straight and somewhat broad, and occasionally slightly pubescent. They are dehiscent, leathery to papery in texture, pale brown (strikingly whitish-grey when mature) and transversely veined. The apex is generally acute.

Field characters Shrubby to medium-sized tree; pale stems; whitish flaking bark; strong blackish hooked thorns; short petiole with squat gland; on sandy soils.

Very similar to *A. erubescens*. The distinguishing features are that *A. fleckii* has shorter petioles (less than 1 cm to first pair of pinnae), a large squat petiolar gland, no glands between the pairs of pinnae, more pairs of pinnae and smaller leaflets, and is generally found on sandy substrates.

Distribution and ecology *A. fleckii* is a western Zambezian domain species associated with the broadly-defined Kalahari Basin in southern Angola, northern Namibia, western Zambia, Botswana, Zimbabwe and the former western Transvaal. In Zimbabwe it has a western distribution at medium altitudes (800-1200 m), but is found as far east as Kwekwe and Kadoma on the central watershed. A shallow-rooted species, it is principally confined to coarse sandy soils including deposits such as old sandy banks close to rivers and coarse-textured sandy colluvial or alluvial soils on granite and gneiss. Perhaps because of its shallow roots it is late coming into leaf and also early deciduous. *A. fleckii* is also common on the Kalahari sands of northern Matabeleland, where it often indicates disturbance or fire. It can be thicket-forming in logged areas or on river banks.

Notes The wood is said to be similar to that of *A. galpinii*. *A. fleckii* is a comparatively frost-tolerant species which recovers well after severe frosts.

The species was named after E. Fleck, a geologist who worked in what is now Namibia between 1888 and 1891. He collected the type specimen near Ghanzi, Botswana.

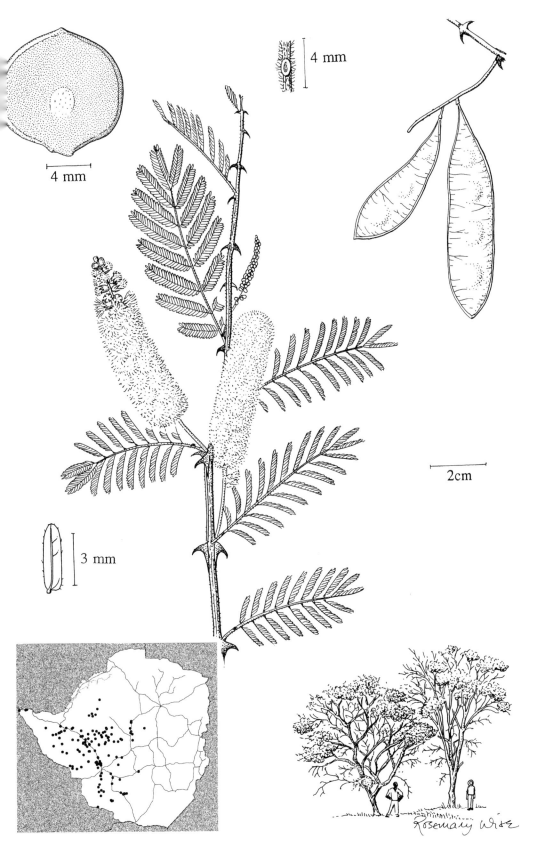

4 mm

4 mm

2cm

3 mm

ACACIA FLECKII

16

ACACIA GALPINII *Burtt Davy*

Common names: monkey thorn; apiesdoring, bladdoring (Afrikaans); umdwadwa, umtungabayeni (Ndebele); umbuia (Ndebele-Gweru); kalaunga (Shangaan); nkotokua (Shona-Zezeru); mfututa (Hurungwe)

Acacia galpinii is the tallest and perhaps largest of Zimbabwe's acacias and is often seen along small rivers in the drier parts of the country.

Description *A. galpinii* is a large erect tree to 30 m or more in height (normally 15-20 m), with a rounded crown; the tallest of the Zimbabwe acacias. Branching is generally high up. Mature trunk diameter is around 40-60 cm. **Bark** is greyish to grey-brown, flaking and paler than most acacias, with a yellowish tinge showing through; it can be corky when young. **Young twigs** are smooth but furrowed, grey-brown to brownish with small pale lenticels. **Thorns** occur in pairs just below the nodes and are strongly hooked and broad-based. They are large (to 1 cm long), strong and blackish in colour, and are often present on the branches; thorns on raised bosses can persist on the trunk. **Leaves** are large (10-15 x 10 cm) with 6-13 pairs of pinnae, each with many medium-sized grey-green leaflets. A small raised gland is seen in the lower half of the petiole. **Inflorescences** are long thin spikes of fragrant cream-yellow flowers. These appear in axillary clusters on the previous seasons' growth in August-September before the leaves; one of the first species to flower. The calyx is red, thus the inflorescence has a distinctive reddish tinge before opening. **Pods** are long (10-25 cm), straight and broad, and pointed at both ends. The valves are brittle, smooth, purplish brown in colour when young, and dehisce on the tree.

Field characters Tall riverine tree; flowers in spikes with reddish tinge, appearing before the leaves; small raised gland more than halfway up the petiole; long broad flat pods.

A magnificent tree when mature and occurring in groves, *A. galpinii* is often confused with *A. polyacantha*, and can be confused with *A. nigrescens* when leafless. *A. galpinii* has less than 13 pairs of pinnae and the petiolar gland is small, stalked and part-way up the petiole, while the gland of *A. polyacantha* is large, squat and situated near the base.

Distribution and ecology *A. galpinii* is a southern African species found in southern Zambia, Malawi, northern and eastern Botswana, Zimbabwe, northern South Africa and eastern Mozambique, with an outlying population in central Tanzania. In Zimbabwe it is fairly widely distributed across the country, principally in drier areas, but nowhere is particularly common. Typically it is a component of riverine woodland with other *Acacia* species, growing as a tall large tree on the river banks, but it can also be found associated with smaller drainage lines, termite mounds or (rarely) scattered through low acacia woodland. It is mostly found on loamy soils or clays derived from goldbelt rocks, seldom on lighter textured soils, except on river banks. *A. galpinii* is a pioneer species in suitable habitats.

Notes The dirty-white sapwood is wide in younger trees while the heartwood is pale brown with an even medium texture. *A. galpinii* possibly gives the highest yield of workable wood of all Zimbabwe's acacias; large planks can be obtained from the trunk (old trees in good condition will yield up to 2.5 m³) and sawlogs can also be obtained from the crown. The heartwood is heavy (800 kg/m³), moderately durable, and of good quality for woodworking, being tough and resilient but not hard. It cuts and seasons well and is suitable for general joinery, both interior and exterior. An excellent finish is obtained just with waxes and oils. The wood has also been used as a mining timber, for fencing, and in waggon construction (Box 16, page 135).

A. galpinii is easy to germinate and establish, and is widely planted as it grows fast. Although frost tolerant, severe frosts often kill off branches and give rise to a stag-headed appearance along some river valleys in western Matabeleland. The tree is said to be comparatively long-lived, and also coppices well when young.

The species is named after Ernest Galpin, a banker and botanical collector. The type of *A. galpinii* was collected in 1920 north of Pretoria near Naboomspruit on Galpin's farm Mosdene.

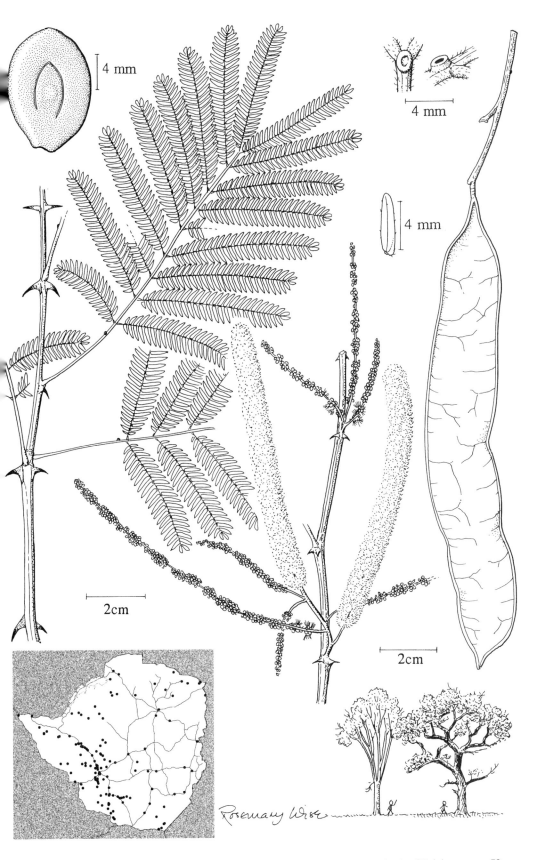

ACACIA GALPINII

ACACIA GERRARDII *Benth.*

Common names: grey-haired acacia, red thorn; rooidoring (Afrikaans); ikope, isanqawe, uhahla (Ndebele)

A widespread species found at medium altitudes and on richer soils under moderate rainfall, *A. gerrardii* is quite variable and not always confidently identified. It is a good indicator of those sites where dry miombo or broadleaved woodland are in equilibrium with mopane or acacia bushland and wooded grassland.

Description *A. gerrardii* is a small to medium-sized tree up to 10 m in height, but often only reaching 5 m. Trunk diameter is 20-30 cm in mature specimens. The ascending robust branches spread in older individuals and the crown is generally narrow and open. **Bark** is dark grey or blackish brown to almost black, rough and fissured. Branches often appear to be clothed in dense green foliage. Younger branches can be smooth and wrinkled like an elephant's trunk. **Young twigs** are robust and covered with a dense, grey-velvety pubescence which later splits to expose a rusty-red inner layer. **Thorns** are straight, very stout, pubescent and paired at the nodes; generally short (up to 1.5 cm), but are sometimes long or recurved. **Leaves** are medium-sized (6 x 4 cm, although they can be much smaller) and tufted so as to appear to be borne on "cushions". There are 5-9 pairs of pinnae each with many small, pubescent leaflets, drying much darker above than below. **Inflorescences** are clustered in the axils of the current or previous seasons' growth and consist of globose heads of white flowers. Flowering is from September to February. The dehiscent **pods** are medium-sized (up to 8-15 x 1.5 cm), markedly curved or sickle shaped, and rounded. The valves are relatively thin and covered in grey velvety hairs, not leathery or woody. In some specimens the pods are almost straight.

Field characters Small tree with ascending branches; young growth thick and robust, seemingly "clothed" in tufted leaves; young twigs densely covered in grey-velvet hairs; long hairs on leaf rachis; pods curved and covered in grey hairs.

A. gerrardii is very variable and difficulties often arise in identification, in particular in distinguishing it from *A. robusta*. The robust young twigs densely covered in grey velvety hairs helps to distinguish most individuals from both *A. robusta* subsp. *robusta* and subsp. *clavigera*. However, when *A. gerrardii* is growing partially shaded among other, taller, trees at vlei margins it can have much thinner twigs with minimal pubescence. The pods of *A. gerrardii* are also hairy and straighter. At times it is difficult to name clearly such specimens and there is a possibility of hybridization with another species, perhaps *A. robusta* subsp. *clavigera*, but not *A. luederitzii* as has been suggested elsewhere.

Distribution and ecology *A. gerrardii* subsp. *gerrardii* is a widespread species being found from KwaZulu-Natal and northern South Africa, through Botswana, Zimbabwe and Mozambique, to tropical West Africa, Sudan and Kenya. In Zimbabwe *A. gerrardii* is widespread at medium altitudes, but rarely outside the range 600-1500 m or in dry areas. It occurs in various types of open woodland or wooded grassland, often on richer soils in mopane-miombo (*Colophospermum mopane-Brachystegia boehmii*) mixed woodland or on vlei margins, and generally in fairly open sites. Termite mounds often support small shrubs of *A. gerrardii*, and in such situations it can be quite gregarious. It is also a common constituent of regenerating or disturbed *Acacia* bushland on soils derived from goldbelt rocks in the Kwekwe-Gweru-Bulawayo-Gwanda-Masvingo area. Here, *A. gerrardii* is characteristically stunted, rarely exceeding 4 m in height. The required soil type appears to be sandy loam or somewhat heavier soils, and it is rarely seen growing on sandy soils.

Notes All populations of *A. gerrardii* in southern Africa belong to subsp. *gerrardii* var. *gerrardii*.

Other recognized varieties of subsp. *gerrardii* are

→

G

D

C

A

B

F

2cm

4 mm

2 mm

2 mm

Rosemary Wise

found in Kenya and Tanzania, and are differentiated by having glabrous young growth or wider pods. The other subspecies, subsp. *negevensis* Zohary, is found only in Israel, Kuwait and Iraq.

The creamy brown sapwood forms a wide ring around the pink-tinged heartwood, from which it is not clearly differentiated. The wood is moderately heavy (900 kg/m³) with a medium to coarse, even texture. It is fairly hard, prone to splitting and fungal staining, needs careful seasoning, and is only moderately resistant to borers and termites. The wood has been used for small furniture, shelving and small carvings, but is not widely utilized. The leaves and bark have been used medicinally as an emetic or inhalant, and the inner bark used for rope. Both leaves and pods are browsed by some wildlife species and also by goats, although tannin levels are thought to be high.

Growth rates are moderately fast. The species has moderately deep roots and only small lateral roots.

The species is named after the English traveller and naturalist W.T. Gerrard, who collected the type specimen in KwaZulu-Natal between 1861 and 1865.

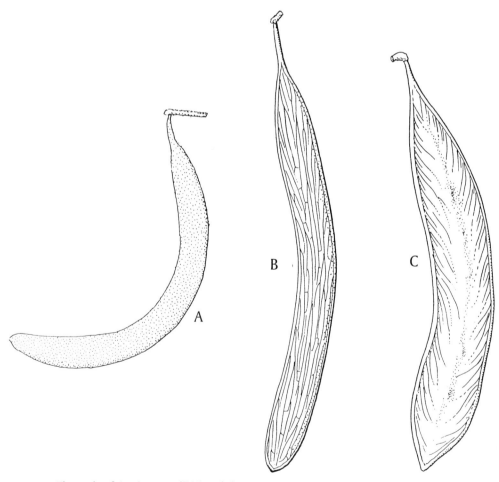

The pods of *Acacia gerrardii* (A) and the two subspecies of *A. robusta,* subsp. *clavigera* (B) and subsp. *robusta* (C), help to distinguish the species (lifesize).

BOX 3 – GROWTH RINGS IN THE ACACIAS

The age of most tree species that grow in temperate climates can be determined by counting the concentric rings in a cross-section of the stem. These rings are defined by changes in cell size or type caused by distinct seasonal growth phases. Such regular patterns are rarely exhibited in stems of trees from tropical climates because growth is comparatively irregular as seasons are less distinct and because meteorological events, such as drought and frost, occur at irregular intervals. The age of most tropical broad-leaved species cannot, therefore, be estimated reliably by counting rings in the stem.

The wood, or xylem, of a tree consists of three types of cell: the strengthening tissue that provides support (fibres), the conducting tissue that transports water (vessels), and the storage tissue that stores food (parenchyma). Most of the parenchyma in *Acacia* species is associated with the vessels and both these are distributed in such a manner that they cannot be associated with annual growth. However, recently it has been found that in some acacias, very fine bands of parenchyma occur independently of the vessels and these bands are now thought to be marginal parenchyma formed at the end of the growing season. In a study on *A. karroo* trees of known age in the Umguza Valley near Bulawayo (Gourlay & Kanowski 1991, Gourlay & Barnes 1994), the numbers of such bands of marginal parenchyma were found to correspond closely with the known age of the trees and were shown to be formed towards the end of each dry season. The cells in these bands are distinct because, under the microscope, they can be seen to be filled with long chains of calcium oxalate crystals. When tree roots take up salty water, excess calcium ions must be removed to maintain the tree's water balance. These ions are combined with oxalic acid to produce insoluble calcium oxalate, which is stored as large prismatic crystals in the wood. It is possible that the high quality of the fuelwood of some acacias might be linked to the presence of these calcium oxalate crystals. It has been suggested that when a piece of fuelwood is set alight, it burns rapidly, producing carbon monoxide which itself is inflammable and raises the flame temperature. When the temperature rises above 370°C, calcium oxalate breaks down and the released oxygen leads to more complete combustion in the wood, which acts as a flame retardant and promotes a glowing combustion similar to that of banked-down coal. Such long-lasting embers are preferred for cooking and heating (Prior & Cutler 1992).

Being able to tell the age of a tree without knowing its history is of crucial value in the study of the productivity and ecology of natural populations. By sampling trees and counting rings, annual wood production per tree at various stand densities can be estimated and used for yield predictions, and also for devising management plans to maximize that yield (Gourlay *et al.* 1996). Such data can also be used to reveal the history of development of a stand – for example, did all the trees start life in the same year and, if so, what were the climatic conditions during that year that led to their successful establishment? If ring widths are measured as well, the effects of rainfall and stand density on growth can also be determined. Sampling need not be destructive because it can be done by removing a core from the standing tree rather than by taking a disc. The alternative to ring counts and measurements would be to record the diameter of every tree every year from the time the trees were seedlings, which would inevitably limit the number of stands that could be studied and lengthen the time taken to get the information.

ACACIA GOETZEI *Harms*

(= *A. welwitschii* sensu Eyles 1916, *A. mossambicensis* sensu Wild 1952)

Common names: purple-pod acacia; chitataunga (Shona-Manyika); mupumbu (Tonga)

A very variable small to large tree, often divided into two subspecies, found across much of Zimbabwe at medium to higher altitudes, but with no particular pattern of distribution. *Acacia goetzei* can look like a small leaflet version of *A. nigrescens*, but the smaller-leaflet form is much more similar to *A. erubescens*. It is not a well-defined species and it is possibly of hybrid origin.

Description *A. goetzei* is a small tree to 5-10 m in height, but occasionally a large tree up to 16 m high with a good length of straight, unbranched bole. The canopy in smaller trees is rather shapeless and narrow and rarely spreads, even in larger individuals. Trunk diameter can be up to 100 cm, but is normally around 60 cm in mature specimens. **Bark** is grey to brownish grey and rough with narrow vertical fissures. Hooked thorns are often seen on small raised bosses on the trunk and main branches. **Young twigs** are generally smooth with a thin splitting epidermis, sometimes pubescent, greyish or grey-brown to brown, and with small orange lenticels. **Thorns** are strong, hooked and paired at the nodes, blackish and up to 5 mm long. **Leaves** are very variable, and have been the basis for subdivision of the species. In what has been termed subsp. *goetzei*, they are medium-sized (6 x 4 cm) with 3-5 pairs of pinnae, each with 3-6 pairs of broad (>3 mm wide) rounded leaflets, distinctly wider towards the apex and sometimes with the terminal leaflets almost flattened at the tip. The base of the leaflets is asymmetric. Small thorns are often present on the rachis. Larger leaflet forms tend to have a pubescent petiole and rachis. In what has been called subsp. *microphylla* the leaves are larger (6-12 x 4 cm) with 4-8 pairs of pinnae each bearing 10-23 pairs of narrower (2 mm wide) parallel-sided leaflets. **Inflorescences** are axillary spikes of creamy white flowers appearing on both young and older growth in September-November, sometimes up to March. **Pods** are wide (>2.5 cm), straight, often with a wavy margin, and dehiscent in April-May. The valves are leathery or somewhat woody, dark brown in colour and smooth.

Field characters Small to large tree, much like *A. nigrescens* in shape; many medium-sized rounded leaflets; leaflet base asymmetric; broad thickened pods.

A. goetzei is such a variable species that it is difficult to differentiate it clearly from others in the *A. nigrescens-A. burkei-A. welwitschii-A. goetzei* complex. No single character separates it out, which is part of the reason why a hybrid origin has been suggested. There appears to be no significant geographical or ecological overlap in Zimbabwe between *A. goetzei*, *A. welwitschii* and *A. burkei*, as presently understood here, but it is doubtful if all would retain a separate identity if a thorough taxonomic study were to be done. In shape and habit, as well as (in many cases) habitat, *A. goetzei* is very similar to *A. nigrescens*. These two species, however, are clearly separated by leaflet size and number – *A. nigrescens* has only 2-3 pairs of pinnae, each with 1 or 2 pairs of large leaflets (1-2 cm wide), while *A. goetzei* normally has significantly more and smaller leaflets per pinna. The raised thorns on the stem of *A. goetzei* are never as conspicuous as the "knob thorns" of typical *A. nigrescens*. The leaflets of *A. welwitschii* are generally rounded with a symmetric base and a dark "foot", but this is not always a clear character. It is often difficult to separate *A. burkei* from *A. goetzei*; *A. goetzei* usually has a smooth rachis, the pods are wider, and the calyx is without hairs.

Distribution and ecology *A. goetzei* has an odd distribution ranging from a scattered occurrence in Angola, across Zambia and Zimbabwe to northern Mozambique and north to the Democratic Republic of Congo, Tanzania, Kenya and Ethiopia. The two recognized subspecies are found in similar areas across much

➔

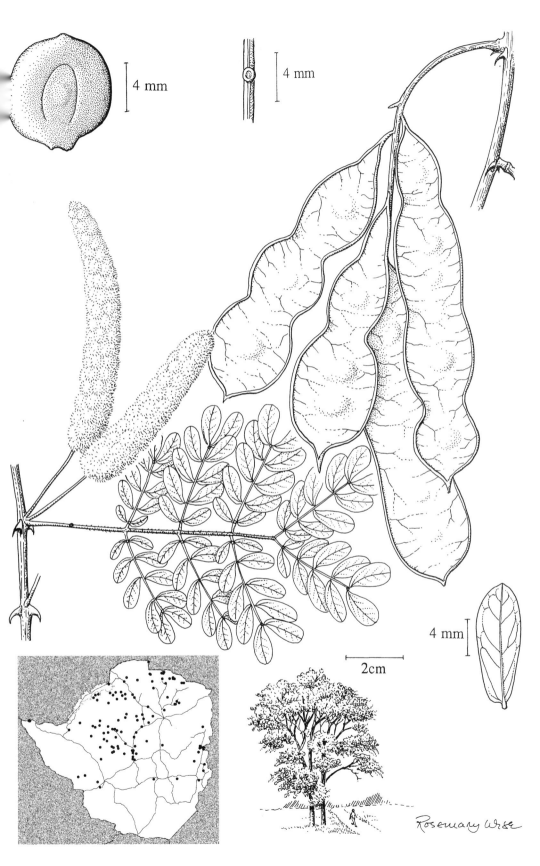

4 mm

4 mm

4 mm

2cm

ACACIA GOETZEI GOETZEI

of that range. In Zimbabwe the species is mostly found at medium altitudes (900-1200 m) from Bulawayo to Mutare, but down to 400 m in the Zambezi Valley. It is quite common in parts of Gokwe and Midlands Province, but scarce in the Bulawayo area.

What has been called subsp. *microphylla* is restricted to the higher altitude and rainfall areas of Karoi, Mvurwi, Harare, Chivhu and Mutare. Subsp. *goetzei* is generally found in mixed dry woodland on moderately fertile shallow or stony soils, often in a similar habitat to *A. nigrescens*. Common associates are *Brachystegia boehmii* and mopane, and it normally occurs as scattered individuals and not in stands. The smaller leaflet form, known as subsp. *microphylla*, is a component of open miombo woodland on less fertile soils, often with such species as *A. amythethophylla*.

Notes Two subspecies have been recognized – subsp. *goetzei* and subsp. *microphylla* Brenan – but here they are treated together. The two are not geographically distinct and fully intergrade, although extremes are clearly separable. At times individuals within the same population have been classified as belonging to different subspecies. Populations in higher rainfall areas show a tendency to larger leaves, more pinnae pairs and narrower leaflets, not rounded or flattened at the tip. It is felt that, at least for Zimbabwe, there is no value in maintaining the differences at subspecies level and it is better to regard them as varieties of little taxonomic significance. There have been suggestions that *A. goetzei* has hybridized with *A. nigrescens*; certainly, a range of intermediates has been recorded. It is possible that *A. goetzei* itself was originally of hybrid origin, perhaps with *A. nigrescens* and *A. galpinii* as the parents, but there is no genetic or chromosome data yet to support this. However, now it is evidently fertile and has an existence of its own, independent of any putative parents. Although the species is not that clearly defined or separable from similar species in the southeast lowveld, it is quite distinct over most of its range in the country.

The wide, dirty yellow sapwood surrounds a yellow-brown to dark chocolate-brown heartwood. This is extremely hard and heavy (1025 kg/m^3) with a fine even texture, and difficult to work. Because of ripples in the grain the wood is difficult to finish by hand. The heartwood is durable and resistant to attack, but less so when in contact with the ground. It is a stable wood, free of seasonal movement, and has been used for structural work, heavy joinery and large items of furniture, as well as in farm construction.

A. goetzei coppices well and often has very straight regrowth. It probably is reasonably long-lived, with a similar longevity to *A. nigrescens*. The taproot is moderately deep with a series of shallow laterals, especially on less well-drained soils.

The specific name refers to the German botanist W. Goetze, who collected the type specimen at Kilosa in Tanzania around 1898. The subspecific name, microphylla, is Greek for small leaves (*micros* - small, *phyllon* - leaf).

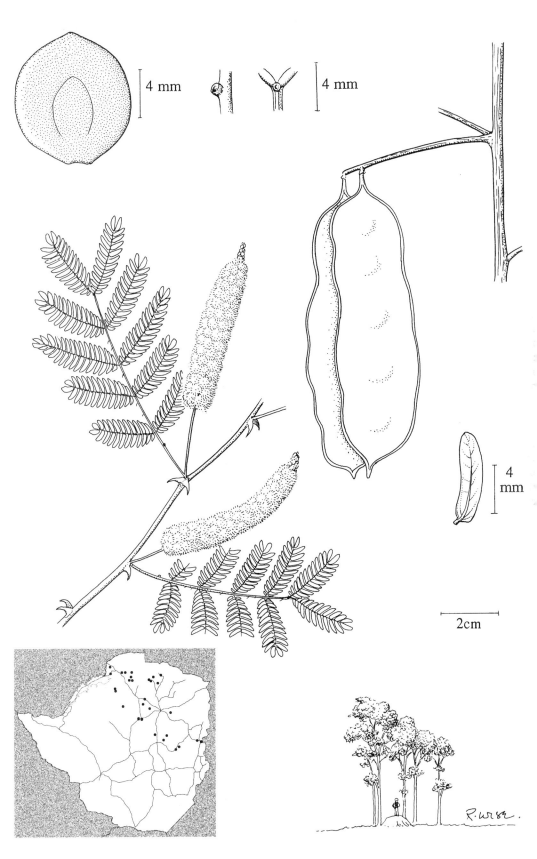

4 mm

4 mm

4
mm

2cm

A. GOETZEI MICROPHYLLA

19

ACACIA GRANDICORNUTA *Gerstner*

Common name: horned thorn

Acacia grandicornuta in many instances is a difficult species to identify confidently. It occurs in the southern lowveld along and away from drainage lines and often has large inflated thorns, hence its name.

Description *A. grandicornuta* is a small tree or spreading bush 2-5 m in height, occasionally a larger multi-stemmed tree to 8-10 m with a rounded irregular crown. Branching is low. The mature trunk can be up to 20 cm in diameter. **Bark** is furrowed, dark grey-brown, sometimes fissured and flaking. Branches smooth and greyish. **Young twigs** are smooth, grey to grey-brown, sometimes tinged orange. **Thorns** are large and stout, partially inflated along their length, straight and paired at the nodes. Some thorns are long (6-10 cm) and distinctly fused and swollen at the base. **Leaves** are small to medium in size (3 x 4 cm), with 1-2 pairs of pinnae, each with relatively few, broad (to 2 mm wide), rounded grey-green glabrous leaflets, the same colour above as below. The rachis is without hairs. Leaves are retained for most of the year. **Inflorescences** are white globose heads clustered in the axils, appearing on new growth irregularly between October and March. **Pods** are dehiscent, curved, medium-sized and narrow (less than 1 cm wide), with smooth and almost shiny purplish-grey valves.

Field characters Shrub or small shrubby tree, sometimes forming thickets; stout straight thorns, often long and inflated; 1-2 pairs of pinnae with broad grey-green leaflets; smooth curved pods.

It is often difficult to separate *A. grandicornuta* from *A. robusta* subsp. *clavigera*. *A. grandicornuta* normally has only 2 pairs of pinnae, while subsp. *clavigera* has 3-5 pairs borne in distinct "cushions". The leaflets in *A. grandicornuta* are not discolorous (they are the same colour above and below), are relatively large and rounded at the ends, and are mostly more than 2 mm wide; the rachis and young growth are hairless. Thorns are better developed in *A. grandicornuta* than in subsp. *clavigera*, and are generally long and at least partially inflated along their length. The pods of *A. grandicornuta* tend to be somewhat thicker in cross-section, grey-brown and very smooth, whilst those of subsp. *clavigera* are flatter, sometimes slightly hairy and with a distinct margin. *A. grandicornuta* is usually a multi-stemmed tree, not single-stemmed or with slender, ascending branches.

Distribution and ecology *A. grandicornuta* is a southern African species found from Botswana eastwards through southern Zimbabwe to southern Mozambique and KwaZulu-Natal, mostly associated with the palaeo-Limpopo Basin. In Zimbabwe it has only been recorded from the southern lowveld where it is associated with the Limpopo, Bubi, Mwenezi and Save rivers. At Sentinel Ranch it is common on calcareous sandstones and on old alluvial terraces. It occurs in clay-rich depressions and along drainage lines, and often forms clumps or thickets. The soils on which it occurs are blackish and range from alluvial fine sandy clay to heavier basalt-derived clays. Stunted mopane is a common associate along with other *Acacia* species such as *A. robusta* subsp. *clavigera*.

Notes *A. grandicornuta* forms part of the difficult *A. robusta* complex; the differences between *A. grandicornuta* and *A. robusta* subsp. *clavigera* are not always easy to apply and the two intergrade so much that it is possibly best to combine them. Ecologically, however, there are some substantial differences – *A. grandicornuta* is always a shrub or multi-stemmed tree that occurs on black clay soils, although often away from alluvium, while subsp. *clavigera* is nearly always confined to riverine and alluvial situations.

In the Kruger National Park in South Africa the pale brown wood is regarded as fairly heavy (770 kg/m³) and hard, although liable to damage by borers. It is said to grow fairly fast but is not cold resistant.

The specific name comes from the Latin for "large-horned" (*grandis* - great, *cornuta* - horned), presumably also the source of the common name (by which it is hardly known). This possibly refers to the curved pods or to the large thorns, neither of which particularly resembles a horn.

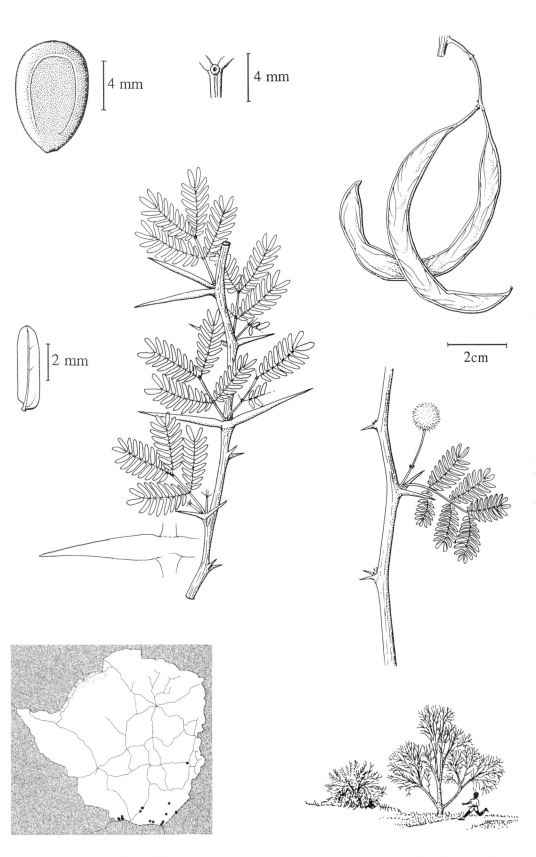

4 mm

4 mm

2 mm

2cm

ACACIA GRANDICORNUTA

20

ACACIA HEBECLADA *DC.* subsp. *CHOBIENSIS (O.B. Mill.) Schreib.*
(= *A. stolonifera* Burch. var. *chobiensis* O.B. Mill.)

Common name: candle-pod acacia

A distinctive riverine shrub of the Upper Zambezi River, often growing half in the water. *Acacia hebeclada* subsp. *chobiensis* has distinctive large erect pods, and occupies a different habitat from the other subspecies.

Description *A. hebeclada* subsp. *chobiensis* is a large, thicket-forming riverine shrub or small tree up to 3 m, branching from the ground and occasionally from underground stolons. **Young twigs** have a dense velvety-pubescent epidermis, splitting to reveal a red-purplish layer underneath, and orangey pustular lenticels. **Thorns** are thick and whitish, generally short and often somewhat curved or hooked; some are straight and much longer (to 7 cm). **Leaves** are medium-sized (6-8 x 4 cm) with 6-14 pairs of pinnae, each with small leaflets. They are clustered at the nodes, often markedly pubescent, and with a small "tooth" at the end of the rachis. The whitish globose **inflorescences** are clustered at the nodes, and appear both on the previous and current seasons' growth around September. **Pods** are very large, distinctive, woody and held upright. They are tardily dehiscent, sometimes remaining on the plant for more than a season, and comprised of rounded woody and shortly-pubescent valves 2.5-4.5 cm wide, each with a series of shallow longitudinal striations. When ripe they are a pale greenish yellow in colour.

Field characters Riparian shrub; curved thorns, not hooked; wide (>2.5 cm) erect woody pods; restricted to the Zambezi River above Victoria Falls.

A. hebeclada subsp. *chobiensis* is unlikely to be confused with any other species in Zimbabwe owing to its habitat and distribution. It is a much larger and taller shrub than subsp. *hebeclada*, with longer internodes and larger leaves and leaflets. The erect pods are bigger and generally wider than 2.5 cm.

Distribution and ecology As its name implies, subsp. *chobiensis* is associated with the Okavango-Chobe-Upper Zambezi river systems, it is found in the Caprivi, northern Botswana, western Zambia and, within Zimbabwe, on the Upper Zambezi River between Kazungula and Victoria Falls. A riverine species, it is restricted to sandy river banks and islands, sometimes growing semi-submerged on island sandbanks or alluvium. The lower branches often touch the ground and make a tent-like refuge for wildlife.

The other subspecies, subsp. *hebeclada,* also occurs in Zimbabwe, but is more widespread and found on the calcium-rich Kalahari sands in Hwange National Park and northern Tsholotsho.

Notes A third subspecies, subsp. *tristis* Schreib., with thinner pods that hang down, occurs in northern Namibia and southern Angola in open bushland on sandy soils. Although the differences between the two subspecies are not always very clear, at least in northern Botswana and the Caprivi, the very different habitats suggest that they are separate taxa.

A. hebeclada subsp. *chobiensis* is considered a threatened species by IUCN owing to its restricted distribution.

The meaning of the specific name is not clear, but seems to refer to having twigs covered in soft hair (Greek: *hebetikos* - juvenile, *klados* - sprout or branch). The subspecific name refers to the Chobe River in Botswana, from where it was first described.

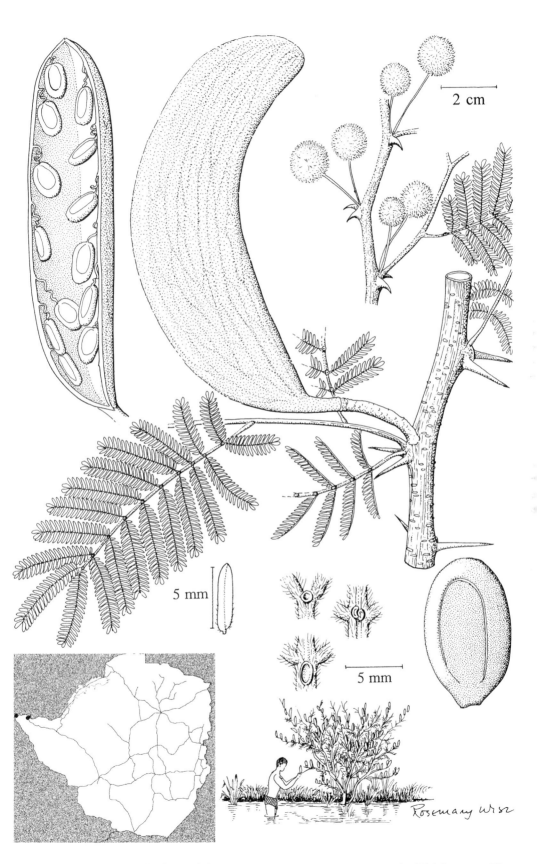

ACACIA HEBECLADA CHOBIENSIS

2 cm

5 mm

5 mm

Rosemary Wise

21

ACACIA HEBECLADA *DC.* subsp. HEBECLADA
(= *A. stolonifera* Burch.)

Common name: candle-pod acacia

A low, spreading shrub of the Kalahari dune system in the Hwange area, *Acacia hebeclada* subsp. *hebeclada* has thick pods held distinctively upright.

Description *A. hebeclada* subsp. *hebeclada* is a small shrub to 1.5 m, branching from the ground and occasionally from underground stolons. The stems are comparatively thick and robust. **Young twigs** have a dense velvety-pubescent epidermis splitting to reveal an orange or brown layer underneath, and orangey pustular lenticels. **Thorns** are thick and whitish, generally short and somewhat curved or hooked on the upper part. A few thorns are almost straight. **Leaves** are small (5 x 3 cm) with 5-9 pairs of pinnae, each with small leaflets. They are clustered at the nodes and are often markedly pubescent. The pale yellowish white, globose **inflorescences** are clustered at the nodes, and appear around September. **Pods** are woody, tardily dehiscent, sometimes remaining on the plant for more than a season, and held distinctively upright. The rounded short-pubescent valves are 1.5-2.5 cm wide, each with a series of shallow longitudinal striations. When ripening they are usually a pale greenish yellow in colour and only split along one side on ripening.

Field characters Small low shrub; curved thorns, not hooked; erect woody pods; associated with old dunes.

A. *hebeclada* subsp. *hebeclada* is unlikely to be confused with any other species in Zimbabwe owing to its restricted distribution and habitat, although it can resemble low shrubs of *A. luederitzii* and *A. gerrardii*. The erect pods are most distinctive and are present on the plant for much of the year.

Subsp. *hebeclada* can be separated from the other subspecies of *A. hebeclada* found in Zimbabwe, subsp. *chobiensis*, as it is a low shrub with shorter internodes, smaller leaves and leaflets, more densely pubescent young growth, and the erect pods are less than 2.5 cm wide. The marked differences in habitat and distribution within Zimbabwe are probably the major differentiating characters.

Distribution and ecology *A. hebeclada* subsp. *hebeclada* occurs in Namibia, Botswana, western Zimbabwe and northern South Africa in the Kalahari Basin. Within Zimbabwe it is found only on calcium-rich Kalahari sands in Hwange National Park and northern Tsholotsho at an altitude of 950-1050 m, usually on clayey deposits in dune slacks. It is a typical Kalahari species that only just enters the country, and is associated with Pleistocene dune fields. Subsp. *hebeclada* is often gregarious and forms small low thickets.

Notes The other subspecies, subsp. *chobiensis*, found in Zimbabwe is associated with the Okavango-Chobe-Upper Zambezi river systems. The habitat and distribution of the two subspecies are so different that confusion is unlikely to arise, but in northern Botswana and the Caprivi gradation between the two is seen.

In Botswana leaf crude protein levels are 13-26%, but prussic acid (cyanide) has been found in both fresh leaves and immature pods.

The meaning of the specific name is not clear, but possibly refers to having twigs covered in soft hair (Greek: *hebetikos* - juvenile, *klados* - sprout or branch).

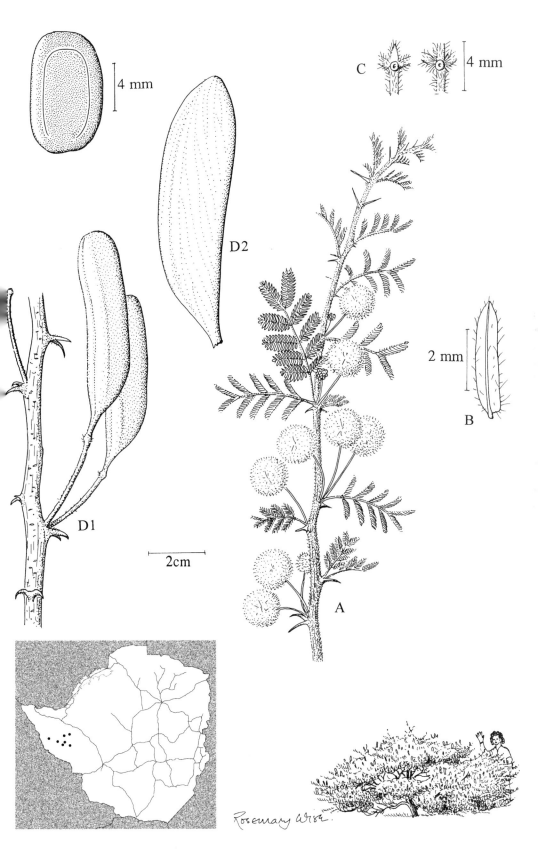

D2

D1

C

4 mm

4 mm

2 mm

B

2cm

A

Rosemary Wise

22

ACACIA HEREROENSIS *Engl.*
(= *A. mellei* Verdoorn, *A. gansbergensis* Schinz)

Common names: red thorn

A rather inconspicuous small tree similar to *Acacia karroo*, *A. hereroensis* is confined in Zimbabwe to the Matopos-Bulawayo area and is usually only noticed when in flower.

Description *A. hereroensis* is a small tree up to 5 m in height, occasionally higher, but more usually a rather inconspicuous shrub. **Bark** is dark greyish brown, rough and fissured. **Young twigs** are purplish brown and pubescent, with many red-brown glands. **Thorns** are hooked in pairs, or sub-opposite, at or below the nodes, sometimes almost scattered. **Leaves** are medium-sized (6 x 3 cm) with 10-14 pairs of pinnae, each with numerous very small pubescent leaflets. There is a conspicuous stalked gland on the petiole. **Inflorescence** is a short axillary spike of cream-coloured flowers appearing on the beginning of the current season's growth in late November to January after the rains, when the plant is quite noticeable. **Pods** are medium sized (6 x 2 cm), brownish, leathery in texture and dehiscent. They are conspicuously densely pubescent and with numerous small brown glands.

Field characters Pubescent glandular twigs; hooked thorns, sometimes more or less scattered; pubescent pods; only in Matopos area and Harare.

It can be confused with *A. caffra* elsewhere in its range, but *A. hereroensis* has a shorter petiole (less than 1.5 cm), smaller leaves and more crowded pinnae, and hairy pods. It is unlikely to be confused with *A. chariessa*, which is a much smaller shrub with slender shoots.

Distribution and ecology *A. hereroensis* is found scattered through Namibia, southeastern Botswana, western Zimbabwe and northern South Africa. In Zimbabwe it has been recorded only from the Bulawayo to Matopos area, particularly on the Agricultural Research Station. There it is nearly always in acacia bushland on red soils derived from schistose goldbelt rocks, often on shallow soil by road cuttings, but occasionally on granite. One small population of eight individuals is known from Marlborough vlei near Mount Hampden in northwest Harare, but these are likely to have been accidentally introduced via seed. There is no sign of regeneration and the site appears disturbed and has been used for camping. In Botswana and the former Transvaal *A. hereroensis* is associated with soils derived from dolomite (limestone), but this is not the case here.

Notes The species is probably under-recorded as it generally occurs with other acacias and is rather inconspicuous, except when in flower.

The specific name refers to Hereroland in Namibia, from where the species was first described. The common name is of unknown origin and inappropriate.

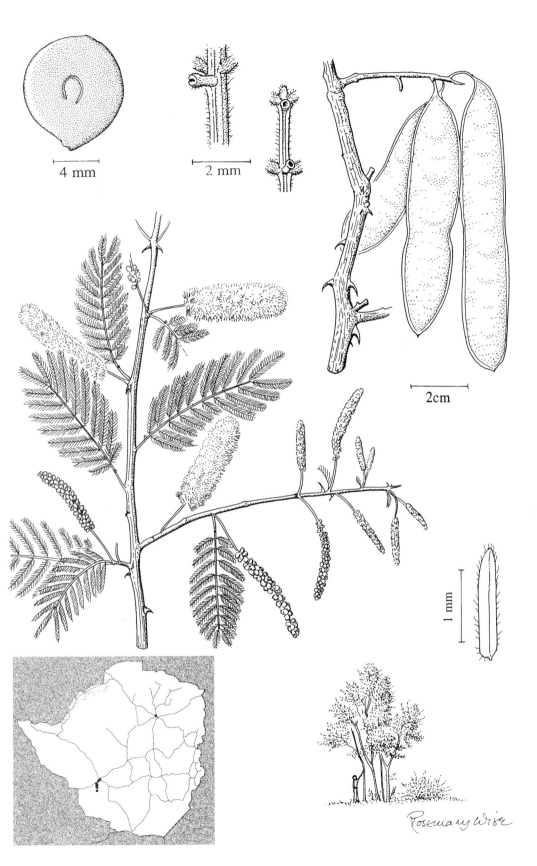

4 mm

2 mm

2cm

1 mm

Rosemary Wise

ACACIA HEREROENSIS

23

ACACIA KARROO *Hayne*
(= *A. natalitia* E. Mey.)

Common names: sweet thorn, mimosa thorn; soetdoring (Afrikaans); isinga (Ndebele); munenje (Shona); butema, gaba (Kalanga)

Acacia karroo is perhaps the commonest and most useful acacia in Zimbabwe. Its upright profile, rich green foliage and strong contrasting colours, particularly when flowering, typify many medium altitude ranching areas in the drier parts of the country.

Description A. *karroo* is a small to medium-sized tree up to 17 m in height, but usually only 4-8 m. Open-grown young trees often have a "skirt" of small dead branches round the stem, which fall as the tree matures to leave a clean bole with a typically wide and rounded crown. Trees in dense stands can be tall and spindly. **Bark** is dark brown to black on the bole, rough and fissured when old, but smoother and often with an orange tinge when young. The trunk is normally 20-30 cm in diameter, but can reach 70 cm. **Young twigs** have a shiny or sticky green appearance on the youngest growth, sometimes with a few small red glands. Older twigs are dark brown, flaking to reveal a reddish underlayer. **Thorns** are long, straight, paired at the nodes, whitish with brown tips. They are normally 2-5 cm long but can be up to 10 cm and sometimes inflated along their length. Such inflated thorns are found on the later part of a season's growth.

Leaves are medium-sized (3-6 x 2-3 cm) with 2-5 pairs of pinnae, each with 8-20 pairs of dark green, smooth, medium-sized leaflets. Trees at higher altitudes can have more pairs of pinnae. **Inflorescences** are numerous globose heads of sweet-smelling golden-yellow flowers clustered at the ends of the current season's branchlets. Flowering can start in November after good rains (the first rains seem to "prime" trees for later flowering), but usually peaks in the second half of December through to January; some trees in favourable situations flower earlier. Second and even third flushes of flowers can occur later in the season depending on the rainfall pattern – flowering seems to be initiated by a period of high rainfall following a drier spell. **Pods** are slender, sickle-shaped, hanging in bunches and becoming twisted after dehiscing on the tree. They are reddish brown when ripe, smooth, and slightly constricted between the seeds.

Field characters Upright profile and curved ascending branches; blackish bark; rusty or orange-red layer underbark on young branches; leaves smooth, almost glossy green; flattened, furrowed rachis; leaflets not overlapping; slender sickle-shaped pods.

A. *karroo* is not normally confused with other *Acacia* species except those of the glandular complex (see Box 4, page 79). However, these species are all shrubs and have sticky glandular young growth and/or small pods covered in small red glands. Compared to other *Acacia* species, the curved ascending branches, glossy rich green leaflets, furrowed rachis and slender pods are quite characteristic.

Distribution and ecology A. *karroo* is the most widespread *Acacia* in southern Africa and occurs from southern Malawi, southern Zambia and southwest Angola to the southern African coast in a multiplicity of habitats. It is, however, absent from the dry interior of Botswana, but not from the arid Karoo. Further north, it is replaced by its ecological counterpart, A. *seyal*. The populations of A. *karroo* found on the north-eastern coast of South Africa behave ecologically quite differently from those elsewhere, and on Bazaruto Island on Mozambique's tropical coastline it is found on the seashore. Those populations are probably a separate species, not yet properly described (see Box 7, page 93). Within Zimbabwe, A. *karroo* is found at medium and higher altitudes up to 1800 m, and rarely is it seen below 1000 m. At higher altitudes trees are generally smaller than elsewhere and inflated thorns are more common.

Here, A. *karroo* is a species of woodland, open woodland and bushland on clay and loamy soils, where it is generally found in association with

→

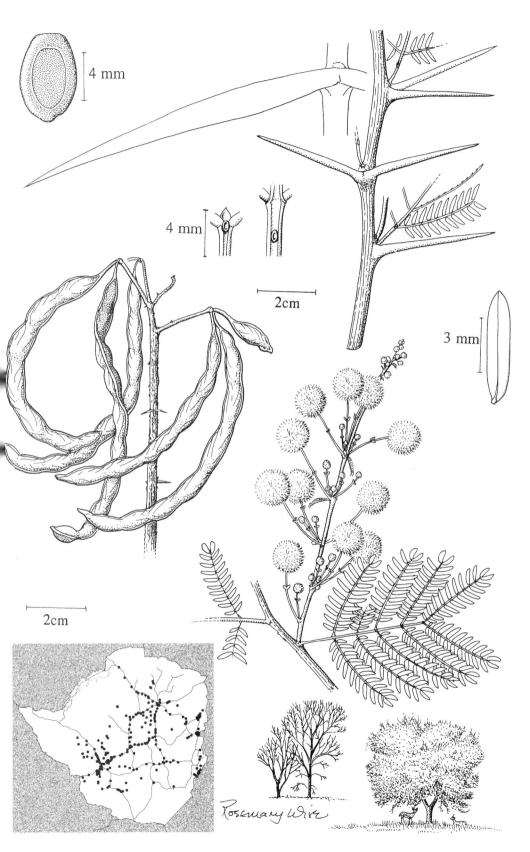

4 mm

4 mm

2cm

3 mm

2cm

Rosemary Wise

ACACIA KARROO

other *Acacia* and some *Combretum* species. It can form dense stands on alluvium along rivers and on red clay soils such as those associated with the footslopes of the Great Dyke. Elsewhere it is common but more scattered, being found along drainage lines and in disturbed areas. It sometimes occurs on black cracking clay soils and the roots appear to be able, at least partially, to withstand root shearing. *A. karroo* is also a component of forest edge woodland, as at Chirinda and other moist forests of the Eastern Highlands. It is tolerant of the severe frosts that occur in the river valleys of Matabeleland, where it is often the dominant species. In all these situations *A. karroo* is on deeper red or blackish nutrient-rich clay soils, and not on sand. Because of this association, the species is generally regarded as an indicator of good agricultural soils and rangeland.

More than most other Zimbabwe *Acacia* species, *A. karroo* is quite plastic in that it can have different forms in different environments. It is also an aggressive pioneer species, readily invading degraded or overgrazed areas.

Notes *A. karroo* is one of the fastest growing of the acacias; individual trees can produce over a cubic metre of wood in 25 years under conditions where few other species, including exotics, could do as well. But it is not a long-lived tree, and decline starts soon after this age with deterioration of the crown rapidly accelerated by heavy infestation by parasitic mistletoes (*Viscum* and *Loranthus* spp.). Few trees live for more than 30-40 years.

Although relatively fast-growing, *A. karroo* produces a wood of surprisingly high density – about 800-890 kg/m³. As a fuelwood, it does not produce long-lasting coals like *Combretum imberbe* or mopane, but it generates a lot of heat and burns very evenly and cleanly with little smoke, therefore is often a preferred fuelwood. It also makes an excellent charcoal. Its ability to coppice means that some form of sustainable utilization is possible. The wood is of medium even texture with very wide and creamy brown sapwood and red-brown heartwood. It is not durable and is prone to splitting and twisting. It is also rapidly attacked by a host of wood-boring insects, especially if there is still any bark attached, and is liable to fungal attack. Leaving logs under water for a year is said to reduce insect attack. Although *A. karroo* produces a tough resilient timber that planes and finishes well, its use is limited by the small size of most trees. It has been used for utility timber and, occasionally, furniture. The inner bark is used for cordage and tanning, and as a dye giving a yellow to brown colour for fabrics and a red colour to leather.

The red-gold gum is collected and sold commercially for use as a gum arabic substitute, from which it is scarcely distinguishable. The edible gum, often chewed by children, is used in the food and pharmaceutical industries, and can also be used as an adhesive. Monkeys and bushbabies also relish it.

A. karroo is an important rangeland tree. It is always associated with sweetveld grasses – those grasses that remain palatable through the dry season. However, *A. karroo* can be invasive in badly managed rangeland, but if the trees are allowed to grow and are then thinned and pruned to allow light to penetrate to the ground, and cattle to have access to the grass underneath, a parkland can develop with a high potential for meat production. In addition, both the pods and foliage provide good browse for cattle and wildlife. The larvae of the emperor moth *Heniocha appollonia* and the butterflies *Anthene amarah*, *A. atacilia*, *Azanzus moriqua*, *A. natalensis*, *A. ubaldus* and *Crudaria leroma*, feed on the foliage.

An infusion of roots of *A. karroo* is used by Ndebele traditional healers against general body pains, and by Shona healers against dizziness, convulsions and gonorrhoea; it is also used as an aphrodisiac. Roots are sometimes placed in chicken runs to reduce parasites. A decoction of the bark has been used as an astringent and emetic and as an antidote to "tulp" (*Moraea*) poisoning in cattle. A mucilage of the gum relieves thrush in the mouth.

Minor uses include the use of thorns as needles, and the flowers are an important source of pollen and nectar for honeybees. The seeds are a coffee substitute when roasted.

Growth is fairly rapid and the species, once established, is drought and frost resistant. It coppices readily. Seeds are readily germinated. As with other similar pioneer species, *A. karroo* often forms even-aged stands (see Box 15, page 131). These stands come about by invasion into a cleared or heavily disturbed site; there is minimal regeneration under the canopy, perhaps owing to excessive shade and moisture competition from grasses.

The species is named after the Karoo region of the former Cape Province of South Africa, where it is often the only tree found. The common name possibly refers to the sweet smell of the flowers, or to the fact that the species presence indicates sweetveld.

BOX 4 – THE GLANDULAR ACACIAS

There is a group of closely-related shrubby acacias in southern Africa which have pods and young growth with small reddish, often sticky, glands. The species that occur in Zimbabwe are *A. borleae*, *A. exuvialis*, *A. nebrownii* and *A. permixta*. Although it doesn't always have these small red glands, *A. karroo* can also be considered to be part of the broader complex (Ross 1971a). Similar species found not far way in South Africa, Botswana and southern Mozambique are *A. swazica* and *A. tenuispina*, while *A. torrei* is known only from central Mozambique.

Features common to the group include slender stems (often somewhat shiny), long straight white thorns, bright green leaflets, yellow globose inflorescences and small flattened curved pods. Important characters in separating the species, in what is a somewhat confusing complex, are the degree of curvature of the pod, presence of glands on the leaf margins, presence of long hairs on the young growth, number of pairs of pinnae, and the position of the involucel on the flower stalk (Verdoorn 1951).

One of the most interesting features of these species is their distribution and its biogeographical implications. All but three (*A. karroo*, *A. nebrownii* and *A. torrei*) are confined to the palaeo-Limpopo Basin (the area drained by the Limpopo River some few million years ago) which stretches from the Makgadikgadi Pans in Botswana, through south-eastern Botswana, southern Zimbabwe and northern South Africa (including the highveld north of Pretoria, the Lebombo Hills and the Kruger National Park), to southern Mozambique. The only species found in the palaeo-Zambezi Basin is *A. nebrownii*.

A. torrei (closely related to *A. borleae*) is known only from the Urema Trough in the Gorongosa area of central Mozambique which, a million years ago or so, was part of the Shire/Lower Zambezi River exiting at Beira. *A. nebrownii* has the widest distribution of any in the group (excepting *A. karroo*), ranging from Namibia across Botswana to both the Zambezi and Limpopo catchments in Zimbabwe. However, it appears as if the Zambezi Basin population, at least within Zimbabwe, differs significantly from that in the Limpopo Basin.

It is likely that the group evolved within the palaeo-Limpopo Basin over the last few million years, perhaps from an ancestral form similar to *A. karroo*. With the increasing aridity of the Basin, different populations adapted to specific dry environments such as black clay soils, gravelly soils and free-draining calcareous outcrops, and became separate species as geographical separation became more pronounced.

If this hypothesis is correct, the group provides a good example of adaptive radiation in a comparatively restricted area. Quite why, or how, *A. nebrownii* became so widespread – in effect "escaped" from the Limpopo Basin – is not known. Whether *A. karroo* was the precursor of this group (Ross 1971a), or a species which subsequently has shown remarkable plasticity and expanded into a whole range of environments, is also open to debate.

24

ACACIA KIRKII *Oliv.*

Common name: flood plain acacia

A medium-sized tree that is apparently associated with clay-rich alluvium deposited in a previous, wetter, epoch, *Acacia kirkii* has a very localized distribution in the west and north of the country. It is characterized by shiny green peeling bark and pods with prominent "warts" over the seeds.

Description *A. kirkii* is a medium sized tree to 8 m, usually branching from the base and with ascending, spreading, arcuate branches, sometimes drooping at the ends. The canopy is open, but with distinctive dark green foliage. Normal stem diameter near the base is 12-20 cm. **Bark** is distinctive with a translucent papery layer peeling off over a shiny green underbark. **Young twigs** are plum coloured and slightly pubescent. **Thorns** are white, straight and paired at the nodes. **Leaves** are clustered, medium-sized (5 x 2 cm) and feathery in appearance, with a very short petiole. There are 6-10 pinnae pairs, each with many very small yellowish green leaflets. The tree appears to hold its leaves for an extended period. **Inflorescences** are globose balls of cream-coloured flowers appearing on old growth around October. The indehiscent, wavy-edged, yellowish brown **pods** are very distinctive, especially when hanging suspended from the branches, and have a raised "wart" over each seed.

Field characters Green stem and peeling bark; dense foliage; hanging pods; wavy-edged pods with distinctive "warts".

The species is unlikely to be confused with any other, especially if pods are seen. It has a superficial resemblance to *A. nilotica*.

Distribution and ecology This distinctive species is found from Kenya and Sudan south to Angola, Namibia, Botswana and northern Zimbabwe. The distribution is curiously restricted, seemingly associated with alluvium of the rift valleys from previous pluvial periods. Within Zimbabwe, *A. kirkii* has a disjunct distribution, being locally common and sometimes forming groves (a) along the Upper Zambezi River above Victoria Falls, (b) along the mid-Zambezi River between the Sapi and Luangwa rivers, and (c) along the lower reaches of the Nata River in Tsholotsho. In each case the species is found with mopane and riparian trees on nutrient-rich, silty, kaolinitic clay to black cracking clays derived from old alluvial or lacustrine deposits, possibly relics of the Pleistocene pluvials. These areas are generally seasonally flooded. Regeneration appears good.

Notes All plants in southern Africa belong to subsp. *kirkii* var. *kirkii*. The other variety, var. *sublaevis* Brenan, and another subspecies, subsp. *mildbraedii* (Harms) Brenan, are found in forested areas in Uganda, eastern Democratic Republic of Congo, Rwanda and northwestern Tanzania under much higher rainfall conditions.

Elephants do a lot of damage to the tree and many specimens show broken, although re-sprouting, branches and stripped bark. The young growth is heavily browsed, perhaps due to its gum content. The indehiscent pods are quite possibly dispersed by elephant via their droppings, so is surprising that the species is not more widespread. A sticky gum is often seen exuding from the stem. Larvae of the butterfly *Charaxes ethalion binghami* feed on the foliage but have not been bred from *A. kirkii* yet in Zimbabwe.

The species is named after Sir John Kirk who collected the type specimen in the Southern Province of Zambia.

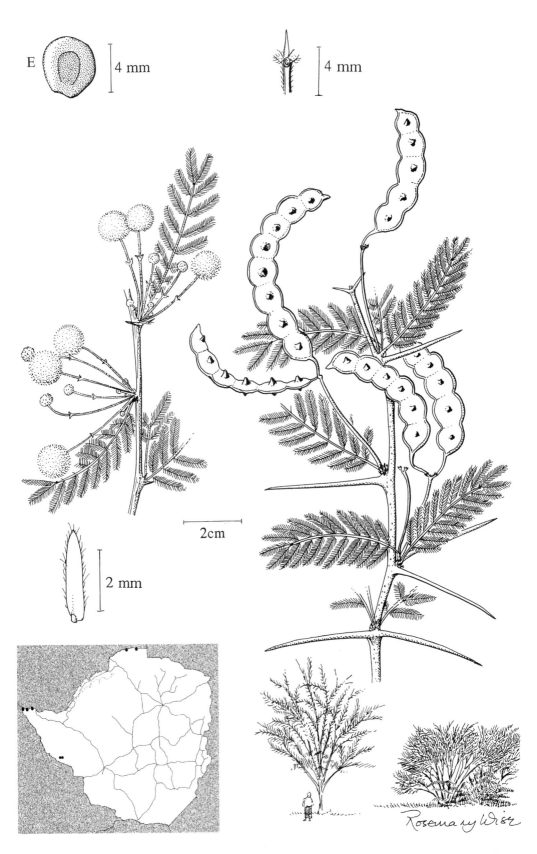

E   4 mm

4 mm

2cm

2 mm

ACACIA KIRKII

Rosemary Wise

25

ACACIA LUEDERITZII *Engl.*
(= *A. retinens* sensu O.B.Miller 1948, *A. uncinata* sensu O.B.Miller 1952)

Common name: kalahari sand acacia

Acacia luederitzii, as its common name implies, is associated with the Kalahari sands of Hwange National Park. The mixture of stout straight and deflexed thorns helps to distinguish it from other species.

Description A. luederitzii is a medium sized tree up to 12 m in height with a rounded crown, often branching from the base. Trunk is normally 15-30 cm in diameter, but can be up to 75 cm. **Bark** is dark brown to greyish, rough and heavily fissured. **Young twigs** are grey to reddish brown and are densely covered in light grey hairs, while older growth is smooth but furrowed. **Thorns** are mostly straight and paired at the nodes but some are shorter and recurved, thus appearing almost hooked. Straight thorns are grey-white, up to 7 cm long, and are often partly inflated. **Leaves** are medium-sized (6 x 4 cm) and softly hairy, normally with 6-8 pairs of pinnae, each with many small leaflets. **Inflorescence** is a globose head of white flowers appearing on the current season's growth around October to February; they are generally clustered at the nodes. **Pods** are dehiscent, grey-brown to purplish brown, straight or slightly curved and rounded at the ends, and ripen in February to May. Valves are stiff and brittle, but not woody, and have longitudinal or oblique veins and fine pubescence on the conspicuously flattened rim.

Field characters Tree of Kalahari sands in Hwange National Park; mixture of long straight and curved thorns; pubescent young growth.
    A. *luederitzii* can be confused with A. *gerrardii* in Zimbabwe, but the latter has thicker and more robust ascending growth and is not found on Kalahari sand. It rarely has recurved thorns and the pods are thinner and curved.

Distribution and ecology A. *luederitzii* var. *luederitzii*, the only variety recorded in Zimbabwe, is otherwise known from western Zambia, Namibia and the former Northern Cape. In Zimbabwe it has been found only in Hwange National Park and northern Tsholotsho communal land on Kalahari sand. Here it grows in open woodland on the slopes of fossil dunes or in dune slacks and on vlei margins; in many respects it is a true Kalahari species. Commonly associated with A. *erioloba* and other *Acacia* species, it is generally found in slightly moister habitats. The trees can be heavily browsed in the park, the lower half of the tree forming a dense bush and developing an hour glass shape.

Notes Another variety, var. *retinens* (Sim) J.H. Ross & Brenan, is found in southeast Botswana, the former Transvaal (including Kruger National Park), southern Mozambique and southwards to KwaZulu-Natal. It is this variety that is normally being referred to under A. *luederitzii* in South African literature. Var. *retinens* is a shrub to 3 m and often has large inflated thorns. The appearance and ecology are substantially different such that they are best regarded as separate species rather than mere varieties. Another species, A. *reficiens* Wawra subsp. *reficiens*, was previously confused with A. *luederitzii*, but they are now kept separate on the basis of details on pubescence and fewer pairs of pinnae. This subspecies of A. *reficiens* is found only in southern Angola and northern Namibia.

The wood is hard and pale brown and makes a good firewood, although not reputedly as long lasting as that from A. *erioloba*. The gum produced is edible, while the leaves contain 10-19% crude protein (figures from central Botswana) and are browsed by elephant.

Growth is relatively slow.

The name refers to the German naturalist and collector August Lüederitz, or his elder brother Adolf, who collected plants in Namibia in the last century.

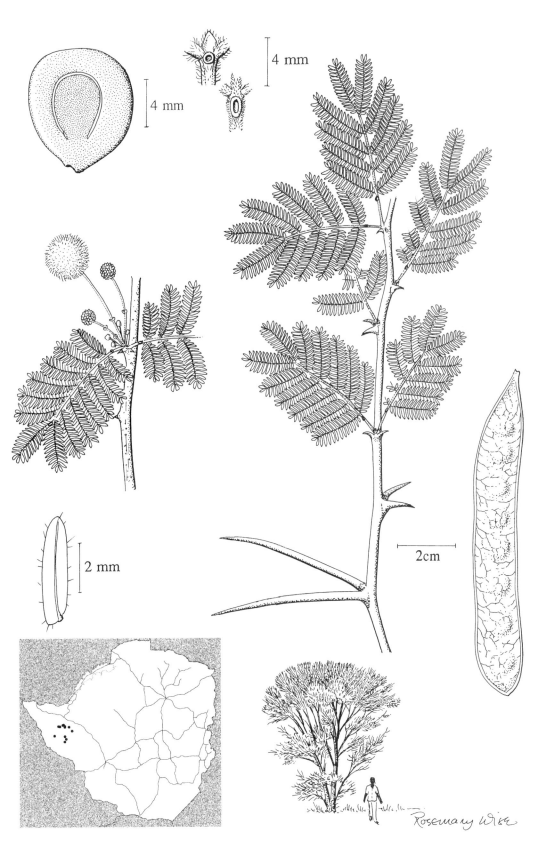

ACACIA LUEDERITZII

Acacias of Zimbabwe   83

ACACIA MELLIFERA *(Vahl) Benth.*
(= *A. detinens* Burch.)

Common names: hook thorn; swaarthaak (Afrikaans); katogwa, muguhungu, mukotokwa, umngaga (Ndebele); mupandabutolo (Tonga)

A small tree or shrub of very localized, scattered distribution, mostly in the western part of the country, *Acacia mellifera* has tough branches with conspicuous white markings and leaves with rounded blue-green leaflets.

Description *A. mellifera* is a small, usually multi-stemmed, tree 4-6 m high, or obconical shrub to 2 m. Some individuals have a main trunk, but branch low. The crown is rounded, sometimes reaching the ground, and the foliage is relatively dense. Stem diameter of mature trees is around 15-20 cm. **Bark** is greyish and fissured; younger branches have greyish smooth bark, often with thorns, leaves and lichen on them. The slash is thin and green underneath, with cream-coloured sapwood. **Young twigs** are rigid, grey to purplish, spiky and hard to break; transverse white lenticels are conspicuous. The strongly attached, hooked **thorns** are small, blackish and paired at the nodes – a vicious plant to get caught in. **Leaves** are medium-sized (3 x 2 cm) with 2-3 pairs of pinnae, each with 1 or 2 pairs of asymmetric, large blue-green leaflets, sometimes almost as large as *A. nigrescens*. **Inflorescences** are white in round to slightly elongate axillary heads, sweet-scented and attractive to insects, appearing in August to October on the previous season's growth before the leaves appear from September onward. **Pods** are relatively small, shortish with an apiculate tip and papery, transversely veined and straw-brown in colour. They are early dehiscent (December-February).

Field characters Small tree with rounded shape; conspicuous white lenticels on young stems; small strong vicious thorns; large blue-green leaflets; papery pods.

Often not noticed from a distance, *A. mellifera* is fairly easily identified from close up. The white lenticels on tough twigs, small thorns and grey-green rounded leaflets separate it from *A. goetzei* subsp. *goetzei* and *A. nigrescens*. Confusion can arise with the hybrid *A. laeta* (see below).

Distribution and ecology The subspecies that occurs in Zimbabwe, *A. mellifera* subsp. *detinens* (Burch.) Brenan, occurs over much of southern Africa from Tanzania south to Angola, Namibia, Botswana, Zambia, Zimbabwe, Mozambique and the former Transvaal. In Zimbabwe it has a scattered distribution, being local and nowhere common, and is normally restricted to patches of a few individuals at low to medium altitudes (300-1200 m). It has been recorded from Dande, Kariba, and Gonarezhou in the north and east, but essentially has a western distribution from Binga and Hwange to Matopos. In the west it is often associated with pans or calcareous clay-rich depressions on Kalahari sands in Hwange National Park and Tsholotsho, an extension of its more widespread distribution in Botswana and the former northern Cape. The species seems to prefer calcareous soils, which may explain its very localized occurrence, and it is also found on sites of old disturbance. At times it can be thicket forming; in Botswana, the former Northern Cape and Namibia it causes severe bush encroachment.

Notes Subsp. *mellifera*, with fewer pinnae and elongate inflorescences, is found only in northern Namibia and Angola, and from Tanzania to the northeast.

Heartwood, almost black in colour, is only found in much older trees. The sapwood is hard and strong, and the wood is very heavy (1100 kg/m³), saws well and has good durability, although it needs careful seasoning. It is resistant to borers, termites and fungi, and has been used for tool and implement handles, perhaps because of its small size.

The pods, leaves and flowers are very nutritious to livestock and game. Crude protein levels of 14-27% have been recorded from leaves

→

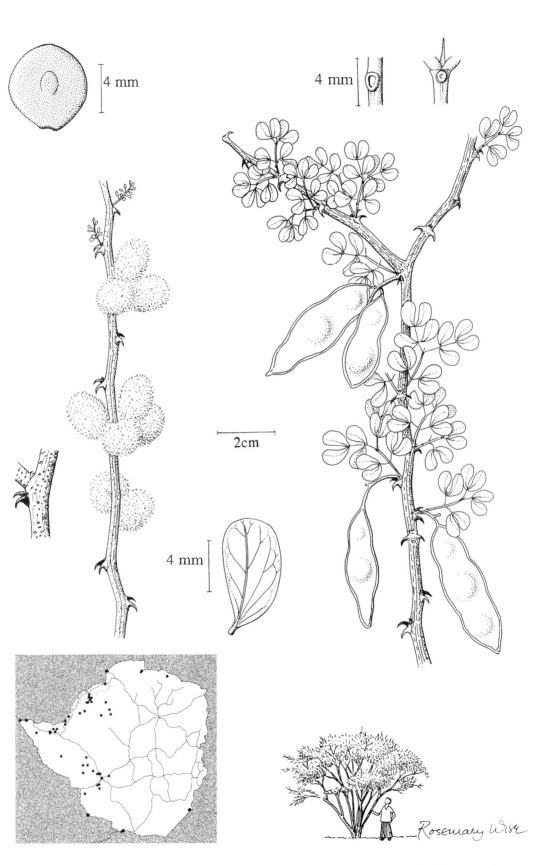

ACACIA MELLIFERA

in central Botswana. A bark infusion is used in parts of Mashonaland as an aphrodisiac. The larvae of the emperor moth *Heniocha dyops* feed on the foliage of *A. mellifera* and some other *Acacia* species.

The growth rate is fairly slow.

The specific name comes from the Latin meaning "honey-producing" (*mel* - honey, *ferre* - to bear) as the flowers are attractive to bees. Owing to its scattered distribution in Zimbabwe it is unlikely to be important for bee-keepers here. The subspecific name comes from the Latin meaning "detaining" (*detineo* - to hold back) and refers to the unwelcome character of the thorns.

"Acacia laeta" At Sentinel Ranch and Nottingham Estates in the far southwest of Zimbabwe along the Limpopo River, a possible hybrid between *A. mellifera* and *A. senegal* has been repeatedly found. Such individuals are closer to *A. mellifera*, but have some of the characteristics of *A. senegal* such as three thorns, more pairs of pinnae (2-4 instead of 2-3 pairs) and more numerous and smaller leaflets (3-5 instead of 1-2 pairs). Various populations of this possible hybrid have been found, always in association with *A. mellifera*. The other parent is most likely to be *A. senegal* var. *leiorhachis*, which occurs in the vicinity and flowers at a similar time (var. *rostrata* flowers much later).

This putative hybrid is a shrub to multi-stemmed tree up to 4 m in height. Young twigs smooth with conspicuous white transversely-arranged lenticels. Hooked thorns at the nodes, paired, single or in threes, but all pointing downwards. Medium-sized leaves with 2-4 pairs of pinnae, each with 3-5 pairs of asymmetric blue-green leaflets. Otherwise it is indistinguishable from *A. mellifera*. It occurs on calcareous alluvial flats and in *Acacia* bushland.

A similar *Acacia* occurs in Tanzania, Somalia and Sudan across to West Africa that has been described under the name of *A. laeta* Benth. This has since been shown to be a fertile hybrid between *A. mellifera* and *A. senegal* var. *senegal*, with a chromosome number of 2n=39. If the hybrid in south-eastern Zimbabwe is found to produce flowers and fertile seed, a case could be made to call it *A. laeta*, although the other parent is a different variety of *A. senegal*. True *A. laeta* has not been recorded south of northern Tanzania. During recent fieldwork two pods with ripe seed were found, but it is too early to draw any firm conclusions.

BOX 5 - USES OF ACACIAS IN COMMUNAL LANDS AND ON SMALL FARMS

Woodlands are a crucial component of most communal farming systems in Zimbabwe. However, population pressure has brought about deforestation and severe land degradation, particularly in the drier parts of the country. People in these areas face great hardships and improving their quality of life depends on maintaining and increasing yields from cultivated crops and, particularly, on realizing more of the potential for livestock production. A great deal of this can be accomplished by re-establishing trees in the evolving farming systems.

Acacia species are a conspicuous element in the natural vegetation in most of the drier parts of Zimbabwe. Many can establish themselves on bare ground, rapidly access water and nutrients deep down in the soil, grow fast and fix nitrogen. It is these attributes that give them their early place in the succession of woody species that naturally colonize and rehabilitate denuded or degraded land in the semi-arid regions of Africa. Acacias also provide multiple products and services including fuelwood, fodder, gums, shade and soil improvement. A large number of the African acacias, therefore, have potential for use in improving animal production through enriching rangeland forage, in restoring fertility in bush-fallows, in inter-cropping with grain crops to increase yields and in woodlots dedicated to fuelwood or gum production.

Acacias have attributes that give them advantages over both the traditionally used slow-growing indigenous species and the exotics that have been introduced to replace them. They are not only drought resistant and fast-growing, but they also have in their thorns a natural defence against browsing animals and are termite resistant; the costs of fencing and insecticide are prohibitive factors for small-scale farmers trying to establish trees. The inherent capacity of many of the acacias to invade is not a problem in the highly populated and intensively-used communal lands where their products are more likely to be welcomed than their presence resented as a hindrance to agriculture.

Compared to a number of countries in other parts of Africa, there is a lack of appreciation of the value of acacias in the communal lands of Zimbabwe, despite their growing contribution to agricultural production through the fodder they provide. There are, however, signs that this is changing. For example, the value of leaving *Faidherbia albida* trees in the cultivated fields is recognized in Binga District, pods of *A. erioloba* are collected and fed directly to cattle throughout its range in Matabeleland, *A. tortilis* pods are collected in Gwanda District and sold to livestock owners for feed at the end of the dry season when grass becomes scarce, and *A. karroo* is becoming recognized for its production of a cash crop of gum and a supply of high quality fuelwood. Many farmers also now recognize the increased productivity that is achieved in grain crops when they are planted in lands cleared of acacia thickets. Recently, a study in the Mutambara Communal Area in the Save Valley (Campbell *et al.* 1994), showed that *Acacia* species gave an increase in productivity over time while only a few other products from the natural woodland even remained stable. Tangible recognition of the value of acacias in agricultural systems is now being demonstrated by communal farmers themselves in the Ntabazinduna Communal Lands near Bulawayo (Clarke 1994) who prune *A. karroo* for livestock forage.

The usefulness of acacias in farming systems can be increased by judicial management of the existing trees, by creating conditions for the existing trees to regenerate themselves, by sowing or planting seeds collected from local trees into the farm or range, by planting seedlings from a source that is more productive than the local material or by introducing an entirely new species into an area. In all these methods, genetic variation can be exploited through selection of superior trees either through removing undesirable individuals or through collecting seed from superior individuals (see Box 1, page 27).

27

ACACIA NEBROWNII *Burtt Davy*
(= *A. rogersii* Burtt Davy)

Common name: water acacia

Acacia nebrownii is the most widely distributed of the shrubby acacias with glandular pods, distinguished by the bright green foliage and slender shiny shoots. It occurs in two different forms – one in the Shashe-Limpopo area and the other in the Kamativi area.

Description *A. nebrownii* is a multi-stemmed shrub to 3 m with slender shoots and an open appearance. **Bark** is smooth and grey-brown. **Young twigs** are purplish to orange-brown, often somewhat shiny and with a grey-translucent peeling epidermis. There are a few scattered reddish glands. **Thorns** are long (6 cm) and slender, straight, white as if whitewashed, and paired at the nodes. **Leaves** are small (1-3 x 2-3 cm) and clustered in the axils forming a "cushion", with 1-3 pairs of pinnae. Leaflets are few and medium, yellowish-green and rounded at the end, sometimes with a small mucronate tip. **Inflorescences** are clustered in the axils of the young growth, with a globose head of bright yellow sweet-smelling flowers appearing from September to November. The involucel is basal or less than halfway up the peduncle. **Pods** are small, broad and curved, covered with small sessile reddish glands.

Field characters Slender-stemmed shrub; 1 or 2 pinnae pairs; short, broad glandular pods; the only glandular acacia (apart from *A. karroo*) in the Zambezi catchment.

The species is clearly separable from most other glandular acacias due to the single (occasionally 2 or 3) pairs of pinnae.

Distribution and ecology *A. nebrownii* is the only glandular acacia that extends beyond the Limpopo basin (see Box 4, page 79). It is found in Namibia, across much of Botswana, in western Zimbabwe and in the former northern Transvaal. In Zimbabwe it has only been recorded from the southwest around Tuli and Beitbridge and in the northwest from Hwange to Milibizi. It is locally common, but not widespread in these areas.

Its ecology appears to be distinctly different in the two areas. In the north *A. nebrownii* is a species of rocky slopes on fine-grained Karoo sediments, possibly with acid soils, in stunted mopane-*Commiphora* savanna. In the south it appears to be more associated with calcareous clays and floodplains with other *Acacia* species, although it can also be found on rocky Karoo-derived soils. Sometimes the species forms thickets close to major drainage lines. In Botswana and Namibia, where the species is more widespread, it is generally associated with calcrete outcrops and fossil river valleys. *A. exuvialis* in Gonarezhou, with which *A. nebrownii* could be confused, is found on rocky soils derived from Cretaceous sandstone – one appears to be the ecological homologue of the other.

Notes Along with the distinct difference in ecology between the two populations, the position of the involucel on the peduncle also differs. The standard taxonomic description of the species puts the involucel as less than one-third of the way up the peduncle, but in the northern population the involucel is consistently higher up the peduncle. This removes one of the main taxonomic differences separating *A. nebrownii* from the other glandular species. Leaves from the northern population normally have two pairs of pinnae, while those from the southern population are distinctly smaller (1 x 1 cm) and rarely have more than one pair of pinnae, each with 3-4 pairs of leaflets. It is possible that there are two subspecies in Zimbabwe, or even two separate species.

The species is named after the botanist N.E. Brown who worked at Kew mostly on African plants, although he never visited the continent.

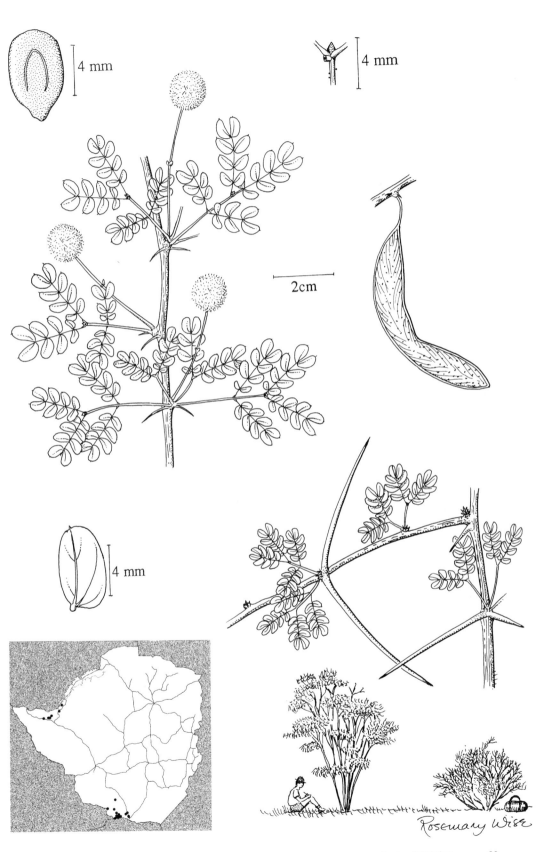

ACACIA NEBROWNII

28

ACACIA NIGRESCENS *Oliv.*
(= *A. pallens* (Benth.) Rolfe)

Common names: knobthorn; knoppiesdoring (Afrikaans); katopa, mupumbu, umhlope, umkayamhlope (Ndebele); gakaunga, mpozva, sinanga (Shangaan); mukotonga, mukuu, nkoho (Shona); moba, mwaba, mukotokoto (Tonga)

Acacia nigrescens is one of the more common and better-known acacias of the hotter, drier parts of Zimbabwe; the white flowers appearing on leafless trees are one of the first sights of spring. This ecologically and economically important species is an indicator of good ranching country and fertile soils, and provides a strong rough timber.

Description *A. nigrescens* is a medium-sized to large tall erect tree up to 16 m in height with a long cylindrical profile and rounded crown. Large, raised, pyramidal woody bosses with a hooked thorn on top are commonly seen on the trunk, particularly on young trees, but are often absent on old individuals. Trunk is normally around 50 cm in diameter on mature specimens, but can reach 75 cm. The slash is red. **Bark** is dark brown to blackish, rough and fissured. On some individuals a yellowish underbark can be seen and on very young specimens the stem is grey. **Young twigs** are relatively thin, greyish brown, and generally smooth with a long distance between the nodes. **Thorns** are strongly hooked and paired at the nodes, broadly based, strong and blackish. **Leaves** are medium in size (7 x 3 cm) with 2-4 pairs of pinnae. Each pinna has 1 or 2 pairs of sometimes pubescent, large (1-2 cm wide) oval, but asymmetric green to blue-green leaflets, the largest of any acacia. The leaves fall in the early to mid dry season and trees are conspicuously leafless until September-October. **Inflorescences** are long spikes of sweetly scented white flowers, reddish in bud, which appear in profusion at the base of young shoots as temperatures rise in August-September with, or just before, the leaves. The dehiscent **pods** are straight, fairly narrow (1-2 cm) and pointed at the tip. The valves are dark brown and smooth, ripening on the tree from December to March.

Field description Erect tree with narrow profile; often leafless for some months in dry season; strong hooked thorns on raised woody "knobs" on trunk and branches; 2-3 pairs of pinnae, each with one or two pairs of large oval leaflets.

Most specimens of *A. nigrescens* are easily identified from the knobby thorns and large leaflets, but confusion can sometimes arise with other large leaflet species such as *A. mellifera*, *A. goetzei* and *A. burkei*. However, *A. nigrescens* rarely has more than 2 or 3 pairs of pinnae, each of which bear 1 or 2 pairs of large rounded leaflets. It is the only species with thorns on large knobs on the trunk, although *A. goetzei* can have smaller knobs.

Distribution and ecology *A. nigrescens* is found from Tanzania southwards to KwaZulu-Natal and west to the Caprivi in Namibia, northern and eastern Botswana. It is primarily a species of woodland and bushland, commonly near rivers and drainage lines, and is rarely found on sandy soils. In Zimbabwe it is widespread at medium and low altitudes, both on shallow soils on rocky hillsides and on alluvial soils in the valleys. However, it is localized and much less common above 1200 m and is not found above 1100 m in the wetter parts of Mashonaland and Manicaland. *A. nigrescens* is an important, occasionally dominant, component of various woodland types on stony or clay-rich soils below 900 m altitude. It seems to require moderately eutrophic conditions and a certain level of available calcium, hence it is common on soils derived from basalt, gneiss and the Basement Complex and uncommon on granite soils. Typical associated species are mopane, *Kirkia acuminata*, *Combretum apiculatum* and other *Acacia* species. Although widespread on such soils, it becomes more common towards drainage lines and can be a large tree in riverine situations. On the central watershed above 1200 m individuals are often rather stunted with more prominent knobs on the stem and larger, pubescent leaflets. ➔

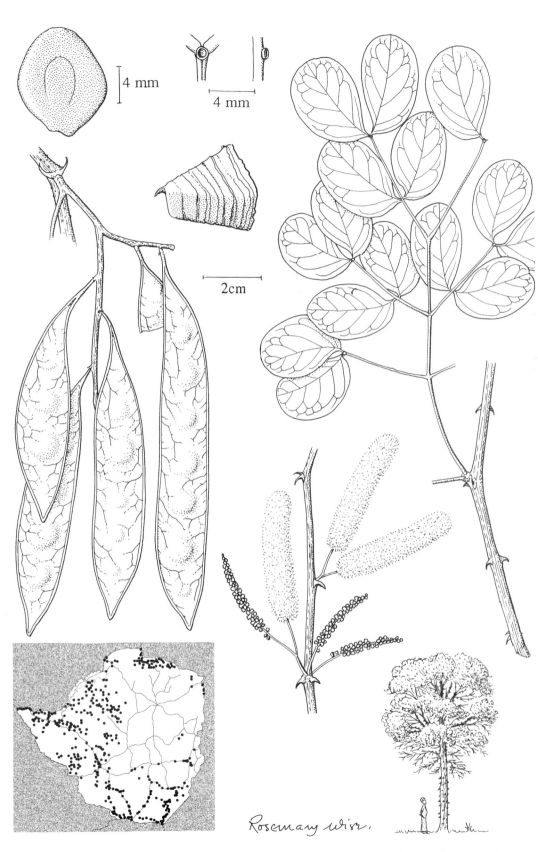

Roscmary Wise.

ACACIA NIGRESCENS

Notes The heartwood, which forms a substantial proportion of most boles, is one of the heaviest and most durable woods; even the sapwood is more durable than that of most acacias. The hard, strong, heavy (1120 kg/m³), dark brown heartwood has a medium to coarse even texture and requires slow seasoning. For such a dense timber it seasons well but often develops cracks. Because of its hardness and uneven crossed grain, it is difficult to work, but provides an excellent finish with only oil or wax. It is difficult to saw and dulls tool edges; sharp tools are required. The heartwood is extremely resistant to borer, termite and fungal attack. *A. nigrescens* can make attractive furniture but is generally considered too heavy for this. The wood has been used for carving, turnery, parquet flooring, railway sleepers and mine props, but its main use is for fence posts and stock handling facilities. The species is ideally suited to this being straight and having a moderate quantity of heartwood when pole-sized. It also provides an excellent firewood (see Box 16, page 135).

The foliage is a good source of browse for wildlife and livestock. Elephant often damage trees in the Zambezi Valley by breaking branches or stripping the bark. The bark is rich in tannin. Larvae of the emperor moths *Heniocha dyops, H. marnois* and the butterfly *Charaxes phaeus* feed on the leaves of *A. nigrescens* and some other *Acacia* species. The only recorded medicinal use is by Shona traditional healers who make an ointment from the burnt roots to treat convulsions.

The species has a slow growth rate and is frost sensitive but drought-resistant. It regenerates well from seed, and moderate germination occurs without pretreatment. The root system is deep with many shallow laterals. It can coppice when young.

The specific name is Latin for "becoming black" (*nigrescere* - to become black) and presumably refers to the thorns or pods.

BOX 6 – "THE ACACIA PENNATA COMPLEX"

The "*Acacia pennata* complex" is a group of mostly climbing or scrambling species with scattered thorns, formerly lumped together as one very variable species – *A. pennata*. However, over the last 50 years this complex has been split up into less variable taxa, most comprehensively by Brenan and Exell (1957), and now comprises 13 different species in mainland Africa (Ross 1979), some of which are also found in Madagascar. True *A. pennata* is now considered to be confined to India, Burma, Sri Lanka and other parts of South East Asia.

This *Acacia* group differs quite substantially from other *Acacia* species and is characterized by what are believed to be primitive features such as a scrambling or climbing habit (many are lianas) and lack of nodulation (Ross 1981). The flowers are globose and in terminal racemes, whilst the pods are mostly indehiscent. In Zimbabwe the group is represented by three species – *A. adenocalyx, A. pentagona* and *A. schweinfurthii*. Two other species,

A. brevispica and *A. kraussiana*, are found within the region in southern Mozambique and Natal.

Unlike all other species of *Acacia*, the majority of species from this group are found only in moist forests, though others in the group (e.g. *A. schweinfurthii* and *A. adenocalyx*) occur in dry forests or thickets. A look at the distribution of the group across Africa (Vassal 1977) shows that most species are found in the higher rainfall areas of the Congo Basin or are associated with coastal forests and thickets. *A. schweinfurthii* is the most widely distributed species, being found throughout the eastern side of the continent in riverine thickets.

The primitive features of this group, and their adaptation to a moist forest environment, suggest they have a long evolutionary history separate from the other members of the subgenus *Aculeiferum*, of which they form part. They are also the only species within the subgenus with globose, not spicate, inflorescences.

BOX 7 – MOLECULAR STUDIES IN THE AFRICAN ACACIAS

Plants are distinguished on the basis of inherent genetic differences between them. Taxonomists have traditionally used morphology and geographic distribution as the basis for their classification. Although this has been very successful in separating taxa at the levels of the family and genus, there are often problems at the variety, sub-species, species and sometimes even generic levels because the environment affects a plant's observable traits and obscures the genetic differences between them.

With the development of laboratory techniques, it has now become possible to identify chemical differences between individual plants at the molecular level and, more recently, even at the level of the genes themselves. These differences are generally unaffected by environment and therefore should provide a more reliable basis for classification. They vary in complexity from the technique of extracting particular enzymes from crushed plant cells (isozyme analysis) to the very precise one of extracting specific lengths of a particular chromosomes from the nucleus of the cell and determining the products from, or even the base sequences in that piece of genetic material (DNA analysis). In all these techniques, the molecular differences are determined by the particular patterns that the extracts produce by a procedure called electrophoresis when they are induced by an electric current to migrate across a gel; molecules of different weights travel different distances before they are fixed and form the characteristic bands that provide a genetic fingerprint. The missing link in these techniques is the ability to relate differences at this molecular level to the morphological differences upon which classical taxonomy is based. Until these links can be made, molecular techniques are seen by taxonomists as providing useful confirmation of otherwise tenuous, and often disputed, differences based on morphological differences rather than definitive evidence of taxonomic status. Comparative field trials that bring diverse populations together into a single environment will be required to establish these correlations, and they still remain the definitive test for the extent to which observed variation is under genetic control in a species.

Biochemical information has been used as supportive evidence for the recent differentiation of *Faidherbia albida* from *Acacia*. DNA studies have indicated that the species is more closely related to the members of the Tribe Ingeae than to those of Acacieae (both in the subfamily Mimosoideae), but the species is without close relatives and therefore considered to be deserving of monotypic generic status. Variation in the isozymes within *Faidherbia albida* has also been studied in a range-wide seed collection to determine patterns of genetic variation within the species (Harris *et al*. 1997). They have shown a marked disjunction between populations from West Africa, Ethiopia/Sudan and southern Africa. West African populations appear to be more diverse than those from Ethiopia and Sudan, which in turn are more diverse than those from southern Africa. The transition between the higher diversity of the northern and eastern populations and the lower diversity of the southern populations is in Tanzania. This kind of information is valuable when drawing up strategies for conserving the full genetic diversity of a species.

The use of molecular methods to investigate variation in *Acacia karroo* has been of particular interest to try to explain whether or not the extraordinary morphological variation within the species over the diverse environments in which it occurs is due to genetic differences. Isozyme analysis has suggested four main groups, the northern, the southern (Karoo), the south-central-eastern (Zululand coast), and the island populations on Bazaruto and Margaruque off the coast of Mozambique (Barnes *et al*. 1996). These differences have also been reflected in the morphology of the trees in comparative field trails near Bulawayo. The differences between the island populations and the rest are so profound that there appears to be a strong case for splitting them off into a separate species. The biochemical and morphological changes from the northern to the southern population types are considerable but gradual, and there appear to be no grounds for creating separate taxa. There is, however, more evidence for a discontinuity between the dune populations of Zululand and those on the rest of the mainland. In a very large study of variation of one particular enzyme (leaf peroxidase) of *Acacia karoo*, five bands were found in the gels and labeled K, L, M, N, and O (Brain *et al*. 1997). The analysis of this huge data set of 4,322 individual trees from 63 populations that represented the complete range of the species, indicated strong regional concentrations of particular types. The K band had a high frequency in the Karoo but was absent from Zululand and Natal, band L was more frequent in the western part of the species' range, but there was virtual fixation of the M band only in the coastal populations of Zululand and Mozambique. Another interesting finding was that variability appeared to be highest under the most adverse climactic conditions. Quite apart from the value of these findings to the taxonomist, these kinds of study can provide information quickly and cheaply on the distribution of genetic variation in a species' range and therefore a basis for sampling when testing the species' potential for domestication.

29

ACACIA NILOTICA *(L.) Delile*
(= *A. benthamii* Rochebr., A. *subalata* Vatke, *A. arabica* (Lam.) Willd.)

Common names: scented thorn; lekkerruikpeul (Afrikaans); isanqawe, umtshanga (Ndebele); changaviha (Shangaan); nombe, mukoka, mungnombie (Tonga)

Acacia nilotica is perhaps the most widespread of Zimbabwe's acacias, although it is most common at medium altitudes. Its low, spreading, rounded crown and constricted black pods are very characteristic, and when in full bloom in the early part of the year mature specimens present a magnificent sight.

Description *A. nilotica* is a small to medium-sized tree about 4-7 m in height with a stem diameter of 20-30 cm, occasionally more. The crown is low, spreading, often quite symmetrical, and characteristically rounded like an umbrella on free-standing specimens. **Bark** is very dark brown to black with deep regular vertical fissures in older specimens. **Young twigs** are grey-brown to dark salmon-pink, finely covered in hairs, and slightly zigzag between the nodes. The greyish epidermis has fine longitudinal cracks revealing a reddish brown inner layer. **Thorns** are moderately long, straight, paired at the nodes and typically pointing slightly backwards. **Leaves** are medium-sized (5 x 3 cm) with 4-8 pairs of pinnae, each bearing many small, closely spaced leaflets on a hairy rachis. Leaflets can be purple-tinged when under stress. The foliage normally remains on the tree into the dry season, and falls later than in some other *Acacia* species. **Inflorescences** are globose heads of yellow flowers clustered towards the end of the current seasons' growth. They are sweet-smelling and appear near the beginning of the rains in October through to January. Individual trees can have two flushes of flowers 2-3 months apart. **Pods** are indehiscent and very distinctive; long (8-15 cm), straight or sightly curved, constricted between the seeds and sometimes likened to a string of beads. When young they are green, but become almost black on ripening and contain a sticky, sweet-smelling gum which is quite noticeable in the early dry season. A tree may have both green and black pods at the same time resulting from the different flowering periods. The pods ripen on the tree and only fall to the ground during the following dry season.

Field characters Low spreading rounded crown; deflexed straight thorns; cracking epidermis on young growth; black indehiscent pods constricted between seeds.

The distinctive pods clearly separate *A. nilotica* from all other *Acacia* species here. When pods are not present, the deflexed thorns, longitudinally splitting epidermis on the young twigs, and small closely-spaced leaflets separate it from *A. karroo* and other savanna species.

Distribution and ecology *A. nilotica* is widespread in tropical and sub-tropical Africa and Asia, extending as far eastwards as India. Of the nine presently recognized subspecies, seven occur in Africa and only two – subsp. *kraussiana* (Vatke) Brenan and subsp. *subalata* (Vatke) Brenan – are present in southern Africa. Subsp. *subalata* is found in western Angola and in Kenya and Tanzania, while subsp. *kraussiana*, the subspecies we are concerned with here, is found in southwestern Angola and northern Namibia and from eastern Botswana and Zimbabwe eastwards to Tanzania, Mozambique and KwaZulu-Natal in South Africa. Subsp. *kraussiana* is found over most of Zimbabwe, particularly at medium altitudes, but rarely above 1500 m.

Within Zimbabwe, *A. nilotica* is found in a wide range of habitats as scattered individuals, and not generally in stands under undisturbed conditions. It occurs in nutrient-rich sites such as termitaria, along drainage lines and on exposures of clay layers as a minor constituent of miombo or similar dry woodlands, along roadsides, as a small shrub in mopane woodland, and even as a stunted shrub in grassland on black cracking clays. It is primarily a species of disturbed areas and can behave as a pioneer in such circumstances, but is not as aggressively invasive as *A. karroo*. The only habitat where its distribution is unlikely to have been greatly influenced by livestock or wildlife is in the

→

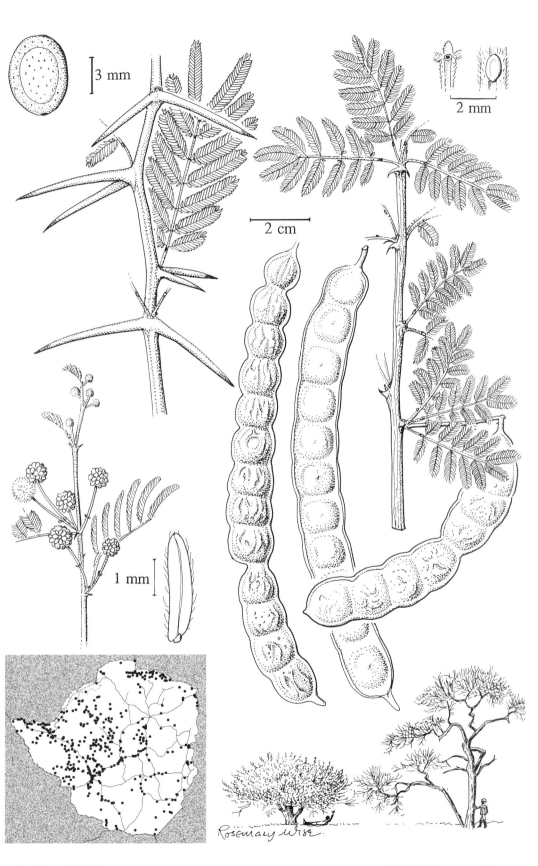

ACACIA NILOTICA

cracking-clay grasslands where it appears to be a component of the vegetation, not just of scattered occurrence. However, many plants in such environments do not reach sufficient size to bear fruit. It is presumably the structure and strength of the rooting system which allows *A. nilotica* to survive on these cracking clays where most woody species would suffer from root shearing and fail to survive. Although requiring moderately fertile soils, *A. nilotica* is less demanding in this respect than either *A. karroo* or *A. nigrescens*. It occurs on a variety of drought-prone heavier soils from red clays to black vertisols under relatively frost-free conditions, and is often found in groves around the sites of old cattle kraals where the animals deposited the seed in their dung. Its widespread distribution pattern is probably due to distribution by cattle and wildlife which eat the pods, and the ease with which it establishes itself from seed.

Notes There are two very distinct ecologies among the African subspecies of *A. nilotica* – one group thrives in savanna or open woodland on dry, heavy soils, whereas the other group is restricted to riverine habitats and seasonally flooded areas. Both groups are restricted to soils of moderate to high fertility. Subsp. *kraussiana* belongs to the former group.

The wide layer of light buff to brown sapwood surrounds a clear deep pink-red dense heartwood with variable markings. The very heavy wood (1100-1170 kg/m³) has a coarse to medium even texture, and is hard and difficult to work. It has a similar hardness to both *A. nigrescens* and *A. erioloba*. The wood seasons well, is very durable, and is resistant to borer and termite attack. Good logs can occasionally be obtained. The wood has been used for mine timber, fence posts, wagons and tool handles, and has also been used for carving, turnery and cabinet-making, although it is difficult to saw and tends to blunt tools. It provides a very good firewood. The bark and pods are rich in tannin, yielding up to 38%, and have been used in tanning.

An edible gum, used in confectionery and as an adhesive, is obtained from the stem, while roasted pods have been used as a flavouring. The tree has many medicinal uses in Zimbabwe – the leaves and roots have been used to relieve colds, ophthalmia, haemorrhages and as a stimulant, while the flower is made into an ointment for wounds.

The greatest economic value of *A. nilotica* is possibly in its use for livestock. Both the leaves and pods are high in protein, and the pods are available into the dry season when they are most needed (see Box 2, page 51). Both cattle and wildlife will attempt to knock down the unripe pods. In southern Matabeleland, 35 kg of pods were obtained from a single average tree in a good season. There appears to be a chemical in the pods, perhaps tannin, that limits animals' intake. The tree is also a useful source of shade as it loses its leaves later in the season than many other species. *A. nilotica* is obviously adapted for animal dispersal, but if concentrations of cattle build up creating disturbed, open habitats, the species will become invasive and form thickets, thus reducing available grass. The larvae of the emperor moth *Cirina forda* feeds on the foliage; these larvae are sometimes eaten by humans.

Growth rate is moderate (reported as fairly slow to fairly fast) and the species establishes readily from seed. Pretreatment is normally required for good germination, but owing to the hardness of the seed coat nicking or some minutes in hot sulphuric acid is recommended. Young trees coppice well. The species is not particularly frost-tolerant. *A. nilotica* is probably longer lived than *A. karroo*.

The specific name is Latin for "of the Nile"; the species was originally described by Linnaeus in 1753 as *Mimosa nilotica* from a specimen collected along the Nile in Egypt. The subspecies was named after C.L. Krauss, a German naturalist and traveller who collected in South Africa, mainly KwaZulu-Natal, in the late 1830s. The common name refers to the sweet-smelling pods.

BOX 8 – CONSERVATION OF ACACIAS

Threats to conservation can be of two main types – habitat loss or loss through over-utilization. Such threats are greatly increased if a species only occurs in small populations or in a restricted area. The majority of *Acacia* species found in Zimbabwe are fairly forgiving in their habitat requirements – indeed many are pioneers that just need a good seed bed, light, and minimal competition for the first year or so to establish. Most are also fairly widely distributed and only a few are confined to specific habitats or localities.

Although some acacias are utilized heavily for rough timber or firewood, or browsed by livestock and wildlife, none in Zimbabwe are really threatened yet by over-utilization. Local extirpation may occur in certain areas, but in most cases scattered individuals still remain. The species under threat are those with a restricted distribution or with very specific habitat requirements, including *A. abyssinica*, *A. burkei*, and the Limpopo Basin populations of *A. erioloba*. These are under threat from habitat loss.

Mountain footslopes of the Eastern Highlands, the habitat of *A. abyssinica*, are increasingly being used for afforestation, agriculture or settlement. This species requires unstable slopes and land slips for regeneration, and stabilizing the landscape will lead to local extinction.

Within Zimbabwe, *A. burkei* is confined to sandy plateau areas around Gonarezhou National Park subject to damage by elephant and fire. The very localized outlying populations of *A. erioloba* in the Maramani/Sentinel area and Gonarezhou National Park are also small. Such areas could be easily cleared for fields or for timber.

Species such as *A. adenocalyx*, *A. caffra*, *A. hebeclada* subsp. *chobiensis*, *A. permixta* and *A. stuhlmannii* are known only from one or two populations in the country, and are thus at risk of localized extinction. *A. adenocalyx* has been found in forested gullies on one hill in the lower Mazoe Valley, an area not subject to heavy land use, but *A. caffra*, confined to a few individuals in and around a construction site on the outskirts of Harare, will possibly soon disappear. It is probably an old introduction to the country, however, rather than fully native. *A. hebeclada* subsp. *chobiensis* is restricted to the riparian fringe of the Zambezi River above Victoria Falls, an area being much affected by tourism development and elephant damage. Changes to flood regime upstream may also modify the distribution and existence of the species.

Perhaps the most threatened species is *A. permixta*, confined to two populations in the southwestern lowveld and of very localized occurrence in adjacent parts of South Africa and Botswana. The main population in Zimbabwe, which is thriving, is on and around Fort Tuli in the Tuli Circle, and the other is on a farm near West Nicholson. Another species with narrowly-defined habitat requirements and only a few populations in the country is *A. stuhlmannii*. This species is limited in southern Africa to a series of populations in the trans-frontier Shashe-Limpopo confluence area, and also near the Makgadikgadi Pans. However, the species does not appear to be under threat and seems to thrive on disturbed land and under heavy browsing pressure.

There are no specific initiatives to conserve acacias in Zimbabwe although many are, of course, protected within existing Protected Areas. None of the species are Specially Protected. The only *Acacia* taxon in Zimbabwe mentioned in the 1997 IUCN Red List of Threatened Plants (Walter & Gillett 1998) is *A. hebeclada* subsp. *chobiensis*, presumably on the basis of its restricted distribution. *A. permixta* and perhaps some others in the glandular complex should also be included using these criteria. No species is mentioned in the World List of Threatened Trees (Oldfield *et al*. 1998). The Sebakwe *Acacia karroo* Botanical Reserve on the Great Dyke near Kwekwe was presumably established to protect a good stand of this common species, but the site now has little botanical value owing to wood cutting (Robertson 1986).

ACACIA PENTAGONA *(Schumach.) Hook.f.*

Common names: gato (Ndau)

Acacia pentagona is very different from all other Zimbabwe species as it is the only one found in rainforest, where it remains in the forest undergrowth, catching the unwary with its small scattered thorns, or becomes a large woody liana climbing into the forest canopy.

Description *A. pentagona* is a tall liana or creeper up to 30 m high, climbing up trunks into the crowns of forest trees. The 5-ribbed stems are 10-15 cm in diameter. **Young twigs** are generally glabrous and red-green to purplish in colour. Long, thin, leafless prickly stems which assist in its climbing habit are often seen arising from the axils. **Thorns** are small, hooked and scattered along the stems, arising from the darker longitudinal bands. **Leaves** are large in size (25 x 15 cm) with a long petiole and 8-15 pairs of pinnae, each with many leaflets. A squat gland is present at the petiole base. Scattered thorns can be found on the rachis. **Inflorescence** is a terminal panicle of white globose heads appearing from October to December. **Pods** are thick, hard and indehiscent with thickened margins, oblong and brown in colour.

Field characters Liana; 5-angled stem; thorny thin stems scrambling over other plants; scattered hooked thorns; thick indehiscent pods; in moist forest.

Distribution and ecology *A. pentagona* is a moist forest acacia widespread from Guinea and Sierra Leone to Uganda and Sudan, south to central Angola, eastern Zimbabwe, western Mozambique and, unusually, also in Madagascar. In Zimbabwe it is found in medium and low altitude rainforests below 1200 m altitude growing in both deep shade and in forest clearings. It is particularly common in Chirinda forest. Exceptionally, at Stapleford and in a forest on Honzo mountain in the upper Honde valley (Watsomba) it grows at around 1400 m.

A. pentagona presumably requires a certain level of light. In dense shade most individuals are stunted and etoliated, but at the edges of forest clearings it climbs into the lower canopy of forest trees.

Notes The species is part of the anomalous "*A. pennata*" complex (see Box 6, page 92) and is reported not to nodulate or fix nitrogen.

The wood is used for implement handles in Chipinge district, and the bark is used for stomach complaints.

The specific name comes from the Greek and refers to the distinctive 5-angled stems (*pente -* five, *gonia -* angle).

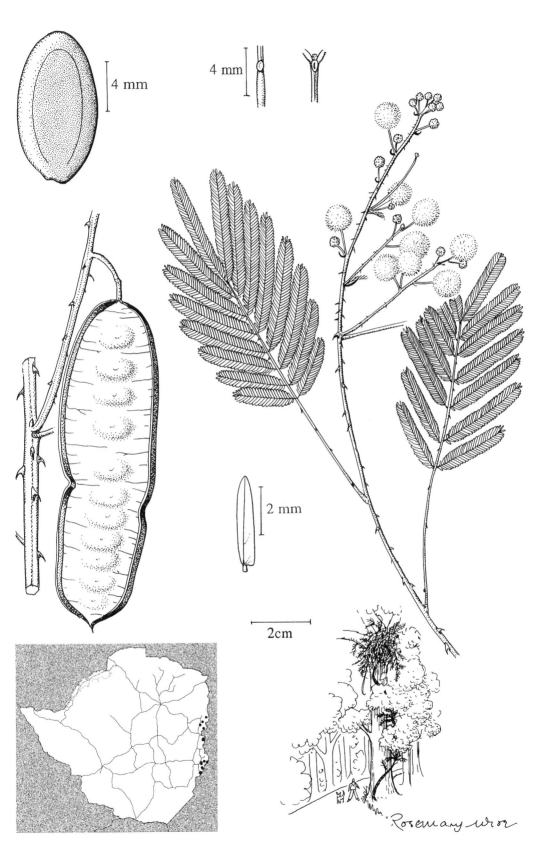

4 mm

4 mm

2 mm

2cm

Rosemary Wroe

ACACIA PENTAGONA

ACACIA PERMIXTA *Burtt Davy*

One of the shrubby glandular species, *Acacia permixta* is among the rarest acacias in the country, confined to two populations in the southwestern lowveld. The long hairs on the young growth are distinctive.

Description *A. permixta* is a shrub to 2 m, often multi-stemmed, with reddish brown stems, somewhat thick and robust for such a small plant. **Young twigs** are pale reddish brown in colour and are distinctly hairy with hairs over 1 mm long. Conspicuous white lenticels are present, but the scattered reddish glands on the stem are much less visible. Older twigs have a splitting greyish epidermis revealing a reddish underlayer, and can be almost hairless. **Thorns** are whitish as if whitewashed, long, straight and paired at the nodes. When young they are somewhat curved. **Leaves** are small (2 x 2 cm) and clustered at the nodes with 2-5 pairs of pinnae, each with a few yellow-green leaflets. Leaflets are slightly hairy with a mucronate tip and very few scattered reddish glands. The leaves appear in early September before those of many other species. **Inflorescences** are scattered, small, axillary globose heads of bright yellow flowers appearing on young growth around September, or even in March to May. The involucel (also seen when in fruit) is near the middle of the peduncle. The reddish brown dehiscent **pods** are small, curved and covered in small reddish glands.

Field characters Shrub to 3 m; rusty-red young growth; long hairs on young growth; glandular pods.

This shrubby species is unlikely to be confused with any other of the glandular complex owing to the distinctive long hairs on the young growth.

Distribution and ecology *A. permixta* is one of the glandular species of the Limpopo basin (see Box 4, page 79). It is found in southwest Zimbabwe, southeastern Botswana and north-western South Africa. Within Zimbabwe it is known only from gravelly basalt soils around Fort Tuli, with one collection from near the Bubi River east of West Nicholson. It is usually associated with stunted mopane and *Combretum* shrubs on old disturbed land, and is surprisingly localized in its occurrence, sometimes forming small clumps. There is a suggestion that it could be an old introduction, brought in by the Pioneer Column from the former Transvaal in animal fodder. However, there is no firm evidence for this.

Notes The very localized distribution of *A. permixta* may be a result of insufficient collecting in suitable rocky basalt habitats, or it may indeed be very rare in the country.

The specific name comes from the Latin and means "much confused" (*permiscere* - to mix together), possibly referring to being confused with other glandular species before it was described.

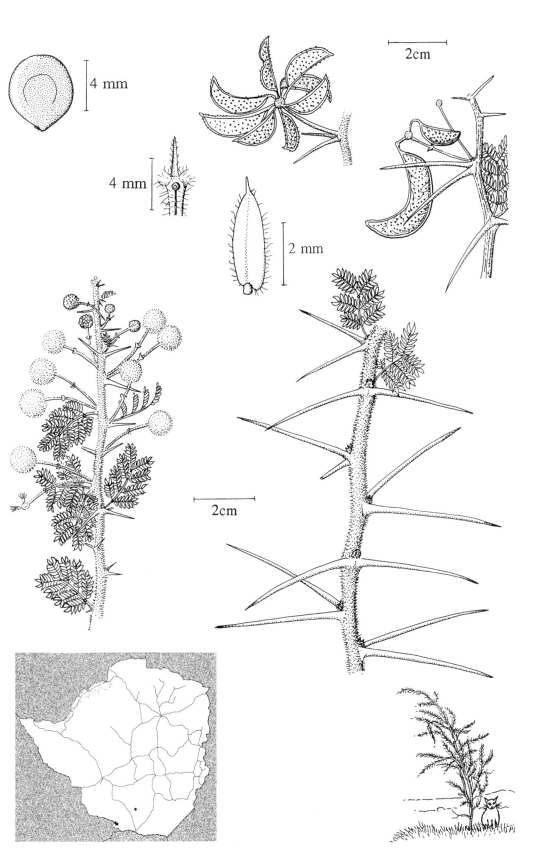

ACACIA PERMIXTA

32

ACACIA POLYACANTHA *Willd.*

(= *A. campylacantha* A. Rich., *A. caffra* sensu Eyles 1916, *A. pallens* sensu Steedman 1925)

Common names: white thorn; witdoring (Afrikaans); umdwadwa, umpumbu (Ndebele); gukwe, kovakova (Shangaan); chikwiku, chiungadzi, mugone, mukwakwa (Shona); luntwele, mumbu (Tonga)

A tall tree with a layered crown and whitish bark, leafless for much of the dry season, *Acacia polyacantha* is widespread along watercourses and in fallows on red clays in higher rainfall areas.

Description *A. polyacantha* is a medium-sized to large tree, generally up to 10 m in height but sometimes as tall as 20 m. The crown is open, becoming characteristically layered and flatter with age. Mature trunk is 50-70 cm in diameter; slash reddish. **Bark** is pale to dark yellow-brown, fissured, peeling off in flakes to reveal the characteristic whitish inner layer, which is very noticeable when the tree is leafless. **Young twigs** are slightly pubescent and pale brown. **Thorns** are hooked, paired at the nodes, straw-brown to blackish, flattened sideways, sometimes large and broad-based. Strongly hooked thorns often persist on the branches and on raised woody bosses on the trunk. Young shrubs can be very thorny, while older trees can become almost thornless. **Leaves** are large (to 20 cm) with 15-30 pairs of pinnae, each with numerous very small pale green leaflets. The petiole is relatively short and has a large flattened oblong gland near the base. Small scattered thorns are often present on the underside of the rachis. **Inflorescences** are axillary and clustered (1-3 together) in the upper leaf axils on the current seasons' growth, and consist of long thin spikes of creamy white flowers which appear with the leaves from September to December. It does not flower early. **Pods** are straight and flat, tapering at both ends, grey-brown in colour. They dehisce on the tree and are often borne in profusion. The smooth valves are fairly thin but not papery.

Field characters Tree with erect profile and layered canopy; pale to whitish bark; hooked thorns often persist on branches; early deciduous; large flattened petiolar gland; profuse pale brown pods opening on tree.

The main distinguishing characters of *A. polyacantha* are the pale coloured bark, almost dirty white at times, and the large conspicuously flattened oblong gland at the base of the petiole, which serves to distinguish it clearly from *A. galpinii*. The erect layered appearance of the crown and whitish stem, coupled with losing its leaves earlier than most *Acacia* species, ensure *A. polyacantha* is readily recognized in the dry season. Although sometimes mistaken at a distance for *A. sieberiana*, the greyish bark, layered crown and hooked thorns help to separate it.

Distribution and ecology *A. polyacantha* subsp. *campylacantha* is found across much of the savanna area of sub-Saharan Africa from Gambia through Sudan and East Africa to northern Botswana, Zimbabwe and northern South Africa. It is principally associated with open woodland and the alluvium of small rivers. In Zimbabwe it is widespread in all but the drier parts of the country, and does not extend (except occasional specimens) into the Limpopo Valley south of Bulawayo and Chiredzi. The incidence of frost as well as suitable soils determines its local distribution. *A. polyacantha* is a pioneer species and is often found in fallow fields and similar disturbed sites on suitable red or black clay soils under moderate rainfall conditions, such as in the Mazowe Valley north of Harare. It is, however, equally at home on alluvial clay soils associated with watercourses and on vlei margins on the highveld granite, where it is generally found in open woodland with a good grass cover underneath. Off the central watershed it can be found on somewhat lighter textured soils. Occasional individuals are seen on sandy alluvium along some lowveld rivers such as in the Zambezi and Save valleys. It is a common species around Harare but very localized in the Bulawayo area, possibly owing to both frost and dryness.

→

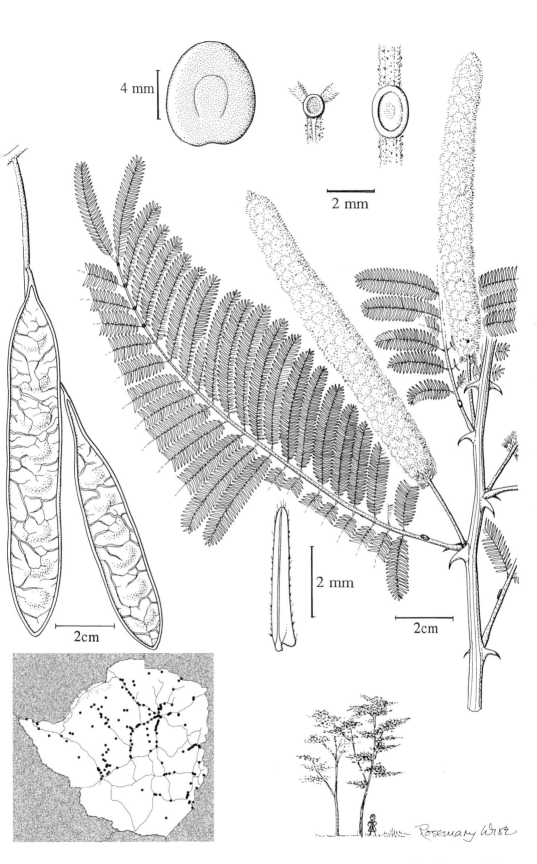

ACACIA POLYACANTHA

Acacias of Zimbabwe **103**

Notes All individuals of *A. polyacantha* in Africa belong to subsp. *campylacantha* (A. Rich.) Brenan; subsp. *polyacantha* is found only in India and possibly Sri Lanka.

The pale yellow-white sapwood is wide and younger trees have very little heartwood. The strong, tough, pinkish brown heartwood has a high resin content and variable colouring and markings (see Box 16, page 135). It is moderately heavy (640-705 kg/m³) with a medium to coarse even texture, and of moderate durability. Prone to splitting it needs to be seasoned slowly. Large logs yield reasonable quantities of heartwood, which is very useful for general woodworking. Although the wood has fair resistance to borer and termite attack, it is highly susceptible to fungi, particularly the sapwood. The wood has been used for rough construction, crates, shelving, etc., but has found only limited usage. Although light it is said to be a good firewood with a high calorific value. The bark has been used for tanning.

The fresh roots have a strong odour and are reputedly a good snake repellant. They are also used as a treatment for snake bite. The edible gum can be used as a substitute for gum arabic in confectionery and as an adhesive. The leaves have been found to have slight antibiotic properties. The larvae of the emperor moth *Heniocha marnois* feeds on the foliage of this and some other *Acacia* species.

A. polyacantha is one of the fastest growing of the acacias and is relatively short-lived with a longevity of 30-40 years. It is readily raised from seed. Like many tropical acacias it is sensitive to both cold and frost, and dies back when frosted. Poorly formed trees can be coppiced when young to improve stem form, and interplanting *A. polyacantha* with more leafy species helps self-pruning and improves timber quality. The root system is essentially shallow with strong spreading subsurface laterals, particularly on heavy soils, and a taproot is also present. The species shows potential for breeding of improved strains for use as firewood or gum production, especially owing to its ease of establishment, rapid growth rate and early maturity.

Owing to its "weedy" nature, *A. polyacantha* can be a problem when it invades fields under high rainfall conditions, such as in the Mazoe Valley. In northern Mozambique fallow cotton fields on red clay soils become heavily invaded with even-aged stands, which then are difficult to remove.

The specific name is Greek for "many thorns" (*polys* - many, *akantha* - thorn), while the subspecific name is Greek for "curved thorns" (*kampylos* - curved).

BOX 9 – GUM ARABIC FROM THE ACACIAS

Gum arabic is an ancient article of international commerce in Africa and the Middle East. It has been used traditionally for the mixing of inks and paints, as an adhesive, in cosmetics, perfumery and in medicine, but today it is most widely known as a food additive. The majority of the world production is used as a flavouring agent, emulsifier, stabilizer, humectant (moistener), surface finishing agent and thickener – its most important property is that it retards sugar crystallization. It is also used in the pharmaceutical industry.

In the specifications of the Joint FAO/WHO Expert Committee on Food Additives (FAO 1990), gum arabic is defined as a dried exudation obtained from the stems and branches of *Acacia senegal* or closely related species; it is not made clear whether this refers to taxonomically or chemically related. The gum consists primarily of high molecular weight polysaccharides and their calcium, magnesium and potassium salts which, on hydrolysis, yield arabinose, galactose, rhamnose and glucuronic acid. Unground gum arabic occurs as white or yellowish-white spheroidal tears of varying size or as angular fragments. It is also available commercially in the form of white to yellow-white flakes, granules or powder.

The increase in the consumption of convenience foods has led to an increase in the use of gum arabic, and concern about a healthy diet has stimulated an interest in thickeners of natural origin. Nevertheless, irregularity of supply and fluctuating prices have caused gum arabic to lose out to synthetic substitutes on the world market with the result that annual gum production has dropped from about 70,000 tons in the 1960s to 25,000 tons today. The 1995 prices were US$4200 per ton for ordinary grade, US$4650 per ton for hand-picked nodules and US$5200 per ton for kibbled ordinary grade ex-Port Sudan, from which 85% of the world production is supplied. The prices have fallen steeply over the past three years and in March 1998 were US$1800, $2200 and $2000 per ton, respectively. The reasons for this fall are not clear. Gum arabic exports constitute 10-15% of the total foreign currency earnings of Sudan. Homogeneity of product and continuity of supply are extremely important; Sudan produces gum with the most consistent quality and uniformity because most of it comes from one species, *A. senegal*, in planted fallows where there has probably been some form of selection operating for many years.

Gums from at least ten species of African acacias have been sources of what is marketed as gum arabic. This has given rise to considerable controversy in the trade, although it is now widely accepted that the source should be *A. senegal* (particularly var. *senegal*) and 18 species belonging to the *A. senegal* complex, mostly occurring in Somalia. Even so, in pure form the chemical constitution of the gums of *Acacia* species from widely disparate groups merge at the boundaries indicating that there are some that could be regarded as closely related gums in regulatory terms. *A. karroo* is the best gum producer in Zimbabwe but the situation in regard to this species is most unsatisfactory; its gum is used regionally as a substitute for gum arabic yet it cannot be exported to Europe or the USA in labelled form.

Gum arabic is a potentially valuable product. With wider acceptance of species source, improved quality control and a more reliable supply, it could provide a cash income for many more resource-poor farmers in Africa.

33

ACACIA REHMANNIANA *Schinz*

Common names: silky acacia; sydoring (Afrikaans); iphucula (Ndebele); mona (Shona-Rusape)

A distinctive small tree with many fine leaflets, hairy growth and orange underbark, Acacia rehmanniana is widespread in the Highveld on vlei margins and in open miombo and acacia woodlands.

Description A. *rehmanniana* is a small to medium-sized tree up to 8 m high, with a stem diameter normally around 15-20 cm. The crown is spreading, rounded and slightly flattened in old trees. **Bark** is conspicuously powdery orange to reddish brown on young trees and on the branches of older trees, but dark brown to black and fissured on the trunk. **Young twigs** are characteristically densely clothed in long golden-yellow hairs, turning greyish and becoming sparser later. The velvety layer splits open on older growth to reveal an orange to rusty-red inner layer. Older growth is often fairly robust.

Thorns are long (up to 5 cm), straight and paired at the nodes. At first the base is often covered in velvety hairs. **Leaves** are medium-sized (6-8 x 2-4 cm) with 20-40 pairs of pinnae, each with numerous very small (1 x 0.3 mm) grey-green pubescent leaflets. **Inflorescences** are clustered towards the end of the current seasons' growth, sometimes looking like a panicle, and consist of globose heads of white flowers. They appear from November to February. **Pods** are flat and straight and dehisce between April and June. The valves are thin, leathery in texture, with wavy longitudinal striations.

Field characters Orange-red older twigs and branches; dense, spreading golden-yellow hairs on young growth; many pairs of pinnae with very small closely packed leaflets.

A. *rehmanniana* is easily confused, if not seen in the field, with both A. *sieberiana* and A. *abyssinica*. The latter two species can be large trees, but A. *rehmanniana* never attains that size. It is also not found above 1500 m altitude or in the lowveld. A. *rehmanniana* can be separated from A. *sieberiana* in the much more numerous pinnae pairs (over 20), smaller leaflets, and the thin non-woody pods. The rusty-red layer on young branches is also characteristic. It is not so easy to separate A. *abyssinica* from A. *rehmanniana*, but the latter has a distinctive, dense yellow pubescence on the young growth, generally smaller leaflets (1 x 0.3 mm) and somewhat smaller leaves (6-8 cm long).

Distribution and ecology A. *rehmanniana* is a southern African species, probably originally confined to the highveld plateau between the Limpopo and Zambezi rivers, from which it has spread to the plateau to the south. It is principally found in Zimbabwe, but extends into north-eastern Botswana around Francistown, and the former northern Transvaal. There is a doubtful record from Choma in southern Zambia. Within Zimbabwe it is restricted to the central watershed mainly between 1000 and 1500 m altitude, where it is locally common but rarely abundant in open woodland and wooded grassland, often associated with other acacia species. The main soil types on which A. *rehmanniana* occurs are clay-rich sites, such as around termitaria, in drier granite landscapes and on red clays and loams derived from the Basement Complex. When apparently found on granite sands it is usually rooted into a clay layer. One of the few acacia species found in miombo or similar broad-leaved woodlands in Matabeleland, it is equally at home in acacia woodland with A. *karroo*.

Notes The wood, even from older trees, consists mainly of slightly fibrous off-white sapwood which is subject to borer attack and not renowned for its mechanical or fuel qualities. The inner bark has been used for rope.

Shona traditional healers rub the roots into the body against headache and pneumonia.

The growth rate is fairly slow and the species is very frost-hardy except when young. The seeds are rounded and thick. A. *rehmanniana* is unusual in that it is resistant to some arboricides.

The specific name refers to the Polish botanist, Anton Rehmann, who collected the type specimen in northern South Africa.

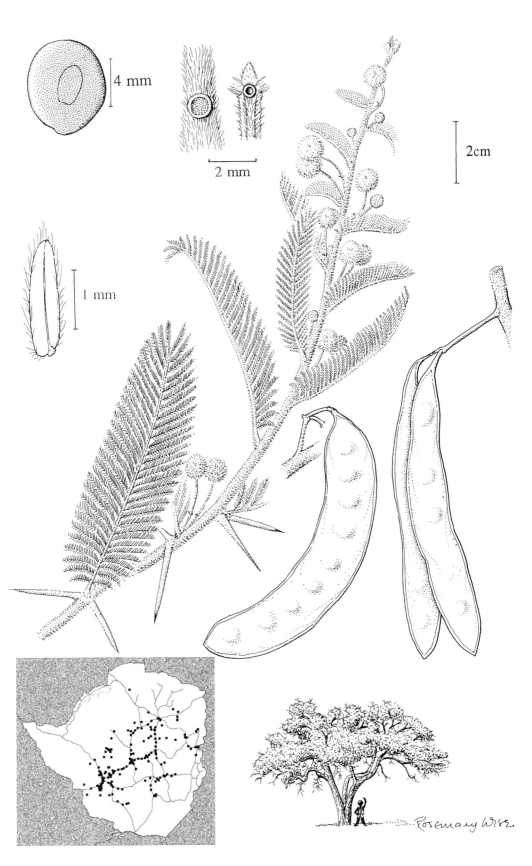

ACACIA REHMANNIANA

34

ACACIA ROBUSTA *Burch.* subsp. CLAVIGERA *(E. Mey.) Brenan*
(= *A. clavigera* E. Mey.)

Common names: splendid acacia; umhlabunga, umgamanzi (Ndebele); sesani, vumbangwenya (Shangaan); mambovu, mundale, munyenyengwa (Tonga)

A common tall riverine tree of lower altitudes in both the Zambezi and Limpopo catchments. Most lowveld rivers have stands of *A. robusta* subsp. *clavigera* along them and drainage lines are often characterized by the green foliage of the species through much of the dry season.

Description *A. robusta* subsp. *clavigera* is a medium to moderately large tree from 10-20 m in height, branching high with an erect habit and partly spreading crown. Trunk is usually 30-40 cm in diameter, but can be up to 70 cm. **Bark** is comparatively smooth, grey-brown to dark brown, sometimes slightly fissured. **Young twigs** are smooth, grey-brown, longitudinally striated and with transverse white lenticels. **Thorns** are straight, paired at the nodes and mostly short (up to 1 cm), erect, divergent, sometimes forward-pointing. Occasionally longer thorns are seen, but at times trees are almost thornless. **Leaves** are tufted at the nodes, sometimes forming "cushions", medium-sized (4 x 3 cm) with 3-6 pairs of pinnae, each with numerous small to medium-sized (1-2 mm wide) green discolorous leaflets. The rachis is pubescent. Trees remain in leaf almost year-round, appearing effectively evergreen. **Inflorescences** are axillary clusters of white globose heads appearing after the leaves in November-February. **Pods** are long, thin (1.3-1.7 cm wide) and curved. The dehiscent ripe pods can be seen up in the canopy almost year-round. Valves are thickened but not woody.

Field characters Tall riverine tree; practically evergreen foliage; short straight thorns; pubescent leaf rachis; thin curved pods.

A. robusta subsp. *clavigera* is readily separated from subsp. *robusta* by being a tall tree, its more slender habit, the significantly smaller (but more numerous) leaflets, and its narrow curved pods. Confusions often arise between subsp. *clavigera* and *A. gerrardii*. Subsp. *clavigera* has smooth, not velvety pubescent, young twigs, and the pods are generally longer, curved and without hairs (see under *A. gerrardii*). The foliage of *A. karroo* is a brighter green and without hairs on the rachis, while the pods of subsp. *clavigera* are tougher and dehisce later. It can be difficult to separate from *A. grandicornuta* in the lowveld, but subsp. *clavigera* has 3 or more pairs of pinnae, a hairy rachis, leaflets distinctly darker in colour above than below, and broader pods.

Distribution and ecology *A. robusta* as a species is found from KwaZulu-Natal northwards to Ethiopia, but subsp. *clavigera* is found only at lower altitudes from northern KwaZulu-Natal and southern Mozambique to southern Zambia, the Caprivi Strip and Malawi. Within Zimbabwe subsp. *clavigera* is found in the frost-free lower parts of the Limpopo catchment (below 600 m) and at somewhat higher altitudes (below 900-1100 m) in the Zambezi catchment.

Subsp. *clavigera* is mostly a component of riverine woodland, often with other *Acacia* species, but can also be found in stands along some larger drainage lines and around pans. It occurs on old alluvium in mopane woodland where moisture levels are sufficient, but then is a weak spindly tree owing to shading. Subsp. *clavigera* can also be found as a minor component of dry forest on heavier-textured soils in such areas, but may well have been brought in by elephants or other animals. Occasionally a woodland of tall spindly trees of subsp. *clavigera* is seen in the Zambezi Valley, probably a result of clearing many years ago and subsequent establishment. Some such "forests" are considered sacred by the local population.

Notes In South Africa confusion arises between subsp. *clavigera* and subsp. *robusta* owing to many individuals with intermediate characteristics, but in Zimbabwe the two subspecies are sufficiently distinct almost to be termed separate species.

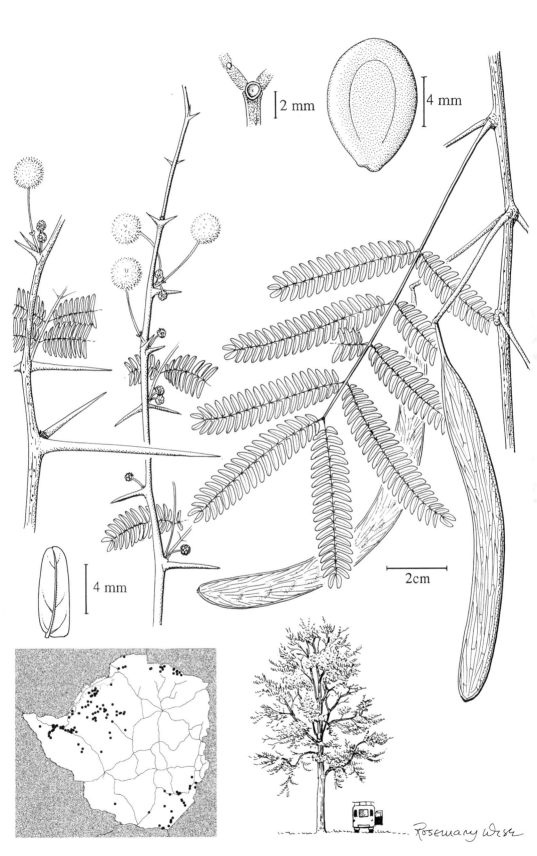

2 mm

4 mm

4 mm

2cm

ACACIA ROBUSTA CLAVIGERA

They do not overlap in appearance, ecology or distribution here.

Another subspecies, subsp. *usambarensis* (Taub.) Brenan, very similar to subsp. *clavigera*, is found from central Mozambique northwards to Kenya, Somalia and Ethiopia. The pods of subsp. *usambarensis* are much narrower and the rachis is without hairs. As both subspecies occur in similar habitats and their distributions overlap, it is possible that these are best considered as varieties and not as subspecies.

A thick ring of white sapwood surrounds the pink-brown hardwood. The wood is fairly heavy (850-880 kg/m³) with a medium to coarse even texture, and is moderately durable though brittle.

It is moderately susceptible to borer and termite attack and highly susceptible to sapstain. The wood has been used for utility furniture and shelving, but is generally unsuitable for working as it warps.

Growth rate is fairly fast and the species regenerates well from seed. The roots are moderately deep with strongly spreading laterals.

The specific name means "strong" in Latin (*robustus* - of hard wood or physically strong) and possibly refers to the robust branches, twigs and thorns of subsp. *robusta*. The subspecific name comes from Latin and means "bearing keys" (*claviger* - the key bearer), presumably referring to the pods as keys, as in ash or sycamore keys.

BOX 10 – GERMINATION OF ACACIA SEED

Nearly all acacias have seeds that develop a very hard coat that is impermeable to water. The mature seed cannot absorb water and start the germination process until the coat is scarified, nicked or cracked without damaging the embryo. In nature this happens when the seed passes through the digestive system of an animal, when it is heated by fire, or through gradual weathering of the coat with the passage of time. Viability of acacia seeds is also likely to be poor as a result of internal damage done by infestation by bruchid beetles (see Box 14, page 125).

To achieve high and uniform germination, seed with bruchid holes must be discarded and the seed coats of the remaining sound seed softened or cracked to allow the endosperm to imbibe water. Various methods of treatment before sowing have been recommended including dropping the seed briefly in boiling water, scarifying with a file, and burning a groove with a red hot wire. However, the most reliable method has been found to be as follows:

(a) wash the seed to remove contaminating agencies or any residual fungicide or insecticide if it has been treated,

(b) place the seed on racks to dry for about 15 minutes,

(c) nick the seed using nail cutters at the micropylar end taking great care not to damage the embryo; there is less danger of this if the seed is nicked at the end opposite the micropyle, but if so the testa (seed coat) tends to be retained and leads to contortion and fungal infection of the cotyledons,

(d) the seeds are then soaked in water for 3 to 12 hours, the precise amount of time depending on the rate of water absorption,

(e) once the seeds are fully imbibed they are placed in a dish on moist filter-paper and placed in a germination cabinet set to run at about 36°C, or in a warm position near a stove or under an iron roof where similar temperatures are reached.

The seed germinates and the root shoot emerges between 6 and 96 hours later, depending on the species. Once the root has emerged, the seeds can be sown with tweezers direct into a pre-dibbled hole in the nursery container – the root is covered with very fine sand. This is done to keep the moisture around the germinating seed and to protect it from direct sun heat. The most advantageous time of the day at which to start this whole process depends upon the speed with which the individual species absorbs water and produces a root. If both are fast (as they are for example with *A. senegal*), seed nicked in the morning can be sown by the evening. The seed leaves emerge above ground 3 to 5 days after sowing.

Provided seed that has bruchid holes or unsound endosperm (brown and spongy instead of white and firm) is discarded before sowing, close to 100% germination and establishment in the containers is possible.

35

ACACIA ROBUSTA *Burch.* subsp. ROBUSTA

Common names: splendid acacia; enkeldoring (Afrikaans); umhlabungu, umgamanzi (Ndebele)

A small dense tree with robust branches and dark green foliage which is often overlooked except when in full flower. *A. robusta* subsp. *robusta* has large stout thorns, the largest of any acacia in Zimbabwe.

Description *A. robusta* subsp. *robusta* is a small to medium-sized tree up to 8 m in height, branching low with an ascending, spreading profile, a bit like an inverted cone. The branches are robust and appear even thicker from a distance as they are densely clothed in deep green leaves. Trunk is from 20-50 cm in diameter. **Bark** is dark brown to black, rough and fissured. **Young twigs** are distinctly thick and robust, purplish to grey-brown, smooth, but with small white lenticels. **Thorns** are straight and paired at the nodes; sometimes they are only 2 cm long, but are often around 4-6 cm, very stout and greyish. Occasionally they reach 10 cm long, the largest of any of the Zimbabwe species. **Leaves** are tufted at the nodes and arise from dense "cushions". They are medium to large (5-10 x 4-6 cm) with 2-4 pairs of long pinnae, each with 10-15 pairs of comparatively large (up to 5 mm wide), well-spaced, oblong, dark green (paler underneath), hairless leaflets. **Inflorescences** are clusters of white globose heads appearing with the leaves in the axils of the previous seasons' growth in August-September. Flowering trees are quite a sight as they are one of the first woody species to come into flower after the dry season. **Pods** are large (up to 15 cm long and 1.7-3 cm wide), robust and woody, ripening in late summer and only tardily dehiscent on the tree. They are mostly straight with rounded ends, sometimes slightly curved, and the thick valves have distinct striations or veining.

Field characters Small tree with robust ascending profile; branches thick and clothed in dark green foliage; robust young twigs; large stout thorns; large woody pods.

A. robusta subsp. *robusta* when it has large stout thorns and woody pods is readily recognized. It can be distinguished from subsp. *clavigera*, *A. karroo*, *A. nilotica* and *A. gerrardii* by a combination of more robust growth, darker foliage, larger leaflets (over 2.5 mm wide) and massive thorns. Subsp. *robusta* can also be confused with *A. grandicornuta*, but it has leaves borne on "cushions", thick young twigs and much larger, wider, thickened pods. There is also a major difference in distribution – subsp. *robusta* is found only at higher altitudes.

Distribution and ecology The species *A. robusta* is found from KwaZulu-Natal northwards to Ethiopia, but subsp. *robusta* is confined to Zimbabwe, eastern Botswana and northern South Africa. Within Zimbabwe subsp. *robusta* is found on the central watershed above 1300 m altitude from Figtree to Bulawayo, Matopos and Inyati. Outlying populations have also been recorded from Gweru, Mvuma and Mt. Buchwa.

The subspecies is found on deep or stony red clay soils derived from the Basement Complex or granite in low open *Acacia* woodland. It is not associated with drainage lines or rocky outcrops. Individuals are normally scattered through the bush, not clumped. Subsp. *robusta* is not a pioneer species, but one more typical of "climax" woodland.

Notes The heartwood is pink-red but quite limited in extent. It is hard and workable, but prone to insect attack. The timber has little value, but it can provide a slow-burning firewood.

Growth rate is fairly slow, but the subspecies makes a good garden tree in frost-prone areas as it is cold and frost-tolerant. The leaves stay on the tree much of the year, and it is probably fairly deep-rooting.

The appearance and thick rounded structure of the seed suggests that they are adapted to survive ingestion by browsing animals, and the species is probably animal dispersed.

The specific name means "strong" in Latin (*robusta* - of hard wood or physically strong) and refers to the robust branches and thorns.

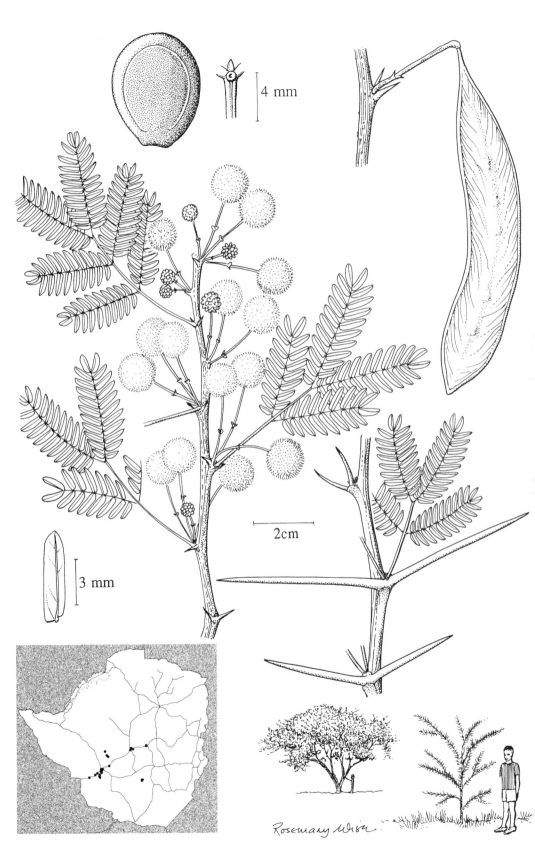

4 mm

2cm

3 mm

Rosemary Wise

ACACIA ROBUSTA ROBUSTA

36

ACACIA SCHWEINFURTHII *Brenan & Exell*

Common names: river climbing acacia; uthathawu (Ndebele); kahe (Shangaan); kandare, rukato (Shona), pfurura (Shona-Pfungwe); gado (Ndau); lubua (Tonga)

A climbing shrub with large leaves and scattered thorns, *Acacia schweinfurthii* is commonly found in riverine woodland at lower altitudes.

Description *A. schweinfurthii* is a liana or scandent shrub climbing up to 20 m in large trees, or forming thickets. When a liana it can have stems up to 5 cm in diameter. **Young twigs** are pale olive-green or brown and smooth. **Thorns** are small, slightly hooked, not paired but scattered along the stem, arising from darker longitudinal bands where the epidermis does not split. **Leaves** are large (up to 20 x 8 cm) with 8-15 pairs of pinnae and a large distinct squat gland just above the conspicuous pulvinus at the base of the petiole. The rachis often has thorns on the underside. Each pinna has many leaflets, which are normally glabrous but sometimes slightly pubescent underneath. **Inflorescences** are terminal or axillary panicles of globose white flowers, appearing on new growth in December and January. **Pods** are distinctly long (to 19 cm) and large, leathery and indehiscent (or tardily dehiscent). They are transversely marked and humped over the seeds, sometimes constricted between them, and the margins are thickened.

Field characters Climbing shrub or liana; pale stem; scattered hooked thorns; large leaves; marked pulvinus and gland at base of petiole; dark longitudinal bands on stem; large pods with transverse veining; riverine woodland.

A. schweinfurthii could be confused with the caesalpinioid climber *Pterolobium stellatum* that is often found in highveld riverine thickets. However, *Pterolobium* has no pulvinus, no longitudinal bands on the stem, and has striking red winged fruits. Confusion with *A. ataxacantha* can arise, but *A. schweinfurthii* has a marked pulvinus on the leaf petiole and a large squat (not small stalked) gland at the base. It is also generally a larger, more robust plant.

Distribution and ecology *A. schweinfurthii* is widespread from Sudan south to the former Transvaal and KwaZulu-Natal. In Zimbabwe it is a species of medium and low altitudes (generally below 1000 m) where it is principally confined to riverine woodland and alluvium, and sometimes termitaria. Occasionally it is found on the central watershed along streams (as at the Hillside dams in Bulawayo), where it may have been introduced. *A. schweinfurthii* can be considered a species of eutrophic soils and can readily tolerate shade. Where it occurs it is often locally abundant and can form almost impenetrable thickets.

Notes Forms part of the anomalous "*A. pennata*" complex of acacias (see Box 6, page 92) which are reported not to nodulate or fix nitrogen. This group seems to be mainly confined to moist and dry forests. *A. schweinfurthii* was often referred to as *A. pennata* (L.) Willd. in early publications before it was split into nine species in 1957.

Brenan (1970) and Ross (1979) recognise two varieties − var. *schweinfurthii* and var. *sericea* Brenan & Exell − the latter having pubescent undersides to the leaflets. Both varieties are said to be found in Zimbabwe but there appears to be no ecological or geographical difference, and it is unlikely that separation can be maintained. Here they are treated together.

Growth rate is fairly fast.

The specific name refers to Georg Schweinfurth, the German botanist and traveller who collected the type specimen in the Sudan.

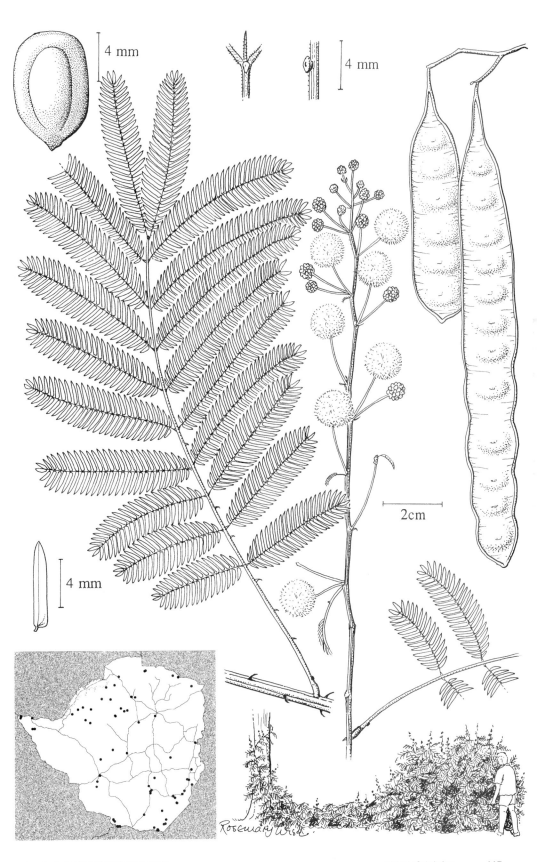

ACACIA SCHWEINFURTHII

37

ACACIA SENEGAL *(L.) Willd.* var. LEIORHACHIS *Brenan*

Common name: three-thorned acacia

The tall, straggly, whip-like shoots of *Acacia senegal* var. *leiorhachis* are a common sight on gravelly basalt soils in the southern lowveld. This variety is also found in the north of the country where it is less distinctive, but the three hooked thorns should ensure confident identification.

Description *A. senegal* var. *leiorhachis* is a distinctive spindly tree to 3-8 m in height or a shrub. The central whip-like stem is tall and erect, often drooping at the tip, and is surrounded at the base by shorter 1-3 m high stems. The bark is distinctive, yellowish and peeling. Stem diameter near the base is generally 8-15 cm, and the slash is creamy brown. **Young twigs** are greyish tinged purplish and smooth. **Thorns** are hooked and in threes at the nodes, two laterals pointing up and the central one pointing down. **Leaves** are medium-sized (6 x 6 cm) with 3-5 pairs of pinnae each with moderate-sized grey-green leaflets. **Inflorescences** are axillary spikes of white flowers appearing early from June to September on older growth before the leaves. The inflorescence axis is glabrous. When older, the flowers look like wet cotton wool. **Pods** are rounded at the tip, light brown in colour, straight and linear-oblong, several times longer than broad. They are dehiscent on the tree, have a leathery to papery texture and can be finely hairy.

Field characters Tall spindly tree with whippy branches; yellowish bark; hooked thorns in threes; inflorescence axis glabrous; long thin pods rounded at end; on gravelly basalt soils.

A. senegal should not be confused with any other species here owing to the distinctive three hooked thorns, two pointing up, one down. Var. *leiorhachis* could be confused with var. *rostrata*, particularly when small or if the adult tree is not seen. The growth form and habitat are usually sufficient to differentiate them, and var. *leiorhachis* flowers very early in the season and has narrower, long pods with no long apical tip.

Distribution and ecology *A. senegal* var. *leiorhachis*, as presently defined, is found from Ethiopia and Kenya south to Zambia, Zimbabwe, Botswana, Mozambique and northern South Africa. In Zimbabwe it is locally common in the Zambezi Basin below 900 m altitude (particularly below 600 m) in the Matetsi, Hwange and the mid-Zambezi Valley areas, and is also found in the Limpopo/Save basin below 600 m altitude from Gwanda through to Gonarezhou and the lower Save River. It is particularly noticeable on the main roads near Beitbridge. In the great majority of cases the species is confined to shallow basalt soils, especially on stony rises and gravelly slopes, but it has also been found on gneissic and even, rarely, on what appear to be shallow sandy soils. Common associates are mopane and species of *Combretum* and *Commiphora*. It is a characteristic component of vegetation on gravelly basalt lithosols, of which it can be considered an indicator.

Notes Although only considered to be varieties at the present, the differences between *A. senegal* var. *leiorhachis* and var. *senegal* in southern Africa make them effectively separate species. The two so-called varieties are very distinct in habit, anatomical characters (flowers, pods), time of flowering and in many ecological aspects such as distribution and soil preference. They are as distinct as most full *Acacia* species here. The taxonomy of the species across its range needs to be rationalized.

The tall, straggly appearance, often with weaver bird nests on the upper branches, makes this species readily identifiable, even at a distance. However, this typical growth form is not common in the Zambezi catchment part of its range where the species is more compact and shorter.

Var. *leiorhachis* appears to hybridize with *A. mellifera* where the two parents occur in the area around the Shashe-Limpopo confluence, resulting

➔

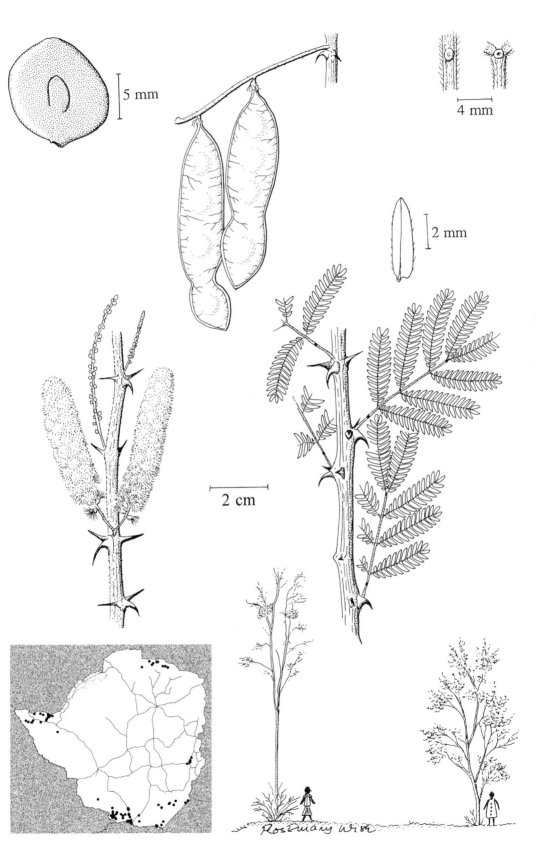

ACACIA SENEGAL LEIORHACHIS

Acacias of Zimbabwe

in what has been called *A. laeta* elsewhere in Africa (see under *A. mellifera*). This hybrid has intermediate characters but is closer to *A. mellifera*.

The wood is hard, heavy (930 kg/m³) and pale brown with no heartwood. It does not appear to be much used. The gum arabic of commerce comes from *A. senegal* var. *senegal* in the Sudan, Ethiopia, Somalia and northern Kenya (see Box 9, page 105). The varieties here do not produce appreciable quantities of gum.

Growth rate is fairly slow, and seed production is low.

The specific name refers to the country Senegal, from where var. *senegal* was first described by Linneaus in 1806 based on specimens collected by the French botanist Michel Adanson. The varietal name *leiorhachis* comes from the Greek for "smooth rachis" (*leios* - smooth, *rhachis* - backbone), and probably refers to the non-pubescent inflorescence axis.

BOX 11 – HYBRIDIZATION IN THE ACACIAS

Hybridization is likely to have been common in the process of speciation of African acacias. About half the species are polyploid, that is they have three or more times the basic haploid set (n) of chromosomes, which in *Acacia* is 13. Polyploid individuals that arise from hybridization are often sexually sterile because, when crossed with diploids, the chromosomes cannot pair and a polyploid arising in a diploid population can only reproduce vegetatively or by selfing. This difficulty is overcome if an ordinary hybrid between two different species containing a set of chromosomes from each parent doubles its chromosome number, in which case this polyploid then becomes a new fertile species because each chromosome has a homologue with which it can pair.

Most of the acacias with non-spinescent stipules from the subgenus *Acueliferum* are diploid with $2n=26$ chromosomes, whereas most of the species with spinescent stipules from the subgenus *Acacia* are polyploid with $2n=52$ chromosomes (see Box 12, page 119). The polyploid species of *Acacia* occupy a greater range of habitats and are more widely distributed than *Acueliferum* species, possibly due to greater genetic plasticity imparted by their polyploid condition.

There is evidence of hybridization among some of the species that occur in Zimbabwe. *A. goetzei* and *A. burkei*, for example, are both very variable species across their southern African range – in leaflet shape, size and number, and also in their ecological preferences. It is suspected that they may both be the result of hybridization with *A. nigrescens* as one of the parents. However, the species are now evidently fertile and able to propagate themselves. An example of a sterile hybrid is the occasional cross between *A. karroo* and *A. rehmanniana* with lemon-coloured flowers and which is also intermediate in other respects. A hybrid between *A. mellifera* and *A. senegal* (possibly var. *leiorhachis*) is commonly found west of Beitbridge. It is still not known whether it flowers and sets fertile seed – if it did the taxon would be very similar to what has been called *A. laeta* in northern and eastern Africa. Although first described in East Africa as a proper species, it was later realized, when the chromosome number was determined as $2n=39$ (triploid), that it was a hybrid between *A. mellifera* and *A. senegal* var. *senegal* (Elamin 1972).

With the research now being undertaken to study the genetic variation between and within African *Acacia* species, great opportunities are opening up for making artificial hybrids. The desirable attributes of pairs of compatible species can be matched to produce trees that will enhance production from the land. The possibility of sterility in the hybrid could prove to be an asset rather than a hindrance in that it might be the most effective way to control invasiveness in the genus.

BOX 12 – NODULATION AND CHROMOSOME NUMBERS OF ZIMBABWE *ACACIAS*

The table below shows which *Acacia* species are known to nodulate, mostly based on work by Corby (1974). Chromosome numbers are given where known, based on various publications (Barnes *et al*. 1996, 1997, Darlington & Wylie 1955, Elamin 1972, Hamant *et al*. 1975, Oballa & Olng'otie 1994, Vassal 1974). Data for *A. ataxacantha* seem rather confused and could be a result of poor experimental recording.

taxon	nodules	chromosome no. (2n) & specimen location
Faidherbia albida	✓	26 (Sudan[1])
Acacia abyssinica	✓	52 (Chimanimani)
A. adenocalyx	no	
A. amythethophylla	✓	26 (Sudan[1])
A. arenaria	✓	
A. ataxacantha	✓	26, 52,104 (?)
A. borleae	✓	
A. burkei	✓	
A. caffra	✓	26 (Natal)
A. chariessa	✓	
A. eriocarpa	n/a	
A. erioloba	✓*	26, 52 (Nyamandhlovu)
A. erubescens	✓	
A. exuvialis	✓	
A. fleckii	✓	
A. galpinii	✓	40 (Matopos)
A. gerrardii	✓	52 (Sudan[1])
A. goetzei	✓	
A. grandicornuta	✓	
A. hebeclada chobiensis	n/a	
A. hebeclada hebeclada	✓	208 (N. Pretoria)
A. hereroensis	✓	
A. karroo	✓	52 (Bulawayo)
A. kirkii	✓	52 (Zaire)
A. luederitzii	✓	
A. mellifera	✓	26 (ssp. mellifera, Sudan[1])
A. nebrownii	✓	
A. nigrescens	✓	26 (N. Transvaal)
A. nilotica	✓	52
A. pentagona	no	
A. permixta	✓	
A. polyacantha	✓	26 (Zambia)
A. rehmanniana	✓	52 (Matopos)
A. robusta clavigera	✓	
A. robusta robusta	✓	52 (N. Pretoria)
A. schweinfurthii	no	26 (Sudan[1])
A. senegal leiorhachis	✓	
A. senegal rostrata	✓	
A. sieberiana	✓	104 (Marondera)
A. stuhlmannii	✓	
A. tortilis heteracantha	✓	52 (Tuli)
A. tortilis spirocarpa	✓	52 (Birchenough)
A. welwitschii	✓	
A. xanthophloea	✓	52

[1] Elamin (1972). * Suggested to be aberrant; does not normally nodulate. n/a data not available

38

ACACIA SENEGAL *(L.) Willd.* var. ROSTRATA *Brenan*

Common names: three-thorned acacia; umhlahlalinye (Ndebele)

Acacia senegal var. *rostrata* is a low spreading shrub with a distinctive shape found on calcareous soils in the southern lowveld, and is closely related to the tree that produces gum arabic north of the equator.

Description *A. senegal* var. *rostrata* is an obconical shrub 2-4 m high, often branching from the base. Crown rounded, sometimes touching the ground. Stem diameter at base is normally 3-10 cm. **Young twigs** are pale, light grey to purplish and slightly pubescent. Persistent dead twigs turn pink-reddish. **Thorns** are hooked and in threes at the nodes, the two lateral pointing up and the middle one pointing down. **Leaves** are medium-sized (5 x 3 cm) with 4-6 pairs of pinnae, each with several small pale green leaflets. **Inflorescences** are white axillary spikes, broad and almost fluffy. These are often profuse, quite conspicuous and handsome, and appear in December on old growth. There are often many visiting insects. The inflorescence axis is pubescent. **Pods** are dehiscent, straight and wide, no more than 3 times as long as broad. They are straw coloured and papery, with a thickened margin and distinct apical tip.

Field characters Obconical shrub; pale grey stems; hooked thorns in threes; inflorescence axis pubescent; broad papery pod with distinct apical tip; on alluvium in lowveld.

The shrubby shape and general appearance clearly separate var. *rostrata* and var. *leiorhachis*, and the different shaped pods should confirm this. At a distance var. *rostrata* can be confused with *A. mellifera*, but the three hooked thorns of *A. senegal* and leaflet size distinguish them (see also *A. laeta* under *A. mellifera*).

Distribution and ecology *A. senegal* var. *rostrata*, as presently defined, is found in Kenya, Somalia and Uganda, with a gap in distribution until the southern African populations in Angola, Namibia, Botswana, Zimbabwe, Mozambique, the former Transvaal, Swaziland and KwaZulu-Natal. In Zimbabwe the subspecies is found only in the Limpopo lowveld (below 600 m altitude) from Tuli across to Gonarezhou and the lower Save River near Birchenough Bridge. The habitat is distinctly different from that of var. *leiorhachis* and the variety is found only on calcareous soils (sometimes with calcium nodules) of alluvial origin associated with the Shashe, Limpopo (plus major tributaries) and Save rivers. However, in the Sentinel Ranch area they can both be found in close proximity. It has not been recorded from the Zambezi catchment, although there is an unconfirmed report from Tsholotsho on the upper reaches of the Nata catchment.

Notes *A. senegal* var. *rostrata* is more closely related to vars. *senegal* and *kerensis* (the former being the variety producing gum arabic in NE tropical Africa) than to var. *leiorhachis* (see Box 9, page 105). However, gum has not been extracted from plants in Zimbabwe.

Varieties of *A. senegal* found in other parts of Africa north of the equator (that are more closely related to var. *rostrata* than to var. *leiorhachis*) are said to be very drought resistant, coppice well, but are not particularly fast growing. They are used as fuelwood and charcoal, as well as for the collection of gum and in soil conservation works. The life for individual trees is estimated at 25-30 years. Natural regeneration in existing stands does not occur, only in fallow lands and on degraded soils. Var. *rostrata* appears similar in this latter respect in Zimbabwe.

The wood is hard, heavy (990 kg/m³) and off-white, with no heartwood.

In northern South Africa var. *rostrata* is reported to be slow growing and frost-sensitive.

The specific name refers to Senegal, from where var. *senegal* was first described by Linneaus in 1806. The varietal name comes from the Latin (*rostratus* - having a beak), referring to the marked apical tip to the pod.

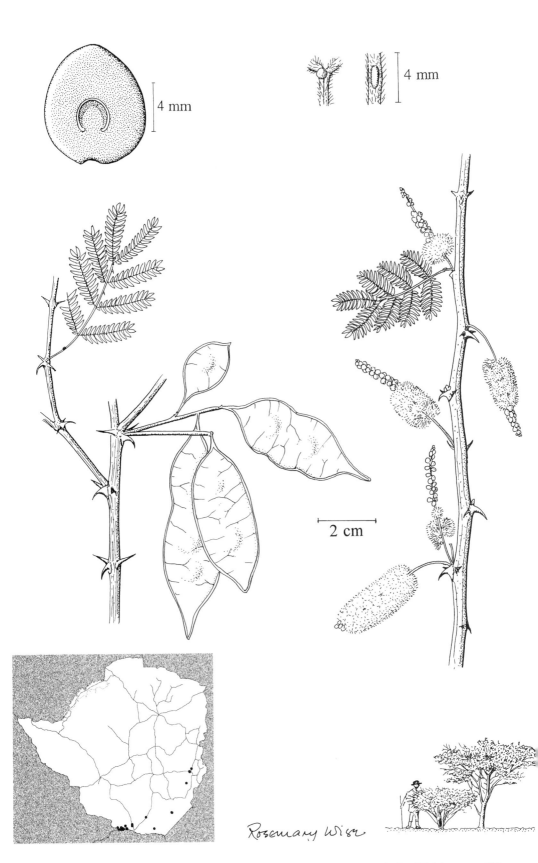

4 mm

4 mm

2 cm

Rosemany Wise

ACACIA SENEGAL ROSTRATA

39

ACACIA SIEBERIANA *DC.*

(= *A. davyii* sensu Boughey 1964, *A. lasiopetala* sensu Suessenguth & Merxmüller 1951, *A. sieberana* var. *vermoensii* (De Wild.) Keay & Brenan, *A. woodii* Burtt Davy)

Common names: paperbark thorn, flat-topped thorn, umbrella thorn; papierbasdoring (Afrikaans); umpumbu, umsasane (Ndebele); hlofungu (Shangaan); impangala, mubovwa, mumpangala (Tonga)

A magnificent tree with a flattened spreading canopy, *Acacia sieberiana* is most common along the central watershed in open areas and along vlei margins. At lower altitudes a different, less-spreading form is encountered.

Description *A. sieberiana* is a medium to large-sized tree up to 15 m in height, usually with a single trunk which can attain a diameter of 75 cm, although normally much less. The canopy is often distinctively flattened but with ascending branches, and the profile is reminiscent of a chanterelle fungus. **Bark** is light grey and somewhat rough, and peels to reveal a yellowish under-layer. **Young twigs** are pale grey to brown, covered in spreading yellow hairs on the current years' growth, but turning greyish later. The epidermis sometimes peels to reveal a yellowish under-layer on older growth. Pustular white lenticels are present on the young growth. **Thorns** are paired at the nodes, straight and up to 5 cm long. Older trees can be practically thornless. **Leaves** are medium to large (8-15 x 4-6 cm) with 8-20 pairs of pinnae, each with many small (3-4 x 1 mm) pale green to yellow-green leaflets. A small tooth is present on the tip of the leaf rachis, often persisting after leaf fall. **Inflorescences** consist of axillary clusters of sweet-smelling white globose heads on long peduncles that appear primarily on young growth around September-December. **Pods** are dark yellowish brown, long (12-25 cm), straight or slightly curved, thick in cross-section with markedly woody valves. They are effectively indehiscent, but do dehisce long after falling to the ground. Although generally smooth, they can be hairy when young.

Field characters Flat spreading crown; flaking bark revealing yellowish under-layer; yellow spreading hairs on young growth; pustular white lenticels on young twigs; thick woody pale brown indehiscent pods.

A. *sieberiana* can be confused with both *A. rehmanniana* and *A. abyssinica* when young, although the size of tree, form and habitat will help separate them in the field. *A. sieberiana* has fewer pairs of pinnae (8-20) than the other two species, and has larger leaflets (3-4 mm long). The woody pods, the remains of which can often be found under the tree, are also very distinctive.

Distribution and ecology *A. sieberiana* occurs from tropical West Africa to Sudan and Ethiopia and southwards through Tanzania to northern Namibia, northern Botswana, Zimbabwe and eastern South Africa. In Zimbabwe it is widespread but is mostly found at medium and higher altitudes above 900 m and in the Zambezi and eastern catchments. Below 900 m altitude and in all but the highest reaches of the Limpopo catchment it is confined to recent alluvial soils and riverine situations. A. *sieberiana* can be found in a variety of habitats ranging from grassland with scattered trees to open woodland; in open grassland it can be a large spreading tree. It is mostly found in higher moisture sites such as the edge of vleis or drainage lines, or in occasionally waterlogged open areas where other trees struggle to survive. The sites are generally on nutrient-poor sandy soils and adjacent to miombo woodland.

Notes All southern African populations of *A. sieberiana* have been classified as var. *woodii* (Burtt Davy) Keay & Brenan. This differs from var. *sieberiana*, which is found from West Africa to Sudan and southwards to Malawi and Mozam- bique, in that the young twigs are hairy, not glabrous, and the branches of the crown are spreading, not ascending. It is not clear if this varietal difference corresponds to the differing

→

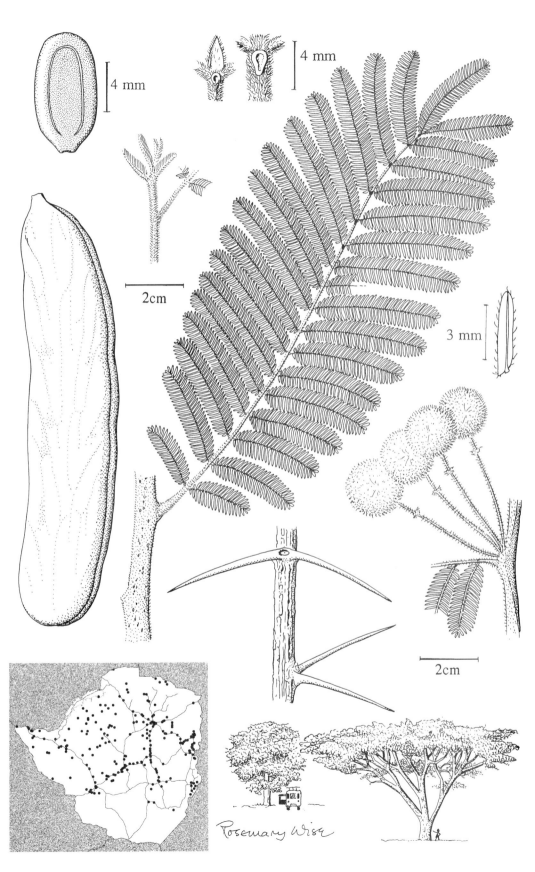

Rosemary Wise

ACACIA SIEBERIANA

forms of the species seen in Zimbabwe – the flat-topped form that grows around Harare and Bulawayo and along the central watershed, and the round-topped form with more yellow bark on the branches that occurs at lower altitudes along large rivers and occasionally on the central watershed as at Kadoma. Specimens from lower altitudes here also have noticeably less hairy, or even glabrous, young growth and fewer pairs of pinnae.

At one time the spelling of the specific name was "sieberana", but recent changes in the International Code of Botanical Nomenclature have made it now correct to spell it "sieberiana".

The majority of wood is a creamy white sapwood; sometimes a very dark brown, narrow heartwood is seen. The coarse-textured sapwood is of medium density (655-720 kg/m^3) and not durable, particularly outdoors. It is one of the softest and lightest of southern African woods. The wood has been used for rough furniture and crates, but moves seasonally. It has only moderate borer resistance and is susceptible to sapstain. It is of little value as firewood, but burns slowly. The pods and foliage are eaten by cattle, but the pods sometimes contain prussic acid when green which can cause fatalities. Pod production could be over 200 kg per tree.

A. sieberiana is a fast-growing tree and easy to establish from seed. It is also cold and frost resistant. The fairly open spreading canopy of highveld specimens, coupled with nutrient input from leaf fall, allow for good grass growth underneath, thus trees are not only attractive but an asset to the farmer. The species is thought to be shallow-rooted; normally individuals lose their leaves fairly soon after the rains finish, but in sites where there is better access to moisture trees can retain leaves for much of the year.

Larvae of the emperor moth *Goodia kuntzei* feed on the foliage.

The species is named after Franz Sieber, a Czech botanist and traveller, who collected the type specimen in Senegal; the variety is named after John Wood, the renowned Natal botanist who collected the varietal type in KwaZulu-Natal.

BOX 13 – ANTS AND ACACIAS

The whistling thorns of the East African plains (e.g. *Acacia drepanolobium)* are some of the best described examples of mutualism between species of *Acacia* and ants found both in Africa and the New World. The *Crematogaster* (cocktail) ants set up their colonies in the swollen thorns after hollowing them out. They enter the thorn chambers through the holes that whistle in the wind, and once in residence the ants incubate their young, tend fungus gardens, and feed on the many leaf nectaries. The acacias benefit because the ants patrol the younger twigs and actively defend them against herbivores, both mammals and insects. In Central America, other *Acacia* species with swollen thorns also harbour ant colonies which, in return for the nectar and protinaceous leaf tips (Beltian bodies) and shelter, attack any herbivores and even prune encroaching vegetation.

Many *Acacia* species without swollen thorns still provide nectar for the ants that are frequently seen patrolling the twigs. It is likely that these ants also reduce insect attack on the trees, although this has not been confirmed experimentally in Zimbabwe.

Insects are also essential in pollinating acacia flowers. An intriguing question is, in species with aggressive ant guards, how do the pollinators have access to the flowers? Recent research on whistling thorns has shown that the ants appear to be deterred from the young flowers only when they are about to open and the pollen released (Willmer & Stone 1997). At this point a volatile chemical signal that can be wiped experimentally from one flower to the next is produced from the flowers. However, the ants will return to patrolling over the flowers shortly after pollination has been effected to deter flower and pod-feeding beetles and seed predators. The outcome is directly improved seed-set in the presence of the ants.

BOX 14 – BRUCHID BEETLES

Seed collected from most Zimbabwe *Acacia* species will have been parasitized to some extent by beetles of the family Bruchidae, often known as bruchids. Their depredations are indicated by small circular exit holes drilled in the seed coat; this generally indicates that the particular seed is no longer viable.

There are more than a thousand species in 60 genera within the bruchid family. The adult beetle can be anything from 1 to 30 mm long (Booth *et al.* 1990). They are major pests of legume seed and are sometimes called pea or bean weevils, although they are not strictly weevils. One group of bruchids lays its eggs on the young green pods. The larvae soon hatch and avoid the toxins in the pod by burrowing immediately through into the seed. Here, they create a chamber and eat away the inner layers until only a thin shell of testa (seed coat) remains. When fully grown, they pupate and the adult beetle emerges after the pod has matured by boring a round exit hole through the seed coat. These bruchid species do not re-infest the seeds after emergence. Another group of bruchids can breed successively and are able to produce many generations on the same stored seed until the food supply is exhausted. The larvae of some species are too large to pupate in the seed and these emerge from the seed and lower themselves on a thin silken thread to pupate in the ground (Southgate 1978).

Many species of the family Bruchidae parasitize acacia seeds. Fourteen of the 61 *Acacia* species in East Africa are known to be hosts to one or more species of bruchid, and the true proportion is likely to be much higher. For example, one bruchid species found in Zimbabwe parasitizes *Acacia tortilis, A. erioloba, A. karroo* and *A. abyssinica,* plus other species outside the country. Predation can destroy all the seed crop, although high rates are normally around 60-70%.

When seed collections from acacias are kept separate by individual trees, it is clear that some have been more susceptible to attack than others. This may be due to differences in the coincidence of flowering and the peak of bruchid activity. On the other hand, there are some early indications from phytochemical investigations that concentrations of certain amino acids, which can differ between individual trees, will determine whether or not a bruchid larva can survive in a seed (Southgate 1978).

Passage of a seed through the gut of a large herbivore is thought to kill any bruchids that might be present. Further, seeds that have emergence holes but which have not been fatally damaged by the beetle's feeding can take up water and germinate soon after being deposited in the dung. Insecticides can be used to treat the seed and prevent re-infestation, while freezing can also kill bruchids within the seed before they have finished feeding. Bruchids do have some value, however, in that they have been used in the biocontrol of some species of Australian acacias that have become serious invaders in exotic situations.

40

ACACIA STUHLMANNII *Taub.*

Acacia stuhlmannii is a distinctive spreading shrub with yellowish-green hairy growth. It forms dense stands in just a few localities on silty soils in the southwestern lowveld.

Description *A. stuhlmannii* is a multi-stemmed shrub 1-3 m in height with stems spreading from the base. Slashed stems have a strong garlicky smell. **Young twigs** are green-yellow, generally quite thick, and covered in long yellow to greyish hairs with conspicuous white pustular lenticels underneath. **Thorns** are long (to 4 cm) and straight, sometimes hairy near the base. **Leaves** are medium-sized (6 x 2 cm) with 6-12 pairs of pinnae and a dense coating of long hairs on the rachis. They appear soon after the first rains. **Inflorescences** are white globose heads, appearing in the axils of both old and new growth in August-October, sometimes before the leaves. Stands are sometimes seen in profuse flower. **Pods** are small and indehiscent, somewhat leathery, and are densely covered with long yellowish hairs. The seeds are hard and rounded.

Field characters Low spreading shrub; local dominance in old fields in Beitbridge area; long shaggy yellowish hairs on twigs and pods. Unlikely to be confused with other species.

Distribution and ecology *A. stuhlmannii* has a very disjunct distribution in Africa, being found around the Shashe-Limpopo confluence in eastern Botswana, the northern tip of South Africa and southeast Zimbabwe, followed by a large gap until Tanzania, Kenya and Somalia, where it is more widespread. Within Zimbabwe it is locally dominant in scattered localities only in the Beitbridge area. The species forms what appear to be even-aged stands along drainage lines on silty soils that are a mixture of basalt and sandstone. Some of the few stands in Zimbabwe are on what were irrigated fields, possibly abandoned due to sodicity. However, stands at these sites have persisted for up to 30 years. The local dominance in these disturbed habitats, to the exclusion of most other shrubs, is quite notable.

Notes There is no information on growth rates or establishment, but growth appears to be fast. *A. stuhlmannii* is thought to be comparatively short-lived. Establishment is presumably episodic when the right conditions are found in fallows. It is browsed by goats and seems to tolerate very heavy browsing pressure.

The species is named after Franz Stuhlmann, a German botanist who later became a senior official in the Tanganyika Administration and set up the Amani Research Institute. He collected the type specimen near Dar es Salaam in Tanzania.

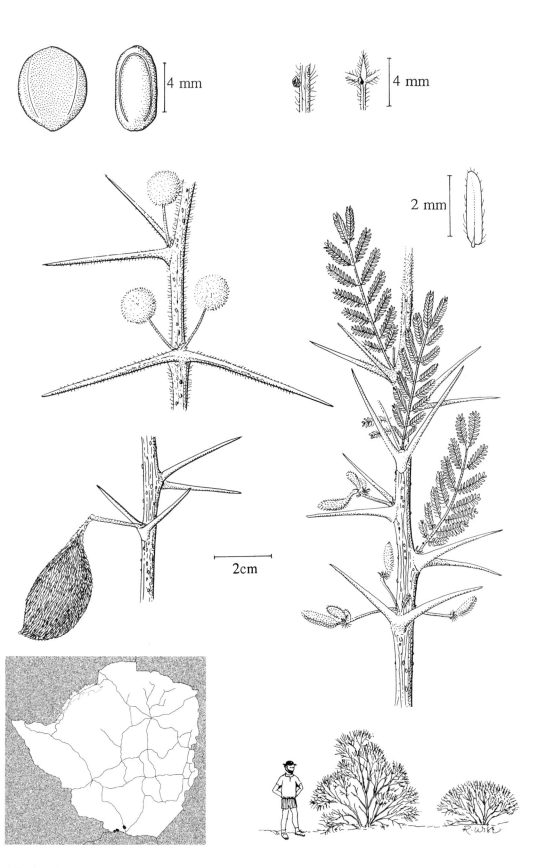

4 mm

4 mm

2 mm

2cm

ACACIA STUHLMANNII

ACACIA TORTILIS *(Forssk.) Hayne* subsp. HETERACANTHA *(Burch.) Brenan*
(= *A. heteracantha* Burch., *A. litakunensis* Burch.)

Common names: umbrella thorn; haak-en-steek (Afrikaans); isanqawe, umsasane, umshishene, umtshatshatsha (Ndebele); sesami (Shangaan)

A widespread, often weedy, tree in the south and west of the country, easily recognized from its mixture of long white and short hooked thorns. *Acacia tortilis* subsp. *heteracantha*, not always clearly distinguished from subsp. *spirocarpa*, is a medium-sized tree associated with old lands, cattle areas and disturbance.

Description *A. tortilis* subsp. *heteracantha* is a small to medium-sized tree, often with a divided trunk, up to 10 m in height, but normally around 4-6 m. It remains a compact bush when heavily browsed. The crown is rounded, but gets flatter in older specimens. **Bark** is quite smooth, dark brown to blackish and vertically fissured. **Young twigs** are slender, purplish brown with small scattered white lenticels. Hairs are generally absent but can be found on some individuals – few and short (<0.25 mm long). Small red glands are absent. **Thorns** occur in pairs at the nodes, and are of two types – long and straight, and short and hooked. The straight thorns are whitish and up to 9 cm in length, and are generally preponderant on young growth close to the ground. The hooked thorns (which are modified stipules, not prickles) are whitish to grey in colour, around 5 mm long, and are mostly found on older growth out of the reach of browsing animals. Sometimes both long straight and hooked thorns are found at a node. **Leaves** are small (2.5 x 1.5 cm), tufted at the nodes, with 2-6 pairs of pinnae each bearing many minute grey-green leaflets. The rachis and petiole are slightly pubescent. **Inflorescences** are axillary clusters of small globose heads of white to pale yellow flowers, appearing on the previous season's growth from November to March, often sporadically following rain. They are very attractive to insects. **Pods** are small and tightly coiled, staying green for some time before ripening straw-brown. They are indehiscent, falling to the ground intact around May to July, and "rattle" when ripe. The pod is without any pubescence or glands and has a "waxy" feel.

Field characters Mixture of long white and short hooked thorns; small leaves and minute leaflets; tightly coiled smooth pods.

A. tortilis as a species is rarely confused with others owing to the mixture of thorn types, but confusion can arise in the separation of the two subspecies. Subsp. *heteracantha* is generally a smaller tree found in disturbed areas away from rivers and with a shrubbier growth form. The young twigs are smooth or only slightly hairy with very short hairs (<0.25 mm long) and are not velvety pubescent. The defining character is the pod – that of subsp. *heteracantha* is tightly coiled, narrower (5-7 mm wide) and without hairs or scattered small red glands, while that of subsp. *spirocarpa* is only laxly coiled like an over-stretched spring, wider (6-9 mm wide), velvety pubescent and covered with small red glands (a hand lens is required). However, individual trees with a mixture of these sets of characters are sometimes encountered in the west of the country.

Distribution and ecology The species *A. tortilis* is found throughout the drier parts of tropical Africa and also in the Arabian peninsula as far north as Israel. Subsp. *heteracantha* is a southern African taxon found only between the Zambezi and Orange rivers and as far west as southwestern Angola. Its distribution in Zimbabwe is still not very clear owing to confusion between the two putative subspecies. The distribution maps given with the illustrations include records attributed to one or other subspecies in the field, while the two maps given after *A. tortilis* subsp. *spirocarpa* on page 134 show the distribution of just herbarium specimens at the National Herbarium, Harare, that have confirmed as being one subspecies or the other solely on the basis of the presence or absence of red glands on the pods. The low number of confirmed records is due to few herbarium

→

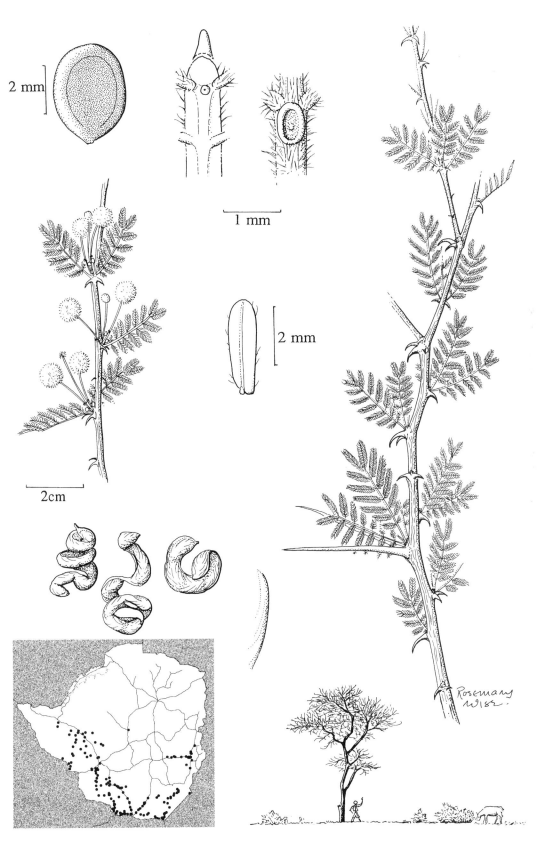

ACACIA TORTILIS HETERACANTHA

specimens having pods. Subsp. *heteracantha* appears to be primarily confined to the Limpopo and Save catchments in Zimbabwe, but is also found in parts of the Gwayi and Nata catchments in the northwest. Scattered occurrences elsewhere appear to be the result of introductions through livestock movement or travellers. It is particularly common in hotter, drier ranching areas around Tsholotsho and Inyati south to Gwanda, Chiredzi and Beitbridge, generally below 1200 m.

Subsp. *heteracantha* is closely associated with livestock and wildlife, which disperse its seeds in their dung. It is principally found in open habitats or disturbed areas in various woodland and bushland types, and can be invasive on old lands. In the Hwange area scattered individuals occur around pans on enriched sandy soils, but it is also encountered in the driest areas on shallow gravelly basalt soils. In the drier parts of the country, subsp. *heteracantha* is one of the few woody plants able to withstand heavy browsing pressure from goats owing to the dense network of long white thorns.

Notes Apart from subsp. *spirocarpa,* the other recognized subspecies of *A. tortilis* are also found north of the equator. Although typical forms of subsp. *heteracantha* and subsp. *spirocarpa* are fairly distinct when pods are seen, and also differ substantively in their ecology and distribution, sometimes apparent intermediates are found. It is a moot point whether the two subspecies are sufficiently distinct to justify that status. On occasion both subspecies are said to occur together, flowering at different times. It appears as if the distribution of subsp. *heteracantha* is determined primarily by wildlife and livestock movement, while that of subsp. *spirocarpa* is more linked to suitable alluvial substrate. Possibly subsp. *heteracantha* has evolved from the other subspecies to accommodate this dispersal mechanism. Further studies are required on the genetic and molecular differences between the two.

The wood is heavy (890-990 kg/m³) and mostly consists of yellowish sapwood. The red-brown heartwood is usually confined to irregular small patches and is very heavy and hard. It seasons well except around the pith. *A. tortilis* makes a good firewood while the inner bark is used for cordage. Young branches are used for bush fencing.

Subsp. *heteracantha* grows moderately slowly and is cold resistant. Its drought resistance is probably a result of a well-developed root system.

The seeds germinate well after some form of scarification and the plant establishes readily, but not in the shade of its parents.

The pods are a much relished source of browse for both wildlife and livestock, particularly goats, and contain up to 17% protein. Seeds are presumably adapted to withstand the mastication and digestive processes and are readily dispersed in droppings. Yield data are not yet available for Zimbabwe, but for maximum production of pods and grass, tree numbers per hectare should be kept low. In some rural areas pods are gathered to feed livestock which have been shown to respond well in meat production. Leafy shoots are also browsed, but the heavy spinescence minimizes this in areas subject to continued browsing pressure. Leaves remain on the plant into the dry season, thus increasing its value as a forage source.

Elsewhere in southern Africa, *A. tortilis* is regarded as a bush encroachment species, reducing the amount of available grass to cattle. This is not generally the case here except on old lands.

The specific name means "twisted" in Latin (*tortilis* - twisted) referring to the coiled pods, while the subspecific name comes from Greek meaning "alternating thorns" (*heteros* - other, *akantha* - thorns) and refers to the two different types of thorns.

BOX 15 – EPISODIC REGENERATION

A feature of some species of *Acacia* is their frequent occurrence in dense stands comprising individuals of similar stature. These even-sized stands are believed to be also even-aged, the result of a comparatively short period of regeneration – a "window of opportunity" – preceeded and followed by lengthy periods where regeneration was not possible or has failed. Such stands are notable for their lack of young regenerating plants and also seem to experience mortality at a similar time. This phenomenon, not just confined to acacias, is termed episodic regeneration or cohort establishment.

The establishment of such uniform stands is thought to be the result of one or more of the following factors: (a) a favourable sequence of climatic factors, such as a good rainfall year/s or a frost-free winter, which allows young plants to establish deep and strong root systems, (b) reduced competition from grass growth for a year or more, (c) lack of fire for sufficiently long so that saplings become strong and tall enough to withstand it, (d) a good seed bed, such as found after ploughing, heavy disturbance or severe flooding, with minimum competition from other woody plants and grasses, or (e) particularly good seed harvest years with widespread dispersal of seed. The most important requirement is probably for a period of reduced competition from other plants such that seedlings can get sufficiently well established. They need a strong root system to gain access soil moisture below the zone utilized by grasses. Lack of moisture is probably the major source of seedling and young plant mortality in acacias, compounded by excessive shading from grass and other herbaceous plants and the weakening effects of frequent fires or browsing.

Acacia species in Zimbabwe notable for their occurrence in even-aged stands include *A. arenaria*, *A. erioloba*, *A. karroo*, *A. polyacantha*, *A. stuhlmannii*, *A. tortilis* subsp. *spirocarpa* and *A. xanthophloea*. It is particularly the pioneer species that show such behaviour, species which can rapidly invade open habitats and cannot tolerate too much competition from other plants. Areas of up to a few hectares of uniform trees or shrubs are often seen with few other woody species mixed in. Sometimes it is obviously an old field site or an area that was subject to devastating flooding some years back, but occasionally the reason is not at all apparent.

Research in the Bulawayo area is now looking at what the mechanisms might be that cause the establishment of uniform stands, and whether such stands are in fact even-aged or just apparently so.

42

ACACIA TORTILIS *(Forssk.) Hayne* subsp. SPIROCARPA *(A. Rich.) Brenan* (= *A. spirocarpa* A. Rich.)

Common names: umbrella thorn; haak-en-steek (Afrikaans); isanqawe, umsasane, umshishene, umtshatshatsha (Ndebele); mukoka, ngoka, muzungu (Tonga)

Often a well-formed tree with a distinctive umbrella-shaped canopy, *Acacia tortilis* subsp. *spirocarpa* is widespread along rivers of the Zambezi and Save River catchments at low altitudes.

Description *A. tortilis* subsp. *spirocarpa* is a medium to large-sized tree up to 20 m in height with a conspicuously flattened umbrella-shaped crown when mature. Trunk usually 30-40 cm in diameter, but can reach 75 cm. **Bark** is dark brown to blackish and vertically fissured. **Young twigs** are slender, generally purplish brown with small white lenticels, densely velvety pubescent with moderately long hairs (>0.25 mm long), sometimes with a few small scattered reddish glands. **Thorns** occur in pairs at the nodes and are of two types – long and straight, and short and hooked. The straight thorns are whitish, up to 9 cm in length, and are more common on younger growth exposed to browsers. The smaller hooked thorns, around 5 mm long, are more common on older growth out of reach of browsing animals. Sometimes a straight and a hooked thorn form a pair at a node. **Leaves** are small (2.5 x 1.5 cm), tufted at the nodes, with 2-6 pairs of pinnae each bearing many minute grey-green leaflets. The rachis and petiole are pubescent with hairs longer than 0.25 mm. **Inflorescences** are axillary clusters of small globose heads of white to pale yellow flowers, appearing on young and older growth from January to April, later than those of subsp. *heteracantha*. **Pods** are small, long and thin (6-9 mm wide), rounded in cross-section and gently coiled like an over-stretched spring, staying green for some time. They are distinctly pubescent with hairs over 0.25 mm long and scattered small red glands (only seen with a hand lens). The pods are indehiscent and fall to the ground when ripe around August/September.

Field characters Tree of drainage lines with an umbrella-shaped canopy; mixture of long white and short hooked thorns; small leaves and minute leaflets; pubescent, curled, indehiscent pods with small red glands.

A. tortilis subsp. *spirocarpa* is often confused with subsp. *heteracantha* (see separate entry). Subsp. *spirocarpa* is generally a tree of sandy alluvium at lower altitudes, the young twigs are distinctly pubescent with hairs longer than 0.25 mm, and the pods are laxly curled with velvety pubescence and small scattered red glands which look like specks of dirt. In the west of the country, however, individuals are found with intermediate characters.

Distribution and ecology Subsp. *spirocarpa* is the most widespread of the four recognized subspecies of *A. tortilis*, occurring from central Namibia, northern Botswana and Zimbabwe northwards to Somalia, Ethiopia and Sudan. As with subsp. *heteracantha,* its distribution in Zimbabwe is not very clear owing to confusions in identification, but it primarily occurs north of the central watershed in the Zambezi catchment, with other major populations in the Save valley. It seems surprisingly localized compared to subsp. *heteracantha*. The subspecies is generally found on sandy alluvium associated with larger rivers below about 1000 m, where it frequently occurs in even-sized stands. These uniform stands are probably the result of flooding events followed by rapid establishment on the bare sandy deposits. It is also found as scattered individuals in riparian woodland, but rarely away from drainage lines.

Subsp. *spirocarpa*, like subsp. *heteracantha*, is a pioneer species that establishes itself in open disturbed areas. This is seen along the Mukumbura River on the northern border with Mozambique where a dense mature woodland with thick undergrowth is found, dominated by *A. tortilis*. Other tree species are slowly gaining dominance and now *A. tortilis* is dying off. Such stands are probably a result of clearing for cultivation some 50 or more years ago.

→

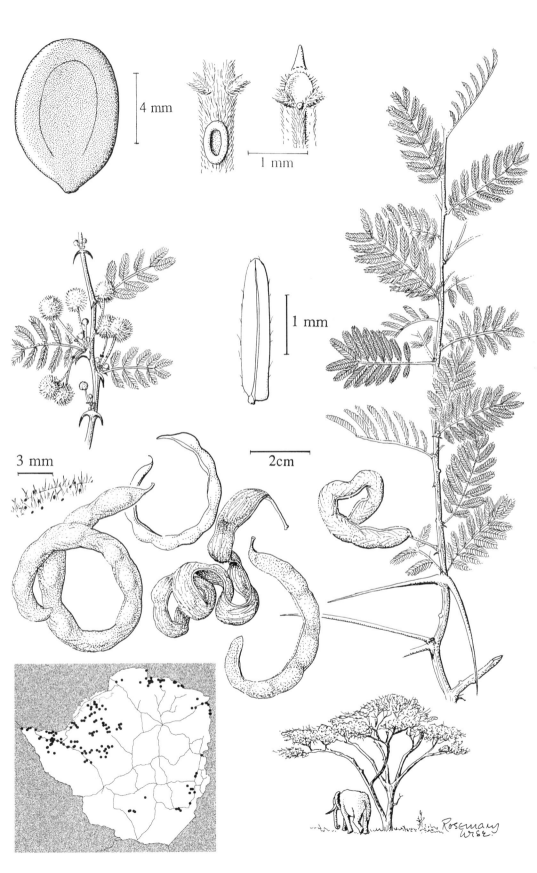

A. TORTILIS SPIROCARPA

Notes Subsp. *spirocarpa* is sometimes subdivided into two varieties – the widespread var. *spirocarpa* and var. *crinita* Chiov. The latter is differentiated by long (1-3 mm) whitish hairs on the pods. Var. *crinita* is recorded from Somalia, Kenya and Tanzania, and has recently been noted in Namibia. It is likely to be just an aberrant form rather than a genetically distinct taxon. The classic flat-topped *Acacia* of the East African savannas is *A. tortilis* subsp. *spirocarpa*, which there appears to occupy the equivalent niches of both subspecies here.

Elsewhere in Africa the subspecies has many uses, but in Zimbabwe, perhaps because of its restricted habitat, few uses have been reported. It provides a good firewood, but the wood is not resistant enough for many construction purposes. The bark is used for cordage, while the pods and leaves are nutritious fodder for both wildlife and livestock; owing to its distribution it is mostly utilized by the former.

Subsp. *spirocarpa* is much faster growing than subsp. *heteracantha*, probably due to its warmer and moister habitat. It is easily raised from seed. Longevity is probably in the order of 50-75 years, after which most individuals are being out-competed by slower-growing trees.

The specific name means "twisted" in Latin (*tortilis* - twisted) referring to the coiled pods. The subspecific name is Greek for "coiled fruits" (*speira* - coil, *karpos* - fruit).

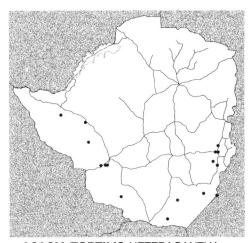
ACACIA TORTILIS HETERACANTHA

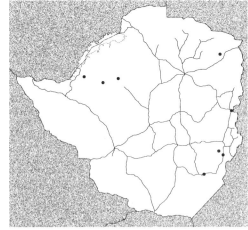
ACACIA TORTILIS SPIROCARPA

Distribution of the two subspecies of *Acacia tortilis* based solely on herbarium specimens with pods.

BOX 16 – WOOD PROPERTIES

To make an evaluation of the suitability of wood from a particular species of tree, the end-use requirements have to be clearly stipulated and the wood also has to be compared to a "standard". In Zimbabwe, the standard used for most wood-working and furniture-making purposes is the heartwood from mukwa (*Pterocarpus angolensis*), while the standard for outdoor construction is often gum (*Eucalyptus*). Wood from various *Acacia* species, if used for these purposes, has both advantages and disadvantages. Wood properties involve a whole suite of (often independent) characteristics, and it is this whole range that has to be evaluated, not just one or two characters. Although the requirements for outdoor farm and interior carpentry uses differ, a common criterion is how long the finished article will last in service.

Most hardwood species contain both heartwood and sapwood. The inner heartwood is generally harder and darker, and contains chemicals that inhibit fungal and insect attack. The outer, paler, sapwood is often prone to attack. For most purposes, it is the heartwood that is used for carpentry or construction because of its durability.

Both the carpenters' workshop and the woodworkers' factory require heartwood planks that are fairly durable, of moderate weight, stable, and workable using standard techniques. Most large acacias with good heartwood formation can be converted to sawn planks if the logs are from well-formed trees. However, there can be considerable variation in ease of sawmilling, a problem which arises more from the hardness of the timber than from abrasive infiltrates. Where there is a large proportion of sapwood in the sawn planks, it is advisable to trim off the outer 25 mm of sapwood which is most prone to insect attack. Unlike mukwa, which shrinks remarkably little on seasoning, acacia planks tend to crack, cup and twist and so require "pin-stacking" and shading while drying out.

The genus *Acacia* provides many useful woods suitable for a variety of purposes, including firewood, fence posts, poles, tool handles and furniture. Those species with irregular or indistinct heartwood and lacking in durability, such as *A. gerrardii*, *A. rehmanniana*, *A. sieberiana*, *A. karroo* and *Faidherbia albida*, are best considered as "all sapwood". The wood of *A. gerrardii* and *A. rehmanniana* is quickly destroyed by fungi and boring insects. Wood from *A. karroo* is strong, of medium weight, and is comparatively easily-worked, but is also rapidly attacked by borers, necessitating protection and quick conversion to planks. *A. sieberiana* and *Faidherbia albida* are available in larger sizes, but there is no clear differentiation between heartwood and sapwood and the wood is comparatively light in weight. As they have some natural immunity to insect attack, they can be used for crating, shelving and cheap interior furniture. None of the "all sapwood" species of *Acacia* are suitable for outdoor construction unless treated with preservative.

Acacia species that have a large proportion of heartwood have good natural durability and are much used for outdoor construction, but there is considerable variation in longevity. For example, *A. polyacantha* and *A. goetzei* may last 10-20 years, *A. nigrescens* and *A. erioloba* can last from 20 to 100 years, while *A. galpinii* and *A. nilotica* are intermediate.

Amongst the durable acacias there is considerable variation in density and hardness. *A. polyacantha* and *A. galpinii* when harvested at maturity can supply large logs with a high proportion of heartwood. Although a bit more difficult to work than mukwa, they can generally be used for the same range of products. Neither are as dimensionally-stable and move to some extent with seasonal changes in humidity, but they have a better natural finish than mukwa when treated with oils or polish alone. The wood of *A. galpinii* has uniform colour and markings that are comparatively consistent from tree to tree, although density does vary. *A. polyacantha*, while in the same weight class, is easier to work but is a timber of greater variation in colour and markings. Its main attribute is its beauty when used "all brown".

The woods of *A. erioloba* and *A. nigrescens* are at the extremes of hardness and difficulty of working. The greatest problem here is with sawmilling, and the use of a bandsaw is recommended after de-barking. Once converted into dimensioned timber, planks can be run through other woodworking machinery to make strong, heavy and beautiful products, but the major use is probably for general purpose farm construction (fencing, kraals, etc.).

Drought, frost, fire and overgrazing affect not only the quality and productivity of a woodland, but also, through their effect on growth rates and stem form, the quality of the wood produced. The land manager can have an effect on the latter two through protection coupled with selective felling or coppicing of poor quality or malformed trees. Natural stands of acacias can be a valuable asset on the farm if managed well, whether the end-use be rough timber for construction or quality timber for woodworking. [Brian Williams]

43

ACACIA WELWITSCHII *Oliv.*
(= *A. delagoensis* Harms)

Common names: mukaya (Shangaan)

One of the taxonomically-difficult species related to *Acacia nigrescens* and *A. burkei*, *A. welwitschii* is a tall riverine tree confined in Zimbabwe to the Chiredzi-Gonarezhou area.

Description *A. welwitschii* is a large tree from 8 to 20 m in height, often with a spreading canopy. Branching is generally low, and the lower branches droop. There is often a certain amount of dieback visible. **Bark** is grey-brown, fissured and flaking, often with a yellowish tinge. Trunk diameter is generally 20-30 cm in many specimens, but can range from 40-70 cm in larger riverine trees. **Young twigs** are glabrous, grey in colour, and with pustular lenticels. **Thorns** are hooked, relatively small, blackish, and paired at the nodes. **Leaves** are medium-sized (4-8 x 3-5 cm) usually with 3-4 pairs of pinnae, each with 3-6 pairs of medium-sized elliptic leaflets. The leaflets are symmetric at the base and often have a darker "foot" (petiolule), especially on drying. **Inflorescences** are terminal white spikes appearing on young growth in November-January. **Pods** are grey-brown to reddish brown, straight, linear-oblong and not constricted, ripening to brown or black. They are leathery in texture, glabrous and dehiscent.

Field characters Strong but small hooked thorns; elliptic bases to medium-sized leaflets; narrow pods.

A. *welwitschii* is difficult to separate from *A. burkei*, which also occurs in the same general area but in a different habitat. From a distance and in habit it greatly resembles the more common *A. nigrescens*, but the numerous and substantially smaller leaflets help distinguish it. *A. welwitschii* is also difficult to separate from *A. goetzei*, but it has narrower pods (less than 2 cm wide), fewer and smaller (less than 4 mm broad) elliptic and symmetric leaflets with a dark "foot", and orange lenticels on the twigs.

Distribution and ecology The subspecies occurring in Zimbabwe is *A. welwitschii* subsp. *delagoensis*, which is also found in Malawi, Mozambique and the former eastern Transvaal. In Zimbabwe it has a curiously restricted distribution and is found only in Chiredzi District along the lower Runde, Chiredzi and Save rivers below about 450 m altitude, an extension of its low altitude distribution in Mozambique and northeastern South Africa. Presumably it is intolerant of frost. Here the species is a riverine tree principally found on enriched or loamy alluvial soils where it can be locally dominant, as along parts of the Chiredzi River.

Notes Only subsp. *delagoensis* (Harms) J.H. Ross & Brenan is found south of the Zambezi. Subsp. *welwitschii*, which has a different appearance with larger leaflets and a longer inflorescence, is confined to northern Angola.

Within Zimbabwe, *A. welwitschii* in its typical tree form is only found adjacent to rivers and drainage lines in the south east. Individuals away from this habitat, if indeed they are *A. welwitschii*, are closer in appearance to *A. goetzei* subsp. *goetzei* with obovate leaflets, asymmetric leaf bases and scattered thorns on the rachis. Although *A. welwitschii* seems a well-defined species, it is possible that *A. goetzei* may hybridize with it.

The wood is hard and heavy (960 kg/m³) with yellow-brown sapwood and black heartwood. It is difficult to work. Growth rate is slow and the species is probably cold-sensitive.

The species is named after the Austrian botanist and explorer Friedrich Welwitsch who collected the type specimen near Luanda in Angola. The subspecies *delagoensis* is named after Delagoa (Maputo) Bay, the area from where it was first described.

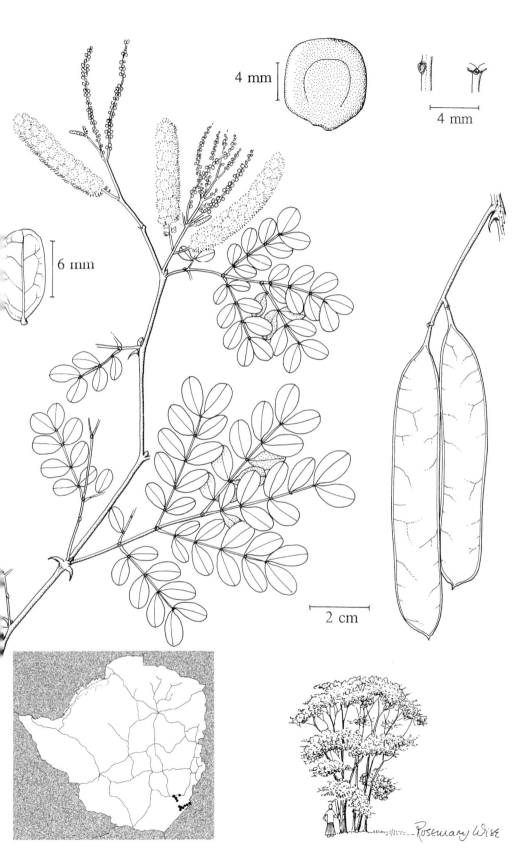

4 mm

4 mm

6 mm

2 cm

ACACIA WELWITSCHII

Rosemary Wise

ACACIA XANTHOPHLOEA *Benth.*

Common names: fever tree; jelenga (Shangaan)

Acacia xanthophloea is unmistakable with its yellow bark and open crown. It is gregarious and rises above most other trees along large rivers in the southern lowveld.

Description *A. xanthophloea* is a medium to large well-shaped tree 10-18 m in height, sometimes emergent above the surrounding riverine woodland. The open canopy casts only a light shade; branching is high. The trunk is tall and straight, not particularly tapering, with a diameter of 30-60 cm when mature. **Bark** is characteristically smooth, powdery and lemon yellow to the base, sometimes with darker flakes remaining. **Young twigs** are slender and yellowish. **Thorns** are long, white, and paired at the nodes. **Leaves** are of medium size with 4-6 pairs of pinnae, clustered on short lateral shoots. The spaced-out leaflets are small and pale yellow-green in colour. The tree comes into leaf later than many acacias. **Inflorescences** are axillary globose balls of fragrant pale yellow flowers, appearing on older growth in August-September, but sometimes as early as June-July. **Pods** are long, straight and thin, and light brown in colour, often with somewhat wavy margins when young. They are indehiscent and break up into segments on the ground.

Field characters Smooth yellow bark; narrow indehiscent pods; lowveld riverine habitat. Unlikely to be confused with other species.

Distribution and ecology This distinctive and well-known species is found over much of eastern and southern Africa from Somalia south to Swaziland and northern KwaZulu-Natal. Within Zimbabwe it is very localized, confined to floodplains close to the Limpopo, Mwenezi, Runde and Save rivers, and some major tributaries at altitudes below about 500 m. It has not been found in the Zambezi basin in this country, but is common in the Shire catchment in Malawi and along the Lower Zambezi below the Shire confluence in central Mozambique – evidence of the geologically-recent river capture of the present-day Middle and Upper Zambezi by the palaeo-Lower Zambezi. The species is gregarious and usually locally dominant, and is found on alluvial black clay soils in what are apparently even-aged stands with little regen-eration underneath.

Notes Establishment seem to be episodic and related to particular flooding events, hence the occurrence of apparently even-aged stands and lack of young plants. Seed production appears to be prolific and the light segments of ındehiscent pod are probably dispersed by wind. However, they are also a favourite food of vervet monkeys. The strange ball-like root parasite, *Sarcophyte sanguinea*, is sometimes associated with this acacia.

The wood is hard, heavy (880-910 kg/m³) and strong, with a coarse, even texture. Heartwood is only present in large specimens. It is moderately resistant and has been used in carpentry, but is prone to splitting. The growth rate is initially fast (up to 7 m height in 3 years) and the species is often used as a garden plant. It is frost-sensitive but can recover from frost damage.

The common name, "fever tree", comes from its incidental association with malarial areas. The specific name is Greek for "yellow bark" (*xanthos* - yellow, *phloios* - inner bark).

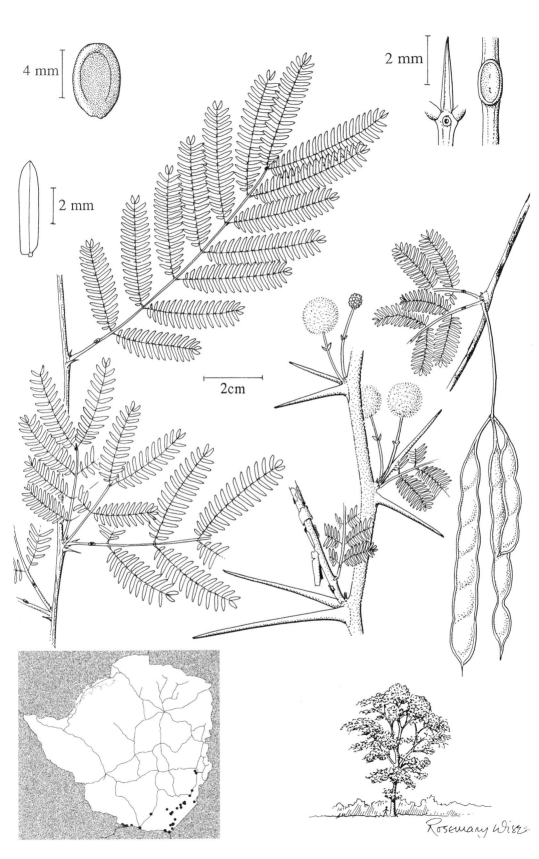

4 mm

2 mm

2 mm

2cm

Rosemary Wise

ACACIA XANTHOPHLOEA

Most of the acacias that have been introduced into Zimbabwe as exotics are from Australia, which is not surprising since over 950 of the 1340 *Acacia* species worldwide occur there. In Australia, the species vary from prostrate shrubs only half a metre high to forest trees over 35 m tall and are widespread throughout the continent, especially in the arid and semi-arid areas. They are collectively known as wattles (Old English, *watul*) because so many of them produce an abundance of small diameter sticks suitable as wattle interlacing for walls, hurdles and roofs. Many economically important products come from the Australian acacias including timber for furniture and construction, wood for fuel, fibre for pulp, tannin from the bark, and fodder from the foliage for domestic and wild animals. For example, *A. aneura* is considered to be one of the most important fodder trees for sheep in Australia. Acacias also play an important role in conservation and maintenance of fertility of the soil, in provision of shade and shelter, and as ornamental plants.

The first Australian species to be introduced to Zimbabwe were *A. mearnsii*, *A. dealbata* and *A. decurrens* (all for tanbark), *A. melanoxylon* (for timber) and *A. podalyriifolia* and *A. baileyana* (as ornamentals). Recently, many more species have been introduced under the auspices of Australian forestry and agricultural aid projects in the search for trees that will provide fodder, fuel and protection in the semi-arid zones. These include *A. acuminata*, *A. ampliceps*, *A. aneura*, *A. aulacocarpa*, *A. auriculiformis*, *A. brassii*, *A. excelsa*, *A. holosericea*, *A. leptocarpa*, *A. ligulata*, *A. mangium*, *A. pubescens*, *A. salicina*, *A. saligna* (previously *A. cyanophylla*) and *A. stenophylla*. The more detailed descriptions given below are limited to seven species that have become naturalized in Zimbabwe, viz. *A. mearnsii*, *A. dealbata*, *A. decurrens*, *A. melanoxylon*, *A. podalyriifolia*, *A. elata* and *A. farnesiana*.

Acacia mearnsii De Wild. (black wattle; previously also known as *A. mollissima* – drawing A on page 141) is a large shrub or small tree to 15 m high that has a limited distribution in the cool southeastern corner of Australia in the states of New South Wales, South Australia and Tasmania. From an economic point of view, the tree is almost ignored in its natural range but it has become very important as an exotic in many parts of the world for the production of fuelwood,

poles, fibre and tannin. *A. mearnsii* has been a species of major importance in Zimbabwe. It was introduced commercially into the mistbelt of the Eastern Districts from South Africa in the early 1920s. There were 600 ha planted by the mid-1940s and this built up to over 30,000 ha by the late 1950s, before synthetic tannins brought about a decline in the tanbark industry. This resulted in a 50% contraction of the plantation area to the climatic zones where the highest quality tannin was produced, the area south of Skyline Junction on the Chimanimani-Chipinge road. However, the wood of *A. mearnsii* is also valuable for poles, pulp, parquet flooring and fuel and, when there is a market for both bark and wood products, it is probably still the most profitable plantation tree to grow in southern Africa.

A. mearnsii has bipinnate leaves with very small leaflets and dark green foliage, hence the common name black wattle. It is easily recognized in November-December when the trees produce masses of yellow-gold globose inflorescences. The species has become naturalized in the Eastern Highlands and is an invader of disturbed grassland and river banks, for example in the Nyanga National Park. After fire, regeneration is very dense and although quite large trees eventually emerge, they lean and fall about and form an impenetrable jumbled forest with a dense canopy under which nothing else will grow. *A. mearnsii* is therefore an unattractive weed (except when in flower) that replaces indigenous species in attractive grassland and on stream banks. It would be a much more serious invader if it were not for its inability to establish itself in the face of competition from the indigenous vegetation unless there has been some disturbance, usually through human activities such as road-making, burning or clearance. This is in marked contrast to *Pinus patula*, another economically important exotic in the Eastern Highlands, which can establish itself direct into undisturbed grassland and forest and will, if it is not checked, eventually colonize most parts of the Eastern Highlands at altitudes over 1750 m.

Acacia dealbata Link (silver wattle – drawing C on page 143) is closely related to *A. mearnsii* and was introduced into Zimbabwe around 1900. Its distribution in Australia is similar to that of *A. mearnsii*, but it extends further north in New South Wales and is probably more cold-hardy. The

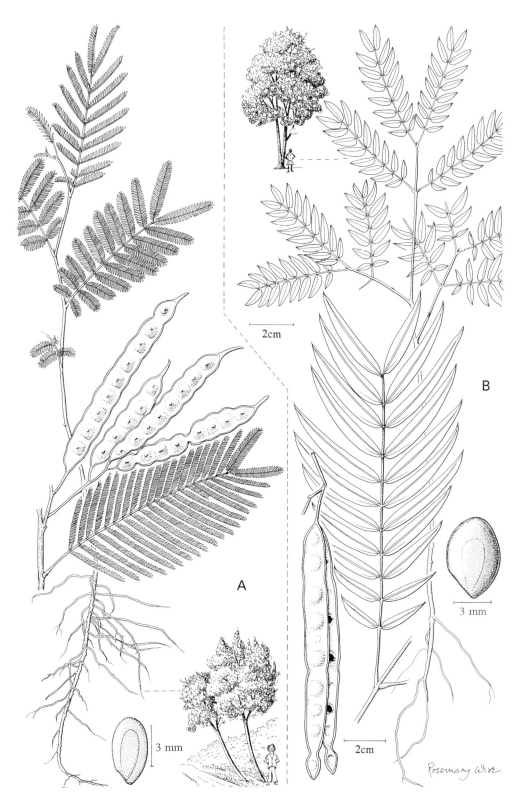

A – *Acacia mearnsii*. B – *A. elata*.

bark was not acceptable for tanning in Zimbabwe and *A. mearnsii* replaced it before *A. dealbata* ever became planted on a commercial scale. It has, however, become naturalized and can be seen in the northern parts of the Eastern Highlands, especially round Juliasdale. Because *A. dealbata* was much less widely planted, it is difficult to tell whether it is as aggressive a colonizer as *A. mearnsii*. Morphologically, it is very similar to that species but can be distinguished from it by its silvery foliage, its broader pods (which are not constricted between the seeds), its whitish not yellowish young growth, and the absence of glands between the top pairs of pinnae.

Acacia decurrens Willd. (green wattle) is closely related to *A. mearnsii* and also native to the southeastern corner of Australia from southern Queensland down to Tasmania. It was introduced into Zimbabwe around 1903 for tannin production, and has become naturalized at Lemon Kop in Chimanimani District. Like *A. dealbata*, it was superceded by A. *mearnsii* because of the latter's superior tannin quality. The identity and nomenclature of green and black wattle are confused but *A. decurrens* has less crowded leaflets than *A. mearnsii* and *A. dealbata* and they are longer in proportion to their width.

Acacia melanoxylon R.Br. (Australian blackwood – drawing B on page 143) is one of the largest acacias in Australia and grows in the southeastern part of the continent from southern Queensland down to Tasmania. Unlike the previous three species, *A. melanoxylon* has bipinnate leaves only in the very young seedling stage, after which wings develop on the leaf rachis and the function of the leaves is taken over by these phyllodes (see drawing).

A. melanoxylon has been planted in the Eastern Highlands only on a very small scale but it became naturalized in the indigenous montane forest fringes soon after it was introduced in the early 1900s. Now fine specimens can be found in indigenous forests such as at Stapleford. Interest in the wood of this species was aroused when it became used as a substitute for the highly prized and highly priced stinkwood, *Ocotea bullata*, from Knysna Forest in South Africa. The best timber came from naturally grown trees rather than from plantations, and this led to a standing order being issued in the 1950s to foresters of the Zimbabwe

Forestry Commission to carry seed around with them and scatter it in moist gullies in the high altitude, high rainfall forest reserves. As a result, the species is now a component of the indigenous montane forest, but is not as serious an invader as *A. mearnsii* or *Pinus patula* because it is not as gregarious and has an ecology more similar to that of the indigenous forest trees.

Acacia podalyriifolia G. Don (pearl acacia – drawing A on page 143) is native to Queensland and the northern New South Wales coast where it is often known as the Queensland wattle. It is a common, short-lived (10-20 years) ornamental shrub to small tree in many gardens all over Zimbabwe, and the pale silvery, grey-green round phyllodes and racemes of yellow globose inflorescences make it very conspicuous. *A. podalyriifolia* has become naturalized in parts of Manicaland, notably near Juliasdale and at La Rochelle in the Mbeza Valley. The seedling starts off life with bipinnate leaves that soon change to phyllodes.

Acacia elata Benth. (cedar wattle – drawing B on page 141) is a large tree that occurs naturally in New South Wales. It has bipinnate leaves with leaflets that are large for an acacia. It was introduced into Zimbabwe as an ornamental and has become naturalized on the John Meikle Forest Research Station and elsewhere on Stapleford Forest Reserve north east of Mutare. It is a handsome tree with terminal panicles of pale yellow globose inflorescences and can grow up to 20 m in height.

Acacia farnesiana (L.) Willd., a thorny pantropical species, has also been introduced into Zimbabwe but does not appear to have naturalized. Its natural range was warm American, but it is now pan-tropical and distributed round the world from the interior of northern Australia to Mexico, Central and South America, southern Europe and the southern USA. It is a small tree cultivated for its flowers from which perfume is made (the essential oil is known as "cassie ancienne") and is reputed to have been cultivated as an exotic in Rome in 1611. Elsewhere, the species produces good turnery wood, posts and fuel, tanbark, high-quality gum, fodder for cattle, and is also used for hedging and sand fixation.

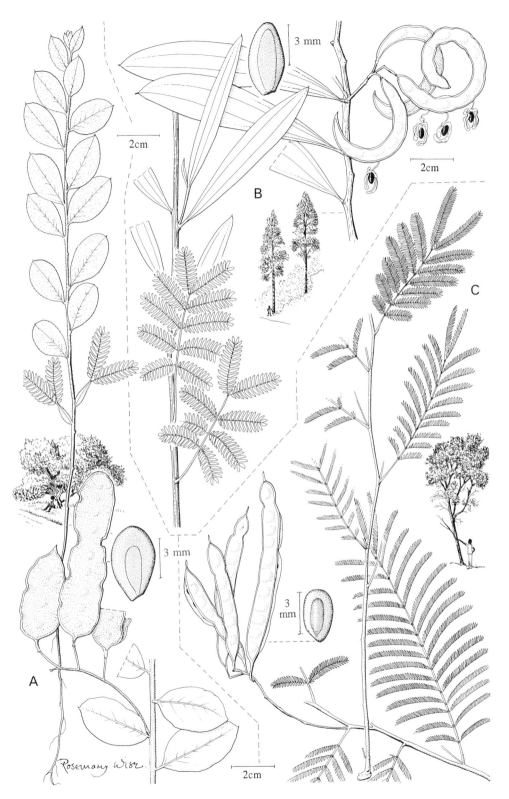

3 mm

2cm

B

2cm

3 mm

C

3 mm

A

3 mm

2cm

Rosemary Wise.

A – *Acacia podalyriifolia*. B – *A. melanoxylon*. C – *A. dealbata*.

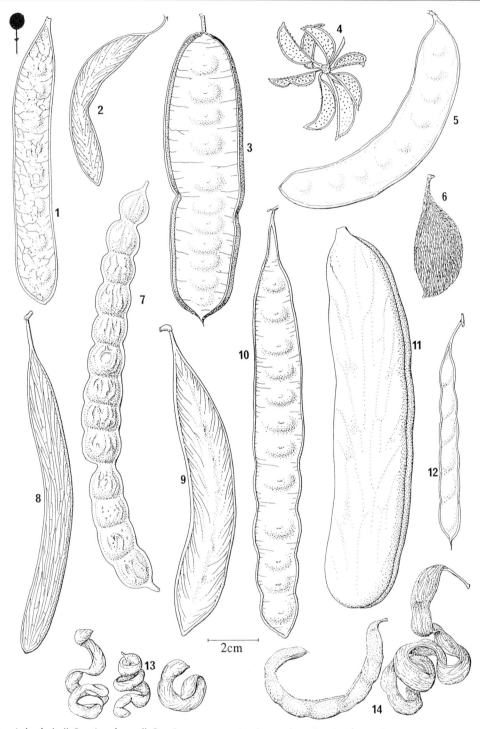

2cm

1 – *A. luederitzii*; 2 – *A. nebrownii*; 3 – *A. pentagona*; 4 – *A. permixta*; 5 – *A. rehmanniana*;
6 – *A. stuhlmannii* 7 – *A. nilotica*; 8 – *A. robusta clavigera*; 9 – *A. robusta robusta*; 10 – *A. schweinfurthii*;
11 – *A. sieberiana*; 12 – *xanthophloea*; 13 – *A. tortilis heteracantha*; 14 – *A. tortilis spirocarpa*.

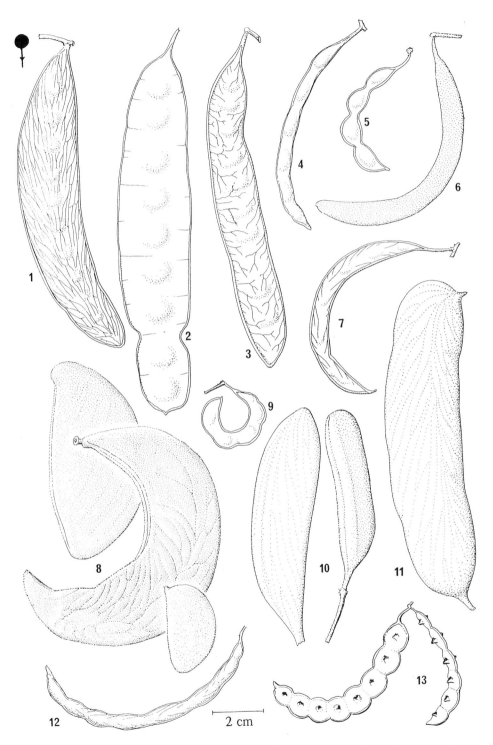

1 – *A. abyssinica;* 2 – *A. adenocalyx;* 3 – *A. amythethophylla;* 4 – *A. arenaria;* 5 – *A. borleae;* 6 – *A. gerrardii* 7 – *A. grandicornuta;* 8 – *A. erioloba;* 9 – *A. exuvialis;* 10 – *A. hebeclada hebeclada;* 11– *A. hebeclada chobiensis;* 12 – *A. karroo;* 13 – *A. kirkii.*

2 cm

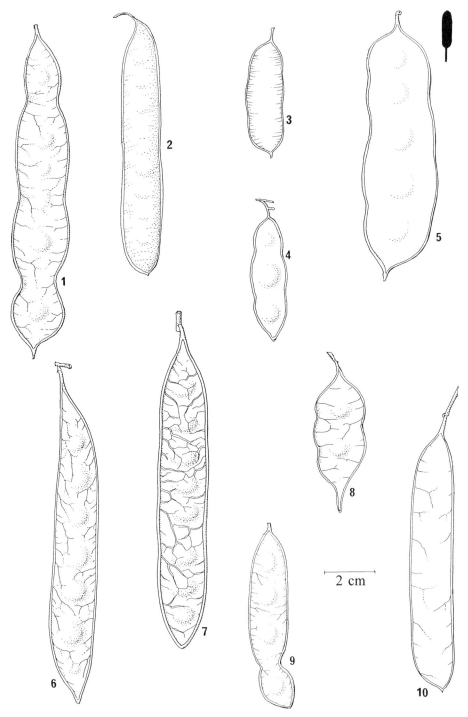

1 – *A. goetzei goetzei*; 2 – *A. hereroensis*; 3 – *A. mellifera* hybrid ("*A. laeta*"); 4 – *A. mellifera*; 5 – *A. goetzei microphylla*; 6 – *A. nigrescens*; 7 – *A. polyacantha*; 8 – *A. senegal rostrata*; 9 – *A. senegal leiorhachis*; 10 – *A. welwitschii*.

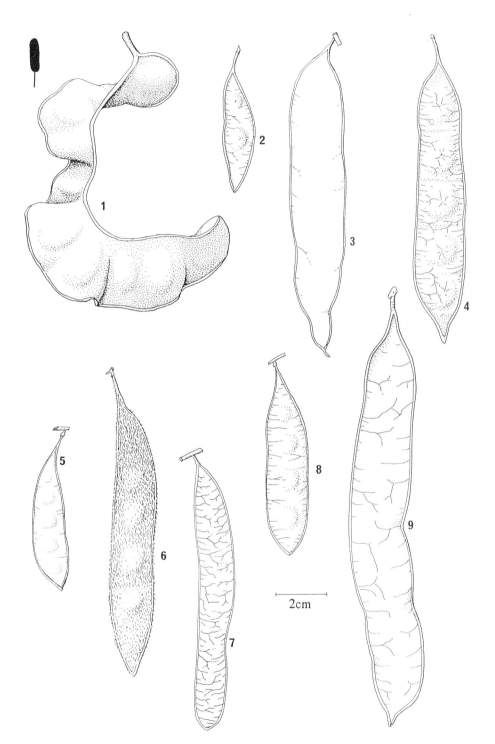

1 – *Faidherbia albida;* 2 – *A. ataxacantha;* 3 – *A. burkei;* 4 – *A. caffra;* 5 – *A. chariessa;* 6 – *A. eriocarpa;* 7 – *A. erubescens;* 8 – *A. fleckii;* 9 – *A. galpinii.*

2cm

List of Acacia Species by Area

Species in brackets are localized or marginal to the region

EASTERN HIGHLANDS
A. abyssinica
A. amythethophylla
A. karroo
A. pentagona
A. polyacantha
A. rehmanniana
A. sieberiana
Australian Acacia spp.

HIGHVELD
(1200-1500 m)
(Faidherbia albida)
A. abyssinica
A. amythethophylla
A. arenaria
(A. ataxacantha)
(A. caffra)
A. chariessa
(A. erioloba)
A. fleckii
A. galpinii
A. gerrardii
A. goetzei subsp. goetzei
A. goetzei subsp. microphylla
A. hereroensis
A. karroo
(A. mellifera)
A. nigrescens
A. nilotica
A. polyacantha
A. rehmanniana
A. robusta subsp robusta
(A. schweinfurthii)
A. sieberiana
A. tortilis subsp. heteracantha

NORTHWEST ZIMBABWE
Faidherbia albida
(A. arenaria)
A. ataxacantha
A. eriocarpa
A. erioloba
A. erubescens
A. fleckii
A. galpinii
(A. gerrardii)
A. hebeclada subsp. hebeclada
A. hebeclada subsp. chobiensis

A. karroo
A. kirkii
A. luederitzii
A. mellifera
A. nebrownii
A. nigrescens
A. nilotica
A. polyacantha
A. robusta subsp. clavigera
A. schweinfurthii
A. senegal var. leiorhachis
A. sieberiana
A. tortilis subsp. heteracantha
A. tortilis subsp. spirocarpa

ZAMBEZI VALLEY
(below 600 m)
Faidherbia albida
A. ataxacantha
A. eriocarpa
A. erubescens
A. gerrardii
A. goetzei subsp. goetzei
(A. kirkii)
A. mellifera
A. nebrownii
A. nigrescens
A. nilotica
(A. polyacantha)
A. robusta subsp. clavigera
A. schweinfurthii
A. senegal var. leiorhachis
A. sieberiana
A. tortilis subsp. spirocarpa

SOUTHEAST LOWVELD
(below 600 m)
Faidherbia albida
(A. ataxacantha)
A. borleae
A. burkei
A. erioloba
A. erubescsns
A. exuvialis
A. galpinii
A. grandicornuta
A. mellifera
A. nebrownii
A. nigrescens
A. nilotica
A. permixta
A. polyacantha
A. robusta subsp. clavigera

A. schweinfurthii
A. senegal var. leiorhachis
A. senegal var. rostrata
A. tortilis subsp. heteracantha
A. tortilis subsp. spirocarpa
A. welwitschii
A. stuhlmannii
A. xanthophloea

LIST OF SPECIES IN GREATER BULAWAYO AREA
(50 km radius)
Faidherbia albida
A. arenaria
A. ataxacantha
A. chariessa
A. erioloba
A. erubescens
A. fleckii
A. galpinii
A. gerrardii
A. goetzei subsp. goetzei
A. hereroensis
A. karroo
A. mellifera
A. nigrescens
A. nilotica
A. polyacantha
A. rehmanniana
A. robusta subsp. robusta
A. schweinfurthii
A. sieberiana
A. tortilis subsp. heteracantha

LIST OF SPECIES IN GREATER HARARE AREA
(50 km radius)
A. amythethophylla
A. ataxacantha
A. caffra - introduction
A. galpinii
A. gerrardii
A. goetzei subsp. goetzei
A. goetzei subsp. microphylla
A. hereroensis - introduction?
A. karroo
A. nilotica
A. polyacantha
A. rehmanniana
A. schweinfurthii
A. sieberiana

List of Acacia Species by Habitat

Species in brackets are localized or marginal to the habitat.

RAINFOREST AND FOREST MARGIN SPECIES
A. karroo
A. pentagona

MIOMBO SPECIES
(A. abyssinica)
A. amythethophylla
(A. gerrardii)
A. goetzii subsp. goetzi
A. goetzii subsp. microphylla
(A. karroo)
(A. nilotica)
A. polyacantha
A. rehmanniana
A. sieberiana

THICKET AND DRY FOREST SPECIES
A. ataxacantha
A. eriocarpa
A. fleckii
(A. nigrescens)
A. nilotica
A. robusta subsp. clavigera
A. schweinfurthii

RIVERINE SPECIES
Faidherbia albida
A. galpinii
A. hebeclada subsp. chobiensis
A. karroo
A. kirkii
A. nigrescens
A. polyacantha
A. robusta subsp. clavigera
A. schweinfurthii
A. sieberiana
A. tortilis subsp. spirocarpa
A. welwitschii
A. xanthophloea

KALAHARI SAND (AND SIMILAR SOILS) SPECIES
A. ataxacantha
A. burkei
A. eriocarpa
A. erioloba
A. fleckii
A. hebeclada subsp. hebeclada
A. luederitzii
(A. mellifera)
(A. nilotica)
(A. sieberiana)
(A. tortilis subsp. heteracantha)

ACACIA DRY WOODLAND SPECIES
A. arenaria
A. chariessa
A. erioloba
A. erubescens
A. fleckii
A. galpinii
A. gerrardii
A. goetzei subsp. goetzei
A. karroo
A. mellifera
A. nigrescens
A. nilotica
A. polyacantha
A. robusta subsp. robusta
A. tortilis subsp. heteracantha

Glossary

Alluvium — soil that is derived from particles deposited by water, e.g. rivers.

Apiculate — refers to leaves or pods; ending abruptly in a short sharp point.

Areole — central area on the flattened sides of a seed, often separated by pale markings.

Axillary inflorescence — inflorescence that arises from an axillary bud, not terminal.

Basement Complex (Gold or Greenstone Belt) — a group of early Precambrian rocks scattered across Zimbabwe consisting of metasedimentary and metavolcanic rocks, some of which yield gold. The soils derived from these rocks include characteristic red clays, a good habitat for some *Acacia* species.

Bipinnate — twice-pinnate.

Bole — cylindrical portion of the trunk of a tree.

Boss — a woody knob on a stem.

Browse — refers to herbivores; the act of eating leaves, pods, etc. from a shrub or tree.

Calcareous — refers to soil; enriched with calcium.

Calyx — the outer parts of a flower; in acacias usually small, fused together and straw-coloured.

Catena — a repeated sequence of soil profiles that is associated with topography.

Chromosome — the microscopic linear bodies containing the genes in the nucleus of the cell. Each species has a fixed number of chromosomes. Diploid cells have a full complement of chromosomes (2n).

Colluvium — soil that is derived from particles deposited by gravity, e.g. at the base of steep hills.

Crenulate — mostly applies to leaves; margins minutely scalloped.

Deciduous — refers principally to leaves; falling at the end of a growth period (e.g. at the onset of the dry season) or at maturity.

Dehiscent — generally refers to pods; opening spontaneously when ripe. The seeds are released from the pod.

Diploid — having two sets of chromosomes in each cell (2n).

Discolorous — refers to leaves; of differing colour above and below.

Dystrophic — environments or soils with comparatively low levels of nutrients (see eutrophic).

Edaphic — pertaining to or influenced by soil conditions or substrate.

Endemic — restricted to a certain region; often used in context of a country.

Epidermis — the outermost protective layer or skin of leaves, roots and stems.

Eutrophic — environments or soils with relatively high levels of nutrients; nutrient-rich (see dystrophic).

Foliar stipule — a stipule that appears almost leaf-like owing to its large size.

Glabrous — without any hairs or pubescence.

Gland — a small protrusion, generally on the leaf petiole, stem or pod, which secretes a fluid that is often sticky. Petiolar glands, or the presence of many sticky glands on the pods and young growth, are important in separating some *Acacia* species.

Glandular — covered with glands (usually very small; a lens is required to see them).

Globose inflorescence (capitate) — an inflorescence arranged in a spherical form or "ball", without a long axis.

Gum — a substance produced by a plant and resulting from breakdown of cells; consists of high molecular weight polysaccharides.

Habit — the shape and form of a plant, e.g. tall tree with a flat top. Many *Acacia* species have characteristic shapes.

Haploid — having a single set of chromosomes in each cell (n).

Heartwood — the darker, harder, central wood of a tree (see sapwood).

Hybrid — a plant which has resulted from a cross between two separate species or taxa. Generally hybrids are sterile and do not produce fertile seed.

Indehiscent — generally refers to pods; not opening spontaneously when ripe. The seeds are retained within the pod.

Inflorescence — a cluster of flowers to form what can appear to be a single flower. Acacias can have spicate (spike-like) or globose (round ball) inflorescences.

Inoculant — *Rhizobia* bacteria suitable for formation of root nodules.

Internode — the portion of stem between two nodes. Nodes are where the leaves and flowers sprout from.

Involucel — the small bracts at the base, or part-way up, the flower stalk (peduncle, q.v.).

Jesse bush — a type of vegetation occasionally seen in dry areas at lower altitudes, generally thicket-like with a dense shrub layer. When undisturbed it is similar to a dry deciduous forest with closed tree canopy, few shrubs and a poorly-developed herbaceous layer.

Kaolinitic clay — clay formed from kaolinite and similar minerals with a high feldspar content, often associated with granite. These soils are often pale in colour, do not crack much when dry, and are not as nutrient-rich as soils from montmorillinitic clay.

Lacustrine — environment associated with, or derived from, lakes and lake deposits.

Leaflet — a unit of a compound or pinnate leaf; a sub-division of a leaf.

Lenticel — a ventilating cell on the stem of a plant, often clearly visible and pustular.

Liana (or liane) — a woody climbing plant.

Micropyle — the small aperture in the seed coat where the pollen tube entered the ovule and close to the embryo root shoot.

Miombo — a woodland type dominated by trees of *Brachystegia, Julbernardia* or *Isoberlinia* species, an important vegetation type in south central Africa.

Monospecific — with only one species.

Montmorillonitic — clay formed from montmorillinite and similar minerals, usually associated with basic and volcanic rocks. These soils are dark in colour, swell when wet and crack when dry, and are more nutrient-rich than soils with kaolinitic clay.

Morphology — to do with the shape.

Mucronate — ending abruptly in a small stiff point; generally refers to leaves.

Naturalized — refers to the presence of a species. Not originating in, but has become adapted to an area and can maintain its population independent of human intervention.

Nodulate — to form root nodules.

Obconical — shaped like an upside-down cone.

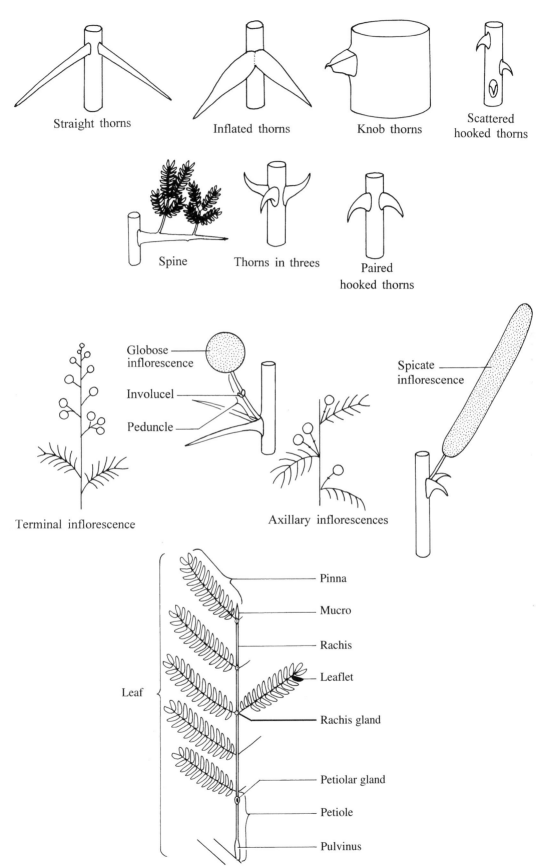

Straight thorns

Inflated thorns

Knob thorns

Scattered hooked thorns

Spine

Thorns in threes

Paired hooked thorns

Globose inflorescence

Involucel

Peduncle

Spicate inflorescence

Terminal inflorescence

Axillary inflorescences

Pinna

Mucro

Rachis

Leaflet

Rachis gland

Petiolar gland

Petiole

Pulvinus

Leaf

Panicle — an inflorescence in which the axis is divided into branches each bearing several flowers.

Parenchyma — soft and relatively undifferentiated (unspecialized) plant tissue.

Peduncle — the stalk on which an inflorescence is carried.

Petiolar gland — a gland situated on the leaf stalk.

Petiole — the stalk of a leaf.

Phenology — the occurrence of periodic biological events such as flowering and leaf fall.

Phyllode — a grossly-flattened petiole that functions as a leaf. Many Australian acacias have phyllodes instead of leaf blades at maturity.

Phytochoria — a broad, geographical area of evolutionally-linked plant species.

Pinna (pl. pinnae) — the primary division of a pinnate leaf. All indigenous acacias have pinnate leaves, ranging from those with just two pinnae pairs to those with over 20 pairs.

Pinnate — a compound leaf with the leaflets arranged on a common rachis.

Pluvial — a lengthy period of time when rainfall was considerably heavier than in preceding and succeeding periods.

Pod — a many-seeded fruit formed from a single carpel and splitting into two valves at maturity; common in legumes.

Polyploid — an organism with more than two chromosome sets, or a reduplication of the basic chromosome number.

Prickle — a sharp outgrowth from the bark (or epidermis), detachable without tearing the wood. *Acacia* prickles are all relatively small and hooked. They are only found in subgenus *Aculeiferum*.

Provenance — a population of trees from a limited area that are probably interbreeding and would be expected to show genetic similarity.

Pubescent — covered with short soft hairs.

Pulvinus — a swelling at the junction of the leaf petiole and the stem which plays a part in leaf movement.

Pustular — like a pustule or excrescence.

Raceme — inflorescence having a common axis.

Rachis — the axis (or petiole) which bears the leaflets of a compound leaf.

Rhizobia — bacteria of the genus *Rhizobia* (or related genera) which form root nodules and often assist in nitrogen-fixation.

Sapwood — the outer, paler and softer wood of a tree (see heartwood).

Scarify — to scratch the surface of a hard seed so that it can imbibe water, and thus germinate, more readily.

Slash — a forestry term to indicate the colour and appearance of tree bark when a cut has been made to expose the innerbark and sapwood.

Species — a taxonomic unit (abbreviated sp.) referring to a group of similar interbreeding, or potentially inter breeding, individuals that are separable principally on morphological characters. It can be subdivided (see subspecies, variety).

Spicate inflorescence (spike) — an inflorescence arranged in the form of a spike, with a long axis.

Spine — a sharp-pointed hardened structure, an outgrowth of the woody tissue, usually with buds on its side. *Acacia* species do not possess true spines.

Spinescent — tending to become spiny.

Stamen — the male part of a flower, carrying the anthers and pollen.

Stipule — small leaf-like appendages (often falling early) at the base of a leaf petiole. In subgenus *Acacia* these are spinescent.

Stolon — creeping stem capable of developing roots, and ultimately a new individual.

Subspecies — a taxonomic unit (abbreviated subsp.), a sub-division of a species, referring to a group of individuals that have certain distinguishing characteristics separating them from other members of the species. There are substantial differences in allocation of sub-specific status among specialists in different groups, but each subspecies should be (a) geographically distinct, (b) populations, not merely morphs (individuals within a population), and (c) different in some degree from other geographic populations. It is likely that many described subspecific and varietal taxa are not valid or should be treated as full species.

Sympatric — the occurrence of two or more closely-related species or subspecies together in the same area. It should be noted that the sympatric occurrence of two subspecies is verging on a contradiction (see subspecies), unless ecologically or behaviourally separated.

Synonym — a taxonomic term for an older name, now superceded owing to amalgamation or splitting of taxa or to the laws of nomenclature.

Tannin — a generic term for complex non-nitrogenous compounds containing phenols and related chemicals found in plants. They are generally mildly toxic with astringent (protein-precipitating) properties; their function appears to be to render plant tissues unpalatable to herbivores.

Taxon (pl. taxa) — a group of organisms of any taxonomic rank, e.g. family, genus, species, subspecies or variety.

Terminal inflorescence — inflorescence that is terminal, beyond which further growth does not occur; not axillary.

Testa — outer coat of the seed.

Underbark — the soft, living part of the bark (or inner bark) underneath the dead, hardened exterior.

Valve — one of two flattened segments of a pod, which separate on dehiscence.

Variety — a taxonomic unit (abbreviated var.), a subdivision of a species, referring to a group of individuals that have certain distinguishing characteristics separating them from other members of the species. It is of lower order than subspecies. As with subspecies, there are substantial differences in allocation of varietal status among specialists in different groups.

Anon. (1982). Australian acacias: the genus *Acacia* in Australia. Leaflet No. 6. Division of Forest Research, CSIRO, Canberra.

Anon. (n.d). *Acacia nilotica, Acacia gerrardii*. Indigenous Trees of Rhodesia Nos. 6 & 7. Natural Resources Board, Salisbury.

Anon. (n.d.). Concise descriptions of timbers: "Our Green Heritage" album competition. Cyclostyled report. Botanical Research Institute, Pretoria.

Armitage, F.B., Joustra, P.A. & Ben Salem, B. (1980). Genetic resources of tree species in arid and semi-arid areas. FAO/IBPGR, Rome.

Aucamp, A.J., Danckwerts, J.E., Teague, W.R & Venter, J.J. (1983). The role of *Acacia karroo* in the false thornveld of the Eastern Cape. *Proceedings of Grassland Society of Southern Africa* 18: 151-154.

Barnes, R.D. & Fagg, C.W. (1995). The potential of the African acacias in agricultural systems in the dryland tropics. Paper presented at the IUFRO 10th World Forestry Congress, August 1995, Tampere, Finland. Congress Report, Vol. 2, pp. 381-390.

Barnes, R.D., Fagg, C.W. & Milton, S.J. (1997). *Acacia erioloba*: monograph and annotated bibliography. Tropical Forestry Papers No. 35. Oxford Forestry Institute, Oxford.

Barnes, R.D., Filer, D.L. & Milton, S.J. (1996). *Acacia karroo*: monograph and annotated bibliography. Tropical Forestry Papers No. 32. Oxford Forestry Institute, Oxford.

Barnes, R.D., Marunda, C.T., Makoni, O., Maruzane, D. & Chimbalanga, A. (1996). African acacias: genetic evaluation. Phase I Final Report. Oxford Forestry Institute, Oxford/Zimbabwe Forestry Commission, Harare.

Bentham, G. (1842). Notes on Mimoseae, with a synopsis of species. *Hooker, London Journal of Botany* 1: 318-392.

Bentham, G. (1875). Revision of the suborder Mimoseae. *Transactions of the Linnean Society of London* 30: 335-664.

Bogdan, A.V. & Pratt, D.J. (1974). Common acacias of Kenya. Ministry of Agriculture, Animal Husbandry & Water Resources, Nairobi.

Boland, D.J. (1984). *Forest Trees of Australia*. Thomas Nelson, Melbourne.

Booth, R.G., Cox, M.L. & Madge, R.B. (1990). IIE guides to insects of importance to man. 3 Coleoptera. International Institute of Entomology/Natural History Museum, London.

Boughey, A.S. (1964). A check list of the trees of Southern Rhodesia. *Journal of South African Botany* 30: 151-176.

Brain, P. (1987). Immunology and phylogeny: a preliminary study of *Acacia*. *South African Journal of Science* 83: 422-427.

Brain, P., Harris, S.A. & Barnes, R.D. (1997). Leaf peroxidase types in *Acacia karroo* Hayne (Acacieae, Leguminosae): a range-wide study. *Silvae Genetica* 46: 88-94.

Brenan, J.P.M. (1956). Notes on Mimosoideae: II. *Kew Bulletin* 2: 185-205.

Brenan, J.P.M. (1957). Notes on Mimosoideae: IV. *Kew Bulletin* 3: 357-372.

Brenan, J.P.M. (1959). Leguminosae, subfamily Mimosoideae. *Flora of Tropical East Africa*. Crown Agents, London.

Brenan, J.P.M. (1970). Leguminosae (Mimosoideae). *Flora Zambesiaca* Vol. 3(1). Crown Agents, London.

Brenan, J.P.M. (1983). Manual on taxonomy of *Acacia* species. FAO, Rome.

Brenan, J.P.M. & Exell, A.W. (1957). *Acacia pennata* (L.) Willd. and its relatives in tropical Africa. *Boletim da Sociedade Broteriana* 31: 99-143.

Bridson, D. & Forman, L. (1992). *The Herbarium Handbook* (revised edition). Royal Botanical Gardens, Kew.

Campbell, B., Clarke, J., Luckert, M., Matose, F., Musvoto, C. & Scoones, I. [compilers] (1995). Local-level economic valuation of savanna woodland resources: village cases from Zimbabwe. IIED Research Series Vol. 3, No. 2. IIED, London.

Carr, J.D. (1976). *The South African Acacias*. Conservation Press, Johannesburg.

Chappill, J.A. & Maslin, B.R. (1995). A phylogenetic assessment of tribe Acacieae. In: *Advances in Legume Systematics 7: Phylogeny* (eds. M. Crisp & J.J. Doyle), pp.77-99. Royal Botanic Gardens, Kew.

Clarke, J. (1994). *Building on Indigenous Natural Resource Management: Forestry practices in Zimbabwe's communal lands*. Earthware Publishing/Forestry Commission, Harare.

Coates Palgrave, K. (1988). *Trees of Southern Africa*. Fifth impression. Struik, Cape Town.

Coe, M. & Beentje, H. (1991). *A Field Guide to the Acacias of Kenya*. Oxford University Press, Oxford.

Coe, M. & Coe, C. (1987). Large herbivores, acacia trees and bruchid beetles. *South African Journal of Science* 83: 624-635.

Coetzee, J.A. (1983). Intimations on the Tertiary vegetation of southern Africa. *Bothalia* 14: 345-354.

Corby, H.D.L. (1974). Systematic implications of nodulation among Rhodesian legumes. *Kirkia* **9**: 301-329.

Corby, H.D.L. (1988). Types of rhizobial nodules and their distribution among the Leguminosae. *Kirkia* **13**: 53-123.

Corby, H.D.L. (1990). The incidence of rhizobial nodulation among legumes dominant in the Flora Zambesiaca area of Africa. *Kirkia* **13**: 365-375.

Darlington, C.D. & Wylie, A.P. (1955). *Chromosome Atlas of Flowering Plants* (second edition). George Allen & Unwin, London, UK.

Davidson, C. & Jeppe, B. (1981). *Acacias: a Field Guide to the Identification of the Species of Southern Africa.* Centaur Publishers, Johannesburg.

Drummond, R.B. (1981). *Common Trees of the Central Watershed Woodlands of Zimbabwe.* Natural Resources Board, Department of Natural Resources, Harare.

Dunham, K.M. (1989). Litterfall, nutrient-fall and production in an *Acacia albida* woodland in Zimbabwe. *Journal of Tropical Ecology* **5**: 227-238.

Dunham, K.M. (1990). Fruit production by *Acacia albida* trees in Zambezi riverine woodlands. *Journal of Tropical Ecology* **6**: 445-457.

Dunham, K.M. (1991). Phenology of *Acacia albida* trees in Zambezi riverine woodlands. *African Journal of Ecology* **29**: 118-129.

Du Toit, J.T., Bryant, J.P. & Frisby, K. (1990). Regrowth and palatability of *Acacia* shoots following pruning by African savanna browsers. *Ecology* **71**: 149-154.

Elamin, H.M. (1972). Taxonomic studies on Sudan acacias. Unpublished MSc thesis, University of Edinburgh.

Elias, T.S. (1981). Mimosoideae. In: *Advances in Legume Systematics* (eds. R.M. Polhill & P.H. Raven), pp.143-151. Royal Botanic Gardens, Kew.

Ernst, W.H.O., Kuiters, A.T., Nelissen, H.J.M. & Tolsma, D.J. (1991). Seasonal variation in phenolics in several savanna tree species in Botswana. *Acta Bot. Neerl.* **40**: 63-74.

Eyles, F. (1916). A record of plants collected in Southern Rhodesia. *Transactions of the Royal Society of South Africa* **5**: 273-564.

Fagg, C.W. & Barnes, R.D. (1995). African acacias: study and assembly of genetic resources. Final report, Project 5655. Oxford Forestry Institute, Oxford.

Fagg, C.W. (1997). Annotated atlas of African acacias. Draft report. Oxford Forestry Institute, Oxford.

Fagg, C.W. & Greaves, A. (1990a). *Acacia tortilis.* Annotated bibliography No. F41. CAB International/Oxford Forestry Institute, Oxford.

Fagg, C.W. & Greaves, A. (1990b). *Acacia nilotica.* Annotated bibliography No. F42. CAB International/Oxford Forestry Institute, Oxford.

FAO (1990). Gum arabic. In: Specifications for identity and purity of certain food additives. FAO Food and Nutrition Paper No. 49, pp. 23-25. FAO/WHO, Rome.

Fanshawe, D.B. (1962). *Fifty Common Trees of Northern Rhodesia.* Natural Resources Board/Forest Dept., Lusaka.

Farrell, J.A. (1964). A Hlengwe-botanical dictionary of some trees and shrubs in Southern Rhodesia. *Kirkia* **4**: 165-172.

Filer, D.L. (1999). BRAHMS, Botanical Research and Herbarium Management System. Introduction to Version 4.6. Oxford Forestry Institute, Oxford.

Friis, I. (1992). *Forests and Forest Trees of Northeast Tropical Africa.* Kew Bulletin Additional Series XV. HMSO, London.

Gelfand, M., Mavi, S., Drummond, R.B. & Ndemera, B. (1985). *The Traditional Medical Practitioner in Zimbabwe.* Mambo Press, Gweru.

Goldsmith, B. & Carter, D.T. (1981). The indigenous timbers of Zimbabwe. Research Bulletin No. 9. Forestry Commission, Harare.

Gourlay, I.D. (1995). Growth ring characteristics of some African *Acacia* species. *Journal of Tropical Ecology* **11**: 121-140.

Gourlay, I.D. & Barnes, R.D. (1994). Seasonal growth zones in the wood of *Acacia karroo* Hayne: their definition and implications. *Commonwealth Forestry Review* **73**: 121-127.

Gourlay, I.D. & Kanowski, P.J. (1991). Marginal parenchyma bands and crystalliferous chains as indicators of age in African *Acacia* species. *IAWA Bulletin* **12**: 187-194.

Gourlay, I.D., Smith, J.P. & Barnes, R.D. (1996). Wood production in a natural stand of *Acacia karroo* in Zimbabwe. *Forest Ecology & Management* **88**: 289-295.

Grobbelaar, N. & Clarke, B. (1972). A qualitative study of the nodulating ability of legume species: list 2. *Journal of South African Botany* **38**: 241-247.

Guinet, P. & Vassal, J. (1978). Hypotheses on the differentiation of the major groups in the genus *Acacia* (Leguminosae). *Kew Bulletin* **32**: 509-527.

Guy, G. & Guy, P.R. (1979). *Some Common Trees and Shrubs of Zimbabwe Rhodesia.* National Museums & Monuments, Bulawayo.

Guy, P.R., Mahlangu, Z. & Charidza, H. (1979). Phenology of some trees and shrubs in the Sengwa Wildlife Research Area, Zimbabwe-Rhodesia. *South African Journal Wildlife Research* **9**: 47-54.

Hamant, C., Lescanne, N. & Vassal, J. (1975). Sur quelques nombres chromosomiques nouveaux dans le genre *Acacia. Taxon* **24**: 667-670.

Harris, S.A., Fagg, C.W. & Barnes, R.D. (1997). Isozyme variation in *Faidherbia albida* (Leguminosae, Mimosoideae). *Plant Systematics & Evolution* **207**:119-132.

Hawthorne, W.D. (1998). MUSICA mapping package, version 1.4. Oxford Forestry Institute, Oxford.

Janzen, D.H. (1966). Coevolution of mutualism between ants and acacias. *Evolution* **20**: 249-275.

Kellerman,T.S., Coetzer, J.A.W. & Naudé, T.W. (1988). *Plant Poisonings and Mycotoxicoses of Livestock in Southern Africa.* Oxford University Press, Cape Town.

Kolberg, H. (1989). Acacias of SWA/Namibia: Tree of the Year 1989. SWA Herbarium, Windhoek.

Lock, J.M. (1989). *Legumes of Africa: a check-list.* Royal Botanic Gardens, Kew.

Miller, M.F. (1994). The fate of mature African *Acacia* pods and seeds during their passage from the tree to the soil. *Journal of Tropical Ecology* **10**: 183-196.

Miller, O.B. (1948). Check-list of the Forest Trees and Shrubs of the British Empire, No. 6, Bechuanaland Protectorate. Scrivener Press, Oxford.

Miller, O.B. (1952). The woody plants of the Bechuanaland Protectorate. *Journal of South African Botany* **18**: 1-100.

Milton, S.J. (1987). Phenology of seven *Acacia* species in South Africa. *South African Journal Wildlife Research* **17**: 1-6.

Mitchell, B.L. (1961). Some notes on the vegetation of a portion of Wankie National Park. *Kirkia* **2**: 200-209.

National Academy of Sciences (1980). *Firewood Crops: Shrub and Tree Species for Energy Production*, Volume 1. National Academy of Sciences, Washington.

National Academy of Sciences (1983). *Firewood Crops: Shrub and Tree Species for Energy Production*, Volume 2. National Academy Press, Washington.

Noy, I. (1988). *Dyeing with Plants in Zimbabwe*. ZIMFEP, Harare.

Oballa, P.O. & Olng'otie, P.A.S. (1994). Chromosome numbers in two African *Acacia* species. *Kew Bulletin* **49**: 107-113.

Oldfield, S., Lusty, C. & MacKinven, A. (1998). *The World List of Threatened Trees*. World Conservation Press, Cambridge.

Orpen, F.C. & Kelly-Edwards, E.J. (1951). Botanical-vernacular and vernacular-botanical names of some trees and shrubs in Matabeleland. *Rhodesia Agricultural Journal* **48**: 165-181.

Palmberg, C. (1981). A vital fuelwood gene pool is in danger. *Unasylva* **33**: 22-30.

Pardy, A.A. (1951-56). Indigenous trees and shrubs of Southern Rhodesia. Various Bulletins, or separates, from the *Rhodesia Agricultural Journal* covering many *Acacia* species.

Pedley, L. (1978). A revision of *Acacia* Mill. in Queensland. *Austrobaileya* **1**: 75-234.

Pedley, L. (1986). Derivation and dispersal of *Acacia* (Leguminosae), with particular reference to Australia, and the recognition of *Senegalia* and *Racosperma*. *Botanical Journal of the Linnean Society* **92**: 219-254.

Prior, J. & Cutler, D. (1992). Trees to fuel Africa's fires. *New Scientist,* 29 August: 35-39.

Raven, P.H. (1983). The migration and evolution of floras in the southern hemisphere. *Bothalia* **14**: 325-328.

Raven, P.H. & Axelrod, D.I. (1974). Angiosperm biogeography and past continental movements. *Annals of Missouri Botanic Gardens* **61**: 539-673.

Reynolds, P. & Cousins, C.C. (1991). *Lwaano Lwanyika: Tonga Book of the Earth*. C. Cousins/Save the Children Fund (UK), Harare.

Robbertse, P.J. (1975). The genus *Acacia* in South Africa. IV - the morphology of the mature pod. *Bothalia* **11**: 481-489.

Robertson, F. (1986). A study of the conservation status of botanical reserves in Zimbabwe. *Zimbabwe Science News* **20**: 102-106.

Robertson, F. (1991). The natural resources of Hwedza Mountain Forest Reserve. *Zimbabwe Science News* **25**: 65-71.

Ross, J.H. (1971a). The *Acacia* species with glandular glutinous pods in Southern Africa. *Bothalia* **10**: 351-354.

Ross, J.H. (1971b). *Acacia karroo* in southern Africa. *Bothalia* **10**: 385-401.

Ross, J.H. (1971c). *Acacia brevispica* and *A. schweinfurthii*. *Bothalia* **10**: 419-426.

Ross, J.H. (1971d) A note on the *Acacia giraffae* x *Acacia haematoxylon* hybrid. *Bothalia* **11**:107-113.

Ross, J.H. (1972). The *Acacia* species of Natal (second edition). Wildlife Protection and Conservation Society of South Africa, Durban.

Ross, J.H. (1973). Towards a classification of the African acacias. *Bothalia* **11**: 107-113.

Ross, J.H. (1975a). Fabaceae: Mimosoideae. *Flora of Southern Africa* Vol. 16(1). Botanical Research Institute, Pretoria.

Ross, J.H. (1975b). The *Acacia senegal* complex. *Bothalia* **11**: 453-462.

Ross, J.H. (1979). A conspectus of the African Acacia species. Memoirs of the Botanical Survey of South Africa No. 44. Botanical Research Institute, Pretoria.

Ross, J.H. (1981). An analysis of the African *Acacia* species: their distribution, possible origins and relationships. *Bothalia* **13**: 389-413.

Rushworth, J.E. (1971). Trees and shrubs of Wankie National Park. Unpublished checklist, Department of National Parks, Wankie.

Rushworth, J.E. (1975). The floristic, physiognomic and biomass structure of Kalahari sand shrub vegetation in relation to fire and frost in Wankie National Park,

Rhodesia. Unpublished MSc thesis, University of Rhodesia, Salisbury.

Shepherd, G. (1976). Indigenous timbers. Natural Resources Board booklet, Salisbury.

Shorter, C. (1989). *An Introduction to the Common Trees of Malawi*. Wildlife Society of Malawi, Blantyre.

Southgate, B.J. (1978). Variation in the susceptibility of African *Acacia* (Leguminosae) to seed beetle attack. *Kew Bulletin* 32: 541-544.

Steedman, E.C. (1925). Trees and shrubs of Southern Rhodesia, part 1. *Proceedings of the Rhodesia Scientific Association* 24: 1-41.

Steyn, D.G. & Rimington, C. (1935). The occurrence of cyanogenetic glucosides in South African species of *Acacia* I. *Onderstepoort Journal of Veterinary Science & Animal Husbandry* 4: 51-63.

Steyn, M. (1994). *S.A. Acacias Identification Guide*. Privately published, South Africa.

Streets, R.J. (1962). *Exotic Forest Trees in the British Commonwealth*. Clarendon Press, Oxford.

Suessenguth, K. & Merxmüller, H. (1951). A contribution to the flora of the Marandellas District, Southern Rhodesia. *Proceedings & Transactions of the Rhodesia Scientific Association* 43: 75-160.

Tame, T. (1992). *Acacias of Southeast Australia*. Kangaroo Press, Australia.

Thomas, P.I. (1970). A Chitonga-botanical dictionary of some species occurring in the vicinity of the Mwenda estuary, Lake Kariba, Rhodesia. *Kirkia* 7: 269-284.

Tietema, T., Merkesdal, E. & Schroten, J. (1992). *Seed Germination of Indigenous Trees in Botswana*. ACTS Press, Nairobi/Biomass Users Network, Harare/Forestry Association of Botswana, Gaborone.

Timberlake, J.R. (1980a). *Handbook of Botswana Acacias*. Ministry of Agriculture, Gaborone.

Timberlake, J.R. (1980b). Vegetation map of South East Botswana. Ministry of Agriculture, Gaborone.

Timberlake, J.R. & Calvert, G.M. (1993). Preliminary root atlas for Zimbabwe and Zambia. Zimbabwe Bulletin of Forestry Research No. 10. Forestry Commission, Harare.

Timberlake, J.R., Nobanda, N. & Mapaure, I. (1993). Vegetation survey of the communal lands – north and west Zimbabwe. *Kirkia* 14: 171-270.

Timberlake, J.R. & Shaw, P. [eds.] (1994). *Chirinda Forest - a visitor's guide*. Forestry Commission, Harare.

Tredgold, M.H. (1986). *Food Plants of Zimbabwe*. Mambo Press, Gweru.

Tybirk, K., Schmidt, L.H. & Hauser, T. (1992). Notes and Records. *African Journal of Ecology* 32: 327-330.

Vandenbeldt, R.J. (1991). Rooting systems of western and southern African *Faidherbia albida* (Del.) A. Chev. (syn. *Acacia albida* Del.) - a comparative analysis with biogeographic implications. *Agroforestry Systems* 14: 233-244.

Van Wyk, B. & Van Wyk, P. (1997). *Field Guide to Trees of Southern Africa*. Struik, Cape Town.

Van Wyk, P. (1984). *Field Guide to the Trees of the Kruger National Park*. Struik, Cape Town.

Vassal, J. (1972). Apport des recherches ontogéniques et séminologiques à l'étude morphologique, taxonomique et phylogénique du genre *Acacia*. *Bull. Soc. Hist. Nat. Toulouse* 108: 125-247.

Vassal, J. (1974). Enumération des nombres chromosomiques dans le genre *Acacia*. *Bulletin of the International Group for the Study of Mimosoideae* 2: 21-29.

Vassal, J. (1977). Distribution maps of African *Acacia* species: *A. seyal, A. albida* and species of the "pennata" group. *Bulletin of the International Group for the Study of Mimosoideae* 5: 31-45.

Vassal, J. (1981). Acacieae. In: *Advances in Legume Systematics*, part 1 (eds. R.M. Polhill & P.H. Raven), pp.169-171. Royal Botanic Gardens, Kew.

Verdcourt, B. (1969). The arid corridor between the north-east and south-west areas of Africa. *Palaeoecology of Africa* 4: 140-144.

Verdoorn, I.C. (1951). South African species of *Acacia* with glandular glutinous pods. *Bothalia* 6: 153-160.

Walter, K.S. & Gillett, H.J. (1998). *1997 IUCN Red List of Threatened Plants*. World Conservation Monitoring Centre/IUCN, Cambridge.

West, O. (1950). Indigenous tree crops for Southern Rhodesia. *Rhodesia Agricultural Journal* 47: 204-217.

White, F. (1983). *The Vegetation of Africa*. Natural Resources Research No. 20. UNESCO, Paris.

Wickens, G.E. (1969). A study of *Acacia albida* Del. (Mimosoideae). *Kew Bulletin* 23: 181-202.

Wild, H. (1952). A guide to the flora of the Victoria Falls. In: *Victoria Falls Handbook* (ed. J.D. Clarke), pp.121-160. Commission for Preservation of Natural and Historical Monuments & Relics, Lusaka.

Wild, H., Biegel, H.M. & Mavi, S. (1972). *A Rhodesian Botanical Dictionary of African and English Plant Names*. Government Printers, Salisbury.

Willmer, P.G. & Stone, G.N. (1997). How aggressive ant-guards assist seed-set in *Acacia* flowers. *Nature* 338: 165-167.

Common & Vernacular Names of Acacias

Alphabetical list of vernacular, English and Afrikaans names based on published records and specimens.

Anaboom (Afr)	Faidherbia albida
Apiesdoring (Afr)	A. galpinii
Apple-ring acacia	Faidherbia albida
Black monkey thorn	A. burkei
Bladdoring (Afr)	A. galpinii
Blade thorn	A. fleckii
Blue thorn	A. erubescens
Butema (Kalanga)	A. karroo
Camel thorn	A. erioloba
Candle-pod acacia	A. hebeclada (both taxa)
Changaviha (Shang)	A. nilotica
Chibatamondoro (Shang)	A. erubescens
Chikwiku (Shona)	A. polyacantha
Chinanga (Shona)	hook thorn acacias
Chisosampotolo (Shang)	A. erubescens
Chitatatunga (Shona-Manyika)	A. goetzei
Chitatsunga (Shona)	A. amythethophylla
Chiungadzi (Shona)	A. polyacantha
Chiungatsikidzi (Shona)	A. amythethophylla
Enkeldoring (Afr)	A. robusta
Fever tree	A. xanthophloea
Flame acacia	A. ataxacantha
Flat-topped thorn	A. sieberiana
Flood plain acacia	A. kirkii
Gaba (Kalanga)	A. karroo
Gado (Ndau)	(see Gato)
Gakaunga (Shang)	A. nigrescens
Gato (Shona)	hook horn acacias
Gato (Ndau)	A. pentagona
	A. schweinfurthii
Giraffe thorn	A. erioloba
Gowe (Ndeb)	A. erubescens
Gukwe (Shang)	A. polyacantha
Grey-haired acacia	A. gerrardii
Haak-en-steek (Afr)	A. tortilis (both taxa)
Hlofungu (Shang)	Faidherbia albida
	A. sieberiana
Hook thorn	A. mellifera
Horned thorn	A. grandicornuta
Ikope (Ndeb)	A. gerrardii
Impangala (Tonga)	A. sieberiana
Ipucula (Ndeb)	A. rehmanniana
Isanqawe (Ndeb)	A. gerrardii
	A. nilotica
	A. tortilis
Isinga (Ndeb)	A. karroo
	straight thorn acacias
Ivikani (Ndeb)	A. arenaria
Jelenga (Shang)	A. xanthophloea
Kahe (Shang)	A. schweinfurthii
Kalahari sand acacia	A. luederitzii
Kalaunga (Shang)	A. galpinii
Kameeldoring (Afr)	A. erioloba
Kandare (Shona)	A. schweinfurthii
Katogwa (Ndeb)	A. mellifera
	A. nigrescens
Kato (Shang)	A. ataxacantha
Katopa (Ndeb)	A. nigrescens
Knob thorn	A. nigrescens
Knoppiesdoring (Afr)	A. nigrescens
Kovakova (Shang)	A. polyacantha
Large-leaved acacia	A. amythethophylla
Lekkerruikpeul (Afr)	A. nilotica
Lubamfwe (Tonga)	A. ataxacantha
Lubua (Tonga)	A. schweinfurthii
Luntwele (Tonga)	A. polyacantha
Mambovu (Tonga	A. robusta clavigera
Mfut'uta (Shona-Hurungwe)	A. galpinii
Mikaya (Shang)	hook thorn acacias
Mimosa thorn	A. karroo
Moba (Tonga)	A. nigrescens
Mona (Shona-Rusape)	A. rehmanniana
Monkey thorn	A. galpinii
Mpozva (Shang)	A. nigrescens
Mubayamhondoro (Shona)	straight thorn acacias
Mubovwa (Tonga)	A. sieberiana
Muchanga (Shona)	A. ataxacantha
Mugone (Shona)	A. polyacantha
Mugowa (Shona)	A. ataxacantha
Mugowa konono (Tonga)	A. ataxacantha
Muguhungu (Ndeb)	A. mellifera
Mujagwe (Tonga)	Faidherbia albida
Mukakanyuro (Shona)	A. ataxacantha
Mukalaunga (Shang)	Faidherbia albida
Mukaya (Shangaan)	hook thorn acacias
Mukoka (Tonga)	A. nilotica
	A. tortilis

Common/local name	Scientific name
Mukombokunono (Tonga)	A. ataxacantha
Mukomborakombora (Shona)	A. ataxacantha
Mukotokoto (Tonga)	A. nigrescens
Mukotokwa (Ndeb)	A. mellifera
Mukotonga (Shona)	A. nigrescens
Mukuu (Shona)	A. nigrescens
Mukwakwa (Shona)	A. polyacantha
Mumbu (Tonga)	A. polyacantha
Mumengami (Shona)	A. amythethophylla
Mumpangala (Tonga)	A. sieberiana
Munanga (Shona)	hook thorn acacias
Mundale (Tonga)	A. robusta clavigera
Munenje (Shona)	A. karroo
Mungnombie (Tonga)	A. nilotica
Munyenyengwa (Tonga)	A. gerrardii
	A. robusta clavigera
Mupandabutolo (Tonga)	A. mellifera
Mupumbu (Ndeb)	A. nigrescens
Mupumbu (Tonga)	A. goetzei
Murangaranya (Shona-Bikita)	A. galpinii
Musavamhanga (Shona)	A. ataxacantha
Mutandanyoka (Shona)	A. amythethophylla
Mutsangu (Shona, Tonga)	Faidherbia albida
Muunga (Shona)	straight thorn accias
Muzunga (Tonga)	A. tortilis
Mwaba (Tonga)	A. nigrescens
Ngoka (Tonga)	A. tortilis spiro.
Nkoho (Shona)	A. nigrescens
Nkotoku (Shona-Zezuru)	A. galpinii
Nombe (Tonga)	A. nilotica
Nyanga flat-top	A. abyssinica
Paperbark thorn	A. sieberiana
Papierbasdoring (Afr)	A. sieberiana
Pfurura (Shona-Pfungwe)	A. schweinfurthii
Purple pod acacia	A. goetzei
Red thorn	A. gerrardii
	A. hereroensis
River climbing acacia	A. schweinfurthii
Rooidoring (Afr)	A. gerrardii
Rukato (Shona)	A. ataxacantha
	A. schweinfurthii
Sand acacia	A. arenaria
Sanddoring (Afr)	A. arenaria
Scented thorn	A. nilotica
Sesani (Shang)	A. robusta
	A. tortilis
Silky acacia	A. rehmanniana
Sinanga (Shang)	A. nigrescens
Soetdoring (Afr)	A. karroo
Splendid acacia	A. robusta (both taxa)
Sticky acacia	A. borleae
Swaarthaak (Afr)	A. mellifera
Sweet thorn	A. karroo
Sydoring (Afr)	A. rehmanniana
Three-thorned acacia	A. senegal (both taxa)
Uhahla (Ndeb)	A. gerrardii
Ulutatau (Ndeb)	A. ataxacantha
	A. chariessa
Umbambangwe (Ndeb)	A. ataxacantha
Umbrella thorn	A. tortilis (both taxa)
	A. sieberiana
Umbuia (Ndeb-Gweru)	A. galpinii
Umdwadwa (Ndeb)	A. galpinii
	A. polyacantha
Umgamanzi (Ndeb)	A. robusta (both taxa)
Umhlabunga (Ndeb)	A. robusta (both taxa)
Umhlahlalinye (Ndeb)	A. senegal var. rostrata
Umhlope (Ndeb)	A. nigrescens
Umhohlo (Ndeb)	see umwhohlo
Umkaya (Ndeb)	hook thorn acacias
Umkayamhlope (Ndeb)	A. nigrescens
Umkotokoto (Lozi)	A. nigrescens
Umlaladwayi (Ndeb)	straight thorn acacias
Umngaga (Ndeb)	A. mellifera
Umpumbu (Ndeb)	Faidherbia albida
	A. polyacantha
	A. sieberiana
Umpumpu (Kalanga)	Faidherbia albida
Umqaqawe (Ndeb)	A. ataxacantha
Umsasane	A. sieberiana
	A. tortilis
Umshishene (Ndeb)	A. tortilis (both taxa)
Umtshanga (Ndeb)	A. nilotica
Umtshatshatsha (Ndeb)	A. tortilis heter.
Umtsungadzi (Ndeb)	A. amythethophylla
Umtungabayeni (Ndeb)	Faidherbia albida
	A. galpinii
Umwhohlo (Ndeb)	A. erioloba
Uthathawu (Ndeb)	A. ataxacantha
	A. schweinfurthii
Vlamdoring (Afr)	A. ataxacantha
Vumbangwenya (Shang)	A. robusta
Water acacia	A. nebrownii
White thorn	Faidherbia albida
	A. polyacantha
Winter thorn	Faidherbia albida
Witdoring (Afr)	A. polyacantha
Woolly-podded acacia	A. eriocarpa

Afr = Afrikaans
Ndeb = Ndebele
Shang = Shangaan

	page
A. **abyssinica** *Benth.*	28
A. abyssinica *Benth.* subsp. abyssinica	28
A. abyssinica *Benth.* subsp. calophylla *Brenan*	28
A. **acuminata** *Benth.*	140
A. **adenocalyx** *Brenan & Exell*	30
A. albida *Delile* (see Faidherbia albida)	24
A. **ampliceps** Maslin	140
A. **amythethophylla** *A. Rich.*	32
A. **aneura** *Benth.*	140
A. arabica *(Lam.) Willd.* (see A. nilotica)	44
A. **arenaria** *Schinz*	34
A. **ataxacantha** *DC.*	36
A. **aulacocarpa** *Benth.*	140
A. **auriculiformis** *Benth.*	140
A. **baileyana** *F. Müll.*	140
A. benthamii *Rochebr.* (see A. nilotica)	94
A. **borleae** *Burtt Davy*	38
A. **brassii** *Pedley*	140
A. brevispica *Harms* (see Box 10)	118
A. buchananii *Harms* (see A. amythethophylla)	32
A. **burkei** *Benth.*	40
A. caffra *sensu* Eyles 1916 (see A. polyacantha)	102
A. caffra var. tomentosa *sensu* O.B. Mill. 1952 (see A. fleckii)	56
A. **caffra** *(Thunb.) Willd.*	42
A. campylacantha *A. Rich.* (see A. polyacantha)	102
A. **caven** *(Mol.) Mol.*	50
A. **chariessa** *Milne-Redh.*	44
A. cinerea *Schinz* (see A. fleckii)	56
A. clavigera *E. Mey.* (see A. robusta subsp. clavigera)	108
A. cyanophylla Lindl. (see A. saligna)	140
A. davyii *sensu* Boughey 1964 (see A. sieberiana)	122
A. **dealbata** *Link*	140
A. **decurrens** *Willd.*	142
A. delagoensis *Harms* (see A. welwitschii)	136
A. detinens *Burch.* (see A. mellifera)	84
A. dulcis *Marloth & Engl.* (see A. erubescens)	52
A. **elata** *Benth.*	143
A. **eriocarpa** *Brenan*	46
A. **erioloba** *E. Mey.*	48
A. **erubescens** *Oliv.*	52
A. **excelsa** *Benth.*	140
A. **exuvialis** *Verdoorn*	54
A. **farnesiana** *(L.) Willd.*	142
A. **fleckii** *Schinz*	56
A. **galpinii** *Burtt Davy*	58
A. gansbergensis *Schinz* (see A. hereroensis)	74
A. **gerrardii** *Benth.*	60
A. **gerrardii** *Benth.* subsp. **negevensis** *Zohary*	62
A. **gerrardii** *Benth.* subsp. **gerrardii**	60
A. giraffae *Willd.* (see A. erioloba)	46
A. **goetzei** *Harms*	64
A. **goetzei** *Harms* subsp. **microphylla** *Brenan*	66
A. **goetzei** *Harms* subsp. **goetzei**	66
A. **grandicornuta** *Gerstner*	68
A. **haematoxylon** *Willd.*	50
A. **hebeclada** *DC.* subsp. **chobiensis** *(O.B. Mill.) Schreib.*	70
A. **hebeclada** *DC.* subsp. **hebeclada**	72
A. **hebeclada** *DC.* subsp. **tristis** *Schreib.*	70
A. **hereroensis** *Engl.*	74
A. hermannii *Baker f.* (see A. arenaria)	34
A. heteracantha *Burch.* (see A. tortilis subsp. heteracantha)	128
A. **holosericea** *G. Don*	140
A. **karroo** *Hayne*	76
A. **kirkii** *Oliv.*	80
A. **kirkii** *Oliv.* subsp. **kirkii** var. **kirkii**	80
A. **kirkii** *Oliv.* subsp. **kirkii** var. **sublaevis** *Brenan*	80
A. **kirkii** *Oliv.* subsp. **mildbraedii** *(Harms) Brenan*	80
A. kraussiana *Benth.* (see Box 6)	92
A. **laeta** *Benth.*	86
A. lasiopetala *sensu* Suessenguth & Merxmüller 1951 (see A. sieberiana)	122
A. **leptocarpa** *Benth.*	140
A. **ligulata** *Cunn.*	140
A. litakunensis *Burch.* (see A. tortilis subsp. heteracantha)	128
A. **luederitzii** *Engl.*	82
A. **luederitzii** *Engl.* var. **luederitzii**	82
A. **luederitzii** *Engl.* var. **retinens** *(Sim) J.H. Ross & Brenan*	82
A. lugardiae *N.E. Br.* (see A. ataxacantha)	36
A. macrothyrsa *Harms* (see A. amythethophylla)	32
A. **mangium** *Willd.*	140
A. **mearnsii** *De Wild.*	140
A. **melanoxylon** *R. Br.*	142
A. mellei *Verdoorn* (see A. hereroensis)	74
A. **mellifera** *(Vahl) Benth.*	84
A. **mellifera** *(Vahl) Benth.* subsp. **detinens** *(Burch.) Brenan*	84
A. **mellifera** *(Vahl) Benth.* subsp. **mellifera**	84
A. mollissima *Burtt Davy* (see A. mearnsii)	140
A. mossambicensis *sensu* Wild 1952 (see A. goetzei)	64
A. natalitia *E. Mey.* (see A. karroo)	76
A. **nebrownii** *Burtt Davy*	88
A. **nigrescens** *Oliv.*	90
A. **nilotica** *(L.) Delile*	94
A. **nilotica** *(L.) Delile* subsp. **kraussiana** *(Vatke) Brenan*	94
A. **nilotica** *(L.) Delile* subsp. **subalata** *(Vatke) Brenan*	94
A. pallens *(Benth.) Rolfe* (see A. nigrescens)	90
A. pallens *sensu* Steedman 1925 (see A. polyacantha)	102
A. pennata *(L.) Willd.* (see A. schweinfurthii & Box 6)	114
A. **pentagona** *(Schumach.) Hook.f.*	98
A. **permixta** *Burtt Davy*	100
A. **podalyriifolia** *G. Don*	142
A. **polyacantha** *Willd.*	102
A. **polyacantha** *Willd.* subsp. **campylacantha** *(A. Rich.) Brenan*	102

A. **polyacantha** *Willd.* subsp. **polyacantha**	104	A. stolonifera *Burch.* var. chobiensis *O.B. Mill.*	
A. **pubescens** *(Vent.) R.Br.*	140	(see A. hebeclada subsp. chobiensis)	70
A. **reficiens** *Wawra* subsp. **reficiens**	82	A. **stuhlmannii** *Taub.*	126
A. **rehmanniana** *Schinz*	106	A. subalata *Vatke* (see A. nilotica)	94
A. retinens *sensu* O.B. Miller 1948 (see A. luederitzii)	82	A. **swazica** *Burtt Davy*	79
A. **robusta** *Burch.* subsp. **clavigera** *(E. Mey.) Brenan*	108	A. **tenuispina** *Verdoorn*	79
A. **robusta** *Burch.* subsp. **robusta**	112	A. **torrei** *Brenan*	79
A. **robusta** *Burch.* subsp. **usambarensis** *(Taub.) Brenan*	110	A. **tortilis** *(Forssk.) Hayne*	
A. rogersii *Burtt Davy* (see A. nebrownii)	88	subsp. **heteracantha** *(Burch.) Brenan*	128
A. **schweinfurthii** *Brenan & Exell*	114	A. **tortilis** *(Forssk.) Hayne*	
A. **schweinfurthii** *Brenan & Exell* var. **schweinfurthii**	114	subsp. **spirocarpa** *(A. Rich.) Brenan*	132
A. **schweinfurthii** *Brenan & Exell* var. **sericea** *Brenan & Exell*	114	A. **tortilis** *(Forssk.) Hayne*	
A. **salicina** *Lindl.*	140	subsp. **spirocarpa** *(A. Rich.) Brenan* var. **crinita** *Chiov.*	132
A. **saligna** *(Labill.) H.L. Wendl.*	140	A. uncinata *sensu* O.B. Miller 1952 (see A. luederitzii)	82
A. senegal *sensu* Wild 1952 (see A. ataxacantha)	36	A. verek *Guill. & Perr.* (see A. chariessa)	44
A. **senegal** *(L.) Willd.* var. **kerensis** *Schweinf.*	120	A. **welwitschii** *Oliv.*	136
A. **senegal** *(L.) Willd.* var. **leiorhachis** *Brenan*	116	A. welwitschii *sensu* Eyles 1916 (see A. goetzei)	64
A. **senegal** *(L.) Willd.* var. **rostrata** *Brenan*	120	A. **welwitschii** *Oliv.*	
A. **senegal** *(L.) Willd.* var. **senegal**	116	subsp. **delagoensis** *(Harms) J.H.Ross & Brenan*	136
A. sieberana *DC.* (see A. sieberiana)	122	A. **welwitschii** *Oliv.* subsp. **welwitschii**	136
A. sieberana *DC.* var. vermoensii *(De Wild.) Keay & Brenan*	122	A. woodii *Burtt Davy* (see A. sieberiana)	122
A. **sieberiana** *DC.*	122	A. **xanthophloea** *Benth.*	138
A. **sieberiana** *DC.* var. **sieberiana**	122	**Dichrostachys cinerea** *(L.) Wight & Arn.*	(see key)
A. **sieberiana** *DC.* var. **woodii** *(Burtt Davy) Keay & Brenan*	122	**Caesalpinia decapetala** *(Roth) Alston*	(see key)
A. spirocarpa *A. Rich.* (see A. tortilis subsp. spirocarpa)	132	**Faidherbia albida** *(Delile) A.Chev.*	24
A. **stenophylla** *A. Cunn.*	140	**Pterolobium stellatum** *(Forssk.) Brenan* (see key)	
A. stolonifera *Burch.* (see A. hebeclada subsp. hebeclada)	72	Vachellia (see A. erioloba)	50